T0074184

ATLANTIS THINKING MACHINES

VOLUME 2

SERIES EDITOR: KAI-UWE KÜHNBERGER

Atlantis Thinking Machines

Series Editor:

Kai-Uwe Kühnberger,

Institute of Cognitive Science

University of Osnabrück, Germany

(ISSN: 1877-3273)

Aims and scope of the series

This series publishes books resulting from theoretical research on and reproductions of general Artificial Intelligence (AI).The book series focuses on the establishment of new theories and paradigms in AI. At the same time, the series aims at exploring multiple scientific angles and methodologies, including results from research in cognitive science, neuroscience, theoretical and experimental AI, biology and from innovative interdisciplinary methodologies.

For more information on this series and our other book series, please visit our website at:

www.atlantis-press.com/publications/books

ATLANTIS
PRESS

AMSTERDAM – PARIS

© **ATLANTIS PRESS**

Real-World Reasoning:
Toward Scalable, Uncertain Spatiotemporal, Contextual and Causal Inference

Ben Goertzel

Novamente
LLC/Biomind LLC
Bernerd Place
MD 20851, Rockville
USA

Nil Geisweiller

yl. Kliment 4
Samokov 2000
Bulgaria

Lúcio Coelho

Rua Guajajaras
1268, apto.506
30180-101
Belo Horizonte
Brasil

Predrag Janičić

Faculty of Mathematics
Studentski trg, 16
11000 Belgrade
Serbia

Cassio Pennachin

Igenesis Av. Prof. Mário
Werneck 2170 / 501
Buritis, Belo Horizonte
30575-180 Minas Gerais
Brasil

ATLANTIS
PRESS

AMSTERDAM – PARIS

Atlantis Press

8, square des Bouleaux
75019 Paris, France

For information on all Atlantis Press publications, visit our website at: *www.atlantis-press.com*

Atlantis Thinking Machines

Volume 1: Enaction, Embodiment, Evolutionary Robotics. Simulation Models for a Post-Cognitivist Science of Mind - Marieke Rohde, Ezequiel A. Di Paolo

ISBNs
Print: 978-94-91216-10-7
E-Book: 978-94-91216-11-4
ISSN: 1877-3273

Contents

Acknowledgements

This book had its origins as a technical report written in 2008 by Novamente LLC for IARPA, under a program managed by Jeffrey Morrisson with the help of Ken Kisiel. So, above all, we would like to acknowledge the vision and practical support of these two most excellent applied scientists, without whom this book would not exist. The book in is current form is not precisely identical to the report we wrote for IARPA, but there is a large amount of overlap.

We also must especially acknowledge those who played a role in the development of the PLN inference system, which arises often in these pages. PLN was created by a large number of people, but perhaps the biggest contributors (aside from Goertzel and Geisweiller who co-authored this book) were Matt Ikle', Ari Heljakka, and Izabela Freire Goertzel, the co-authors of the PLN book, and Joel Pitt who became involved later. André Senna and Welter Silva also deserve particular thanks for their leading roles in developing the Novamente Cognition Engine and OpenCog frameworks in which the current PLN implementation exists.

Thanks are also due to Jeffrey Epstein for a research grant supporting Ben Goertzel's research, during part of the time period the original IARPA report was being written, and also during part of the time period the report was being turned into this book.

And, thanks go to Zeger Karssen of Atlantis Press for clearly understanding the need for a book such as this one ... and being patient with our inordinately long delays in producing the final manuscript.

Chapter 1

Introduction

The general problem addressed in this book is how to effectively carry out reasoning, knowledge discovery and querying based on huge amounts of complex information about real-world situations. Specifically we conceive "real-world reasoning" here mainly as "massively scalable reasoning involving uncertainty, space, time, cause and context." Of course there are other important aspects to reasoning about the real world we live in, e.g. the hierarchical structure of much of the human world, and we will briefly touch on some of these here as well. But for the purposes of this book, when we mention "real-world reasoning" or RWR, we're mostly talking about uncertainty, spacetime, cause, context and scalability.

The RWR problem is critical in at least two respects: as part of the broader pursuit of artificial general intelligence (AGI) (Goertzel & Pennachin, 2006; Goertzel *et al.*, 2006a; Goertzel & Bugaj, 2008; Hart & Goertzel, 2008), and in terms of the practical information processing needs that have arisen in current society.

On the AGI side, it is obvious that every human brain ingests a huge amount of knowledge each waking hour, and somehow we manage to query and analyze our huge, dynamic internal data stores. No AGI design can possibly succeed without some way to effectively carry out intelligent judgment and discovery based on these data stores. AGI also has other aspects, e.g. procedure learning and goal refinement (to name just two), but RWR is certainly a huge part of the puzzle.

On the practical information processing side, anyone who lives in a developed country these days is aware of the tremendous amount of data continually being gathered about all manner of aspects of the human and natural worlds. Much of this data is discarded shortly after it's gathered, but much of it is retained in various repositories. However, even when the data is retained, it is rarely utilized to anywhere near the full extent possible, because our state-of-the-art technologies for storing, querying, mining and analyzing very large data stores are still very primitive and simplistic (not only compared to what is in principle possible, but compared to what we know to be possible based on contemporary mathematics and computer science).

In these pages we review a class of approaches to handling these RWR problems using uncertain, spatiotemporal, contextual and causal logic. Uncertain logic is not the only possible approach to the RWR problem, but we believe it's one very promising approach, and it's our focus here. While the first RWR-capable logic system has yet to be constructed, we make an argument, via detailed review of the literature and the state of the art and suggestion of some original ideas, that the time is ripe for their construction.

The book is intended to serve two purposes: to provide a reasonably accessible overview of the RWR problem and the available technologies and concepts for its solution; and to provide a sketch of one possible avenue toward solution.

Toward the "overview" goal, we review a number of concepts and technologies – some recently developed, some more classical – that address aspects of the RWR problem. While our treatment centers on formal logic, we also introduce material from other areas such as graph databases, probability theory, cognitive architecture and so forth as appropriate.

After reviewing a variety of other logical approaches, we present our own approach to real-world reasoning, which is based on the Probabilistic Logic Networks (PLN) framework (Goertzel *et al.*, 2008); and give some detailed suggestions regarding how one might address the scalable real-world inference problem effectively via integrating PLN with other ideas and technologies described. Our goal in this regard is not to propose a particular highly-specific technical solution, but rather to describe a class of possible solutions that might be described as "scalable spatiotemporal uncertain logic systems". In this vein, in the later chapters we give a number of detailed examples showing the kinds of results one might expect to obtain by approaching a large knowledge store containing information about everyday human activities with the Probabilistic Logic Networks inference framework that we have developed in prior publications.

1.1   The Advantages of a Logical Approach

There are many advantages to the logic-based approach relative to others, some of which will be alluded to as the text progresses, but perhaps the largest advantage is its relative representational transparency. That is, if the knowledge stored in a knowledge base, and the patterns recognized in this knowledge base, are represented in a logical format, then it is reasonably tractable for humans to inspect this knowledge and these patterns. This is a major practical advantage in terms of allowing hybridized human/artificial intelligence – and, given the comments made above about the interesting but erratic performance of AI algorithms in our domain, this seems a very important point.

Given the advantage of logic-based approaches in terms of representational transparency, the only reason to choose an opaque approach over a logic-based approach would be if the opaque approach were dramatically superior in its capabilities. However, this currently seems not to be the case: in fact the evidence so far seems to indicate that logic-based approaches are the most powerful ones in this sort of context.

Some theorists have argued against logic-based approaches to real-world data on the grounds that there are problems with "grounding" logical symbols in real-world data (the so-called "symbol grounding problem" (Goertzel *et al.*, 2006a)). However, these objections do not hold up to scrutiny. It is true that logic-based approaches cannot function adequately for real-world applications unless the logical symbols used are explicitly associated with observed data-patterns, but there are well-understood technologies for making such associations. Historically, many logic-based AI systems have been used in an "ungrounded" way, not containing components that directly connect the logical terms used with real-world observations – but this is a problem of poor system architecture, not a flaw of the logic-based approach in itself.

1.2 Main High-Level Conclusions

To give a small hint at what is to come, the main conclusions at the end of our investigation are that

- the logic-based approach has the in-principle power to solve the problem of querying and analyzing very large scale spatiotemporal knowledge bases, in a manner respecting the contextual and causal knowledge contained therein
- there is a significant amount of scientific and technological knowledge in the literature regarding nearly every aspect of the application of logic-based technology to this problem
- the Achilles heel of current relevant logic-based technology is scalability
- the keys to achieving scalability in this context are conceptually understood – adaptive inference control and attention allocation – but have not been explored nearly as thoroughly as they need to be

- it seems likely that special techniques may be useful for adaptively controlling real-world scalable inference as opposed to inference in other domains (e.g. mathematical theorem proving)
- one viable way to achieve scalable real-world reasoning may be to use the Probabilistic Logic Networks framework, perhaps within an integrative AGI design like OpenCog which provides flexible means for adaptive inference control

We thus suggest that a critical focus of research should be on the development of methods for *exploiting the specific statistical structure of real spatiotemporal data, to adaptively guide logical inference methods* in performing query and analytical processing.

1.3 Summary

We now briefly review the chapters to follow, summarizing the main themes and ideas to be introduced.

1.3.1 *Part I: Representations and Rules for Real-World Reasoning*

Part I of the book reviews a host of approaches described in the literature for representing and reasoning about real-world knowledge, including temporal, spatial, contextual and causal knowledge.

Chapter Two reviews many of the varieties of formal logic that have been developed during the last century, with a focus on those approaches that appear most relevant to the large-scale information-management problem. We begin with a basic review of predicate and term logic, and then move on to subtler variations such as modal logic (the logic of possibility) and deontic logic (the logic of obligation). We also discuss the methods that logic systems use to actually draw logical conclusions based on the information provided to them: forward chaining, in which information items are combined exploratorily to come to new conclusions; and backward chaining, in which a question is posed to the system and it then seeks to find the answer using multiple logical inference steps based on the information at its disposal.

Chapter Three considers various methods of handling uncertainty in formal logic, including fuzzy sets and logic, possibility theory, probability theory, and imprecise and indefinite probabilities. Uncertainty management is critical to our target application, because a great percentage of real-world data is uncertain, and most of the conclusions one can draw based on real-world data are also uncertain. So, logic systems that only deal with absolute truth or falsehood are not going to be very useful for our target application. But, the literature contains a huge number of different methods for dealing with uncertainty – and one of our conclusions is that there isn't necessarily a single best approach. Rather, a practical solution may integrate more than one approach, for instance using both fuzzy and probabilistic methods as appropriate. Figures 1.1 and 1.2 from Chapter Three illustrate several of the possible methods for representing time within logic:

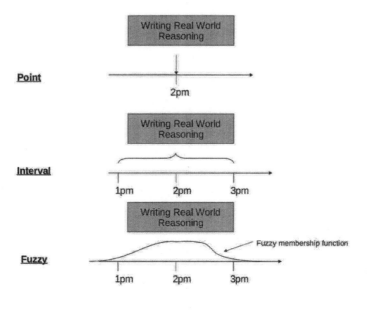

Fig. 1.1

Chapter Four grapples with the various ways logicians and computer scientists have devised to represent time within logic. This is a core issue for our current pursuit, because a large percentage of real-world knowledge involves time. The most standard method for handling time within logic is Allen's interval algebra, which treats time-intervals rather than points as the atomic temporal entities, and enumerates a set of rules for combining and reasoning about time-intervals; but it suffers the deficit of being crisp rather than explicitly handling uncertainty. So we review several methods of extending interval algebra to deal with uncertainty, including methods involving fuzziness, probability, and combinations of the two. Figure 1.3 from Chapter Four illustrates the logical relationships between time intervals specified by Allen's interval algebra:

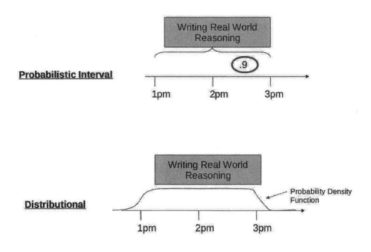

Fig. 1.2

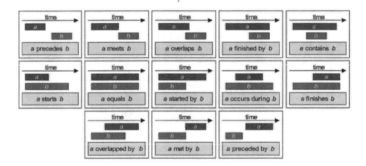

Fig. 1.3

And the Figure 1.4, also from Chapter Four, is a graphical representation of some temporal relationships between events, using a probabilistic variation of Allen's interval algebra:

Continuing the theme of its predecessor, Chapter Five deals with temporal inference, reviewing the multiple methods presented in the literature for incorporating time into logic. These include methods that simply treat time like any other logical information, and also methods that give time a special status, including reified and modal techniques. We conclude that methods giving time a special status are likely to be dramatically more efficient, and express a particular favor for reified techniques compatible with Allen's interval algebra (discussed above) and its variations. We give some concrete examples of temporal inference regarding peoples' daily activities.

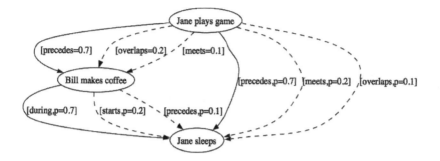

Fig. 1.4

For instance, one of the example problems we consider involves a query regarding "which people were in the same place as Jane last week," and a knowledge base with the following information:

- Susie and Jane use the same daycare center, but Jane uses it everyday, whereas Susie only uses it when she has important meetings (otherwise she works at home with her child).
- Susie sends a message stating that Tuesday she has a big meeting with a potential funder for her business.

Given this information, inference is needed to figure out that on Tuesday Susie is likely to put her child in daycare, and hence (depending on the time of the meeting!) potentially to be at the same place as Jane sometime on Tuesday. To further estimate the probability of the two women being in the same place, one has to do inference based on the times Jane usually picks up and drops off her child, and the time Susie is likely to do so based on the time of her meeting. We show in detail how temporal inference methods can be used to carry out this commonsense inference, and other similar examples.

Chapter Six builds on the treatment of time and presents an analogous discussion of a more complex subject, space (critical to our core theme as a substantial percentage of real-world knowledge involves spatial as well as temporal information). We review the Region Connection Calculus, which models the logic of space in terms of a fixed set of logical relationships between logical terms that correspond to spatial regions. As this is a simple but limited technique, we then consider more complex approaches to representing space in logic, including directional calculus, and occupancy grids as utilized in robotics (which are extremely general yet also resource-intensive, and so should only be used when

simpler methods fail). The following diagram, drawn from Chapter Six, depicts the relationships between various spatial regions and spatially distributed phenomena (NTPP
stands for Non-Tangential Proper Part, and O stands for Overlapping; these are spatial-
relationship predicates drawn from the Region Connection Calculus formalism):

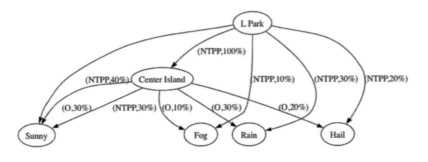

Fig. 1.5

Next, as well as time and space, another critical aspect of real-world reasoning is context. Nearly all real-world knowledge implicitly or explicitly gains its meaning from the
specific context in which it is understood by human knowledge producers and consumers to
exist. So if logical methods are to be applied effectively to real-world data, it is important
that they explicitly represent contextuality. In Chapter Seven, we review a number of approaches to representing contextuality in logic, and give detailed examples of several. We
also consider one example of context representation that is particularly acutely relevant to
our application area: the use of contextual logic to handle user modeling. If different users
of an information system have different biases and interests, then a logic based system can
pay attention to this and give them different information via treating each user as a separate
context and then doing contextually-biased reasoning.

In addition to context representation, Chapter Seven treats contextual inference, reviewing a number of techniques presented in the literature, and again finding favor in those
methods that explicitly represent context as a special relationship within the base logic.
We give a concrete examples of contextual inference applied to practical problems regarding people and their interrelationships. One example we consider involves the following
assumptions:

- Alison is an accountant who is also a musician. Alison is emotional in the context of
  music, but not in the context of accounting. She frequently mentions Canadian place

names in the context of music (maybe she's a Canadian music fan), but not in the context of accounting.

- Bob is in a similar situation, but he frequently mentions Canadian related stuff in both the music and accounting contexts.
- Clark is also in a similar situation, but he frequently mentions Canadian related stuff only in the accounting context, not the music context.
- People who have a lot to do with Canadian people, and a lot to do with money, have a chance of being involved in suspicious log trafficking activities.

We then show how contextual inference methods can be used to estimate the probability that Clark may be involved with log trafficking.

Chapter Eight turns briefly to causal reasoning, reviewing the multiple formalisms used to represent the notion of causality, and connecting causation to probabilistic and inductive reasoning.

1.3.2 *Part II: Acquiring, Storing and Mining Logical Knowledge*

Our focus in this book is doing logical reasoning on real-world knowledge, and this is a large and critical topic – but, once one has a large store of real-world knowledge in logical format, reasoning per se is not the only thing that must be done with it. Part II, a brief interlude at the center of the book, consists of three short chapters which lightly touch three other important issues to do with large stores of logical knowledge: acquiring logical knowledge via transforming real-world data, storing and querying large volumes of logical knowledge, and mining patterns from large logical knowledge stores. Each of these topics could be a book in itself, and here we only roughly sketch the main problems involved and give some pointers into the literature.

Chapter Nine very briefly reviews existing relevant literature, discussing the use of natural language processing technology to map text and voice into sets of logical relationships; and the use of image processing and heuristic algorithms to create logical relationships out of tables, graphs and diagrams. For instance, the following diagram drawn from Chapter Six shows some logical relationships that current NLP technology can extract from the simple sentence "Gone for dinner with Bob":

Another key question that must be answered if logic-based methods are to be applied to massive real-world data stores is: how can a huge amount of logical knowledge be stored and manipulated? This is not a question about logic per se, it's a question about modern computer systems, database and database-like technologies, and so forth. In Chapter Ten,

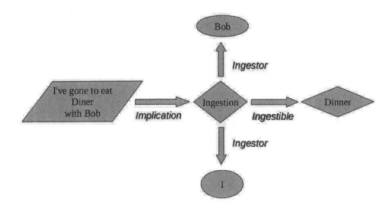

Fig. 1.6

we review a number of current technologies, including relational databases, RDF triple-stores, object databases, and hypergraph and graph databases. Our conclusion is that at present the latter form the best option, and we give some specific examples of how to translate complex logical knowledge into the specific format required for a graph database. The following table, drawn from Chapter Ten, summarizes some of our findings in more depth:

Technology	Strengths	Weaknesses
Relational DBs	• Mature, enterprise grade solutions • Ease of integration with other systems	• Poor conceptual fit for logical information storage • Inadequate model for reasoning • Complex scalability
Object-Oriented DBs	• Better conceptual fit than relational DBs (still not perfect) • Mature solutions	• Single data model • Small ecosystem • Not designed for reasoning

Continued on next page

continued from previous page

Technology	Strengths	Weaknesses
Graph DBs	• Flexible, dynamic data model • Good performance and scalability • Designed with data analysis in mind	• Less mature than competing technologies
Hypergraph DBs	• Best data model fit • Designed with reasoning and data analysis in mind	• Alpha stage technology
RDF Triplestores	• Semantic web friendly • Adequate data model for some inferences	• Less mature technology • Rigid data model
Document-oriented DBs	• Flexible data model • Performance and scalability • Rapidly maturing solutions	• Not adequate for reasoning and analysis • More work is left for application layer
Column-oriented DBs	• Very flexible, dynamic data model • Performance and scalability • Rapidly maturing solutions	• More work is left for application layer • Not designed for reasoning
Key-value DBs	• Extremely good performance and scalability • Mature and rapidly maturing solutions	• No data model, leaving most work for application layer • Not designed for reasoning

Chapter Ten turns to one of the most important applications desirable to carry out on large data stores – "data mining" (also known as "information exploitation", "pattern discovery", etc.). Most existing datamining techniques are either specialized for relational databases, or don't scale beyond small knowledge stores. We review here some specific datamining algorithms in depth. One conclusion drawn is that, for datamining to really be effective in this context, it will need to be hybridized with inference. Datamining technology, in itself, will always find too many potentially interesting patterns for any human user to want to explore. So logical inference technology is needed to filter the results of datamining, either via interaction with the datamining process, or via postprocessing.

1.3.3   *Part III: Real World Reasoning Using Probabilistic Logic Networks*

The second major of the book provides a detailed exploration of the applicability of one particular logical framework, Probabilistic Logic Networks, to real-world reasoning problems. This part is different from the previous ones, in that it comprises primarily original work, rather than literature survey and summary.

Chapters Twelve and Thirteen summarize Probabilistic Logic Networks (PLN), the particular uncertain logic system called which several of the authors (Goertzel and Pennnachin and Geisweiller) and their colleagues have developed over the last years (and published extensively on elsewhere). We outline the basic mechanisms via which PLN deals with a variety of aspects of inference, including term and predicate logic, extensional and intensional inference, and contextual, causal, spatial and temporal inference.

Chapter Fourteen turns to the specific problem of inference about changes in large knowledge bases. We consider several concrete examples including the following causal inference scenario:

- Before March 2007, Bob never had any Canadian friends except those who were also friends of his wife.
- After March 2007, Bob started acquiring Canadian friends who were not friends of his wife.
- In late 2006, Bob started collecting Pokemon cards. Most of the new Canadian friends Bob made between March 2007 and Late 2007 are associated with Pokemon cards
- In late 2006, Bob started learning French. Most of the new Canadian friends Bob made between March 2007 and Late 2007 are Quebecois.

We show in detail how a PLN inference engine, combining temporal inference with causal inference and numerous other aspects, can attempt to answer the question: What is the probable cause of Bob acquiring new Canadian friends who are not also friends of his wife?

Chapter Fourteen also considers spatial inference in the context of change analysis, giving particular attention to the incorporation of the Region Connection Calculus (RCC) into PLN. It is shown how a fuzzy/probabilistic version of RCC may be used together with a fuzzy/probabilistic version of Allen's interval algebra to carry out commonsense inferences about the causes of peoples' activities and relationships, based on knowledge involving time and space. To exemplify the practical use of these ideas, we extend the example of Bob and his Pokemon cards, from the previous chapter, to include the case where some of Bob's friends live near Canada but not actually in Canada, and the inference system has to deal with the notion of "fuzzy Canadian-ness" as related to spatial geometry. The following figure illustrates the fuzzy spatial membership function corresponding to Canada, used in the example inference:

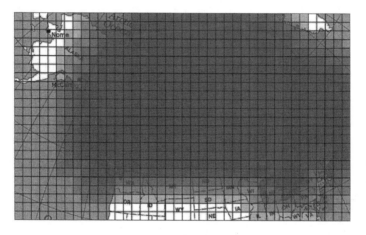

Fig. 1.7

Finally (before Chapter Sixteen which is a brief conclusion), Chapter Fifteen confronts the thorny conceptual and algorithmic issue of inference control: determining which inference steps to take, in which order, in order to answer a question, filter a datamining results list, or carry out an analysis. Far from being "merely an efficiency issue," inference control actually hits many of the deepest issues of AI, including the "frame problem" (briefly stated, that AI systems tend to lack tacit background knowledge about what questions not to bother asking because their answers are supposed to be obvious, or are irrelevant). We discuss a number of specific techniques that may be able to achieve effective inference control in the context of inference on large stores of spatiotemporal logical knowledge, including techniques that hybridize logic with other AI methods such as activation spreading. Here the discussion broadens from logic per se to the topic of "cognitive architectures" and general AI systems, the point being made that the integrative architectures underlying many such systems exist largely in order to provide effective, scalable inference control. As an example, the OpenCog cognitive architecture in which the PLN inference system is embedded is briefly considered.

PART I

Representations and Rules for Real-World Reasoning

Chapter 2

Knowledge Representation Using Formal Logic

Now we begin to dig into the nitty-gritty of our subject matter. Before discussing querying and analysis of complex, heterogeneous spatiotemporal and contextual knowledge, we must discuss representation of temporal knowledge (as well as, to a certain extent, spatial knowledge)... and before that, we must address knowledge representation in general.

In the course of our investigation we must work through a number of difficult questions regarding knowledge representation, including:

- Which of the many species of uncertain logic to use as the basis for our knowledge representation
- How specifically to represent temporal knowledge?
- How specifically to represent spatial knowledge?
- What is the best low-level (e.g. graph) representation of logical knowledge for efficient storage and processing?

"Logic" itself is not a monolithic entity; it comes in many different flavors. At the highest level, there is the dichotomy between predicate logic and term logic (and there are also systems that hybridize the two, e.g. (Goertzel *et al.*, 2008; Wang, 2006a)). There are also many types of logical system within each of these broad categories, some of which will be reviewed later on.

The material in this chapter becomes somewhat formal and technical, for which we apologize to the reader who lacks the relevant taste or experience; but which unfortunately seems unavoidable if we are to give a serious treatment of our topic. The reader lacking appropriate expertise may either consult relevant background material (Copi & Cohen, 1998), or less ideally, skim this material and proceed to the later chapters, some of which will be quite clearly comprehensible without grasp of these preliminaries, some less so.

2.1 Basic Concepts of Term and Predicate Logic

Term logic, or *traditional logic*, was founded by Aristotle and was the dominating logical framework until the late nineteen century. Term logic uses subject-predicate statements of the form "S is P" (for instance, "Socrates is a man"). There are singular and universal terms (the former correspond to unique subjects). There are just four forms of propositions in term logic:

- Universal and affirmative (e.g. "All men are mortal")
- Particular and affirmative (e.g. "Some men are philosophers")
- Universal and negative (e.g. "No philosophers are rich")
- Particular and negative (e.g. "Some men are not philosophers").

New conclusions are derived from premises by *syllogisms*. Aristotle introduced fourteen syllogisms, of which we will give just two here for illustrative purposes:

- *(Barbara)* If every M is L, and if every S is M, then every S is L. (for instance, "if every man is mortal, and if every philosopher is a man, then every philosopher is mortal")
- *(Celarent)* If no M is L, and if every S is M, then no S is L. (for instance, "if no philosopher is rich and if every poet is a philosopher, then no poet is rich").

Syllogisms provide a method for deduction – deriving new facts from already proved facts. In addition there are rules for induction and abduction:

- *(Induction)* If every M is L, and if every M is S, then every S is L. (for instance, "if every poet is mortal, and if every poet is a philosopher, then every philosopher is mortal")
- *(Abduction)* If every L is M, and if every S is M, then every S is L. (for instance, "if every poet is mortal, and if every philosopher is mortal, then every philosopher is poet")

Notice that the induction and abduction rules do not neccesarily derive true statements. Nevertheless these are important forms of inference in the face of insufficient evidence, in modern AI reasoning systems as well as in classical Aristotelian term logic (Dimopoulos & Kakas, 1996). Induction and abduction are omnipresent in human commonsense inference.

Put simply, induction aims at *generalization*. In the above example ("if every poet is mortal, and if every poet is a philosopher, then every philosopher is mortal"), the first premise yields that all philosophers that are also poets are mortal, but then it is generalized to conclude that all philosophers are mortal. Yet, it is possible that there are some philosophers that are not poets, so potentially not mortal, so the above generalization rule does not neccesarily lead to true conclusions.

Similarly, abduction aims at *explanation*. In the above example, the explanation for the fact that "every philosopher is mortal" may be that it is because "every philosopher is a poet".

In the late nineteenth century, classical term logic was the subject of criticism, for its weak expressive power and the limited forms of reasoning it permitted. For example, in classical term logic from "every car is a vehicle" one cannot infer "every owner of a car is an owner of a vehicle." In that period, predicate logic was designed, and it still serves as a basis for most mathematical and philosophical formal reasoning. However, modern theorists have extended classical term logic in various ways (Englebretsen & Sommers, 2000; Wang, 2006b), so that there are now term logics which equal predicate logic in expressive power. There are also systems that hybridize term and predicate logic, such as our own Probabilistic Logic Networks framework (Goertzel *et al.*, 2008), which will be discussed below. Advocates of term logic often argue that it more closely matches the patterns of human commonsense reasoning.

In standard *predicate*, or *first-order logic*, statements have arbitrary propositional form (involving conjunctions, disjunctions, negations, …) and arbitrary use of quantifiers (for instance, "for every man, there is a woman, such that for every man, …"). Modern variants of term logic provide this same expressive flexibility.

Pure predicate logic is a framework in which one can describe other theories. This framework is defined by the set of axioms and the set of inference rules (such as "if P and if P yields Q, then Q"). The proofs are sequences of derivation steps based on these axioms and rules. For example, one can represent in predicate logic and derive "not every man is a philosopher if and only if there is a man such that it is not a philosopher". For first-order logic there are also inductive and abductive rules, not used in mathematical theorem-proving, but for uncertain reasoning, most often in AI. First order logic is also used as a basis for many specific logics, including modal, deontic, temporal and spatial logics as will be discussed below.

2.2 Review of Propositional Logic

In order to explain predicate logic in more depth, we must begin with a simpler variant called "propositional logic." Propositional logic can express simple facts while first-order logic (or predicate logic) also involves quantification and more complex statements. In this sense, first-order logic subsumes propositional logic. Both propositional and first-order logic have many practical applications beyond the ones considered here, in describing different processes and concepts. Most important perhaps are applications in computer science, ranging from chip design (Aehlig & Beckmann, 2007) to natural language processing (Meulen, 2001).

Both propositional logic and first-order logic have three important aspects:

- syntax – describing well-formed formulae and their basic properties;
- semantics – describing *meaning* of well-formed formulae;
- deduction – describing systems for syntactically deriving new formulas from other formulas (with no respect to their meaning).

We now give a brief mathematical exposition of these three aspects.

First, syntax. Let P be an infinite, but countable set, whose elements will be called *propositional letters* or *atomic propositions*. The set of *propositional formulas* is defined by the following rules:

- all elements of P are propositional formulas;
- $\perp$ and $\top$ are propositional formulas (which as we will see below, are normally taken to semantically represent False and True)
- if A is a propositional formula, then so is $\neg A$ (which is normally taken to represent the negation of A)
- if A and B are propositional formulas, then so are $A \wedge B$, $A \vee B$, $A \Rightarrow B$, $A \Leftrightarrow B$ (which are normally taken to represent And, Or, and implication and equivalence)
- each propositional formulas is obtained by a finite number of applications of the above rules.

Next, semantics. A valuation v is defined as a mapping from P to the set $\{0, 1\}$. That is, a valuation assigns either 0 or 1 to any propositional letter. An interpretation I_v is an extension of a valuation v, mapping propositional formulas to the set $\{0, 1\}$, defined in the following way:

- $I_v(\perp) = 0$;
- $I_v(\top) = 1$;
- $I_v(p) = v(p)$, if p belongs to P;
- $I_v(\neg A) = 1 - I_v(A)$;

- $I_v (A \wedge B) = \min(I_v (A), I_v (B))$;
- $I_v (A \vee B) = \max(I_v (A), I_v (B))$;
- $I_v (A \Rightarrow B) = \max(1 - I_v (A), I_v (B))$;
- $I_v (A \Leftrightarrow B) = 1$, If $I_v (A) = I_v(B)$ and $I_v (A \Leftrightarrow B) = 0$ otherwise.

The above semantics is referred as to Tarski's semantics (that he introduced in (Tarski, 1994)). Put simply, this allows the interpretation of propositional formulas like

$$A \wedge (\neg B \vee (C \Rightarrow A))$$

as having truth values drawn from the set $\{0, 1\}$ (given the truth values for A, B and C), with 0 usually interpreted as meaning False and 1 as meaning True.

A formula A is satisfiable if there is a valuation v such that $I_v (A) = 1$ (otherwise, it is *unsatisfiable* or inconsistent, aka self-contradictory). A formula A is a tautology if for an arbitrary valuation v $I_v (A) = 1$. If a formula A is a tautology, then we denote that by $\models$ A.

For example, it holds that $I_v(p \vee q) = 1$ in a valuation v such that $v(p) = 1$, $v(q) = 0$ – so the formula $p \vee q$ is satisfiable. On the other hand, the formula $p \vee \neg p$ is tautology.

The problem of checking the satisfiability of a formula made of conjunctions of disjunctions of literals (variables or negations of variables) is decidable (there is an effective algorithm for solving it) and is called SAT. SAT is on of the most important NP-complete problems. Programs for testing satisfiability are called SAT solvers. There are different methods for checking satisfiability of a formula: the simplest is based on truth-tables (i.e. tabular enumeration of all possible combinations of values for the formula's variables, and evaluation of the truth value of the formula for each combination). Other include Davis-Putnam-Logmann-Loveland (DPLL) procedure, and modern solvers – DPLL-based, resolution-based solvers, tableaux-based solvers etc. Modern SAT solvers can decide propositional formulas with thousands variables and clauses (Lynce & Marques-Silva, 2002).

2.2.1 *Deduction in Propositional Logic*

There is a number of inference systems for propositional logic. Most of them are actually restrictions of inference systems for first-order logic. Hilbert-style inference system consists of the following axiom schemes (Mendelson, 1997):

(A1) $A \Rightarrow (B \Rightarrow A)$
(A2) $(A \Rightarrow (B \Rightarrow C)) \Rightarrow ((A \Rightarrow B) \Rightarrow (A \Rightarrow C))$
(A3) $(\neg B \Rightarrow \neg A) \Rightarrow ((\neg B \Rightarrow A) \Rightarrow B)$

and the inference rule *modus ponens*: A, A$\Rightarrow$B $\vdash$ B.

A *proof* or a *derivation* in a Hilbert system is a finite sequence of formulas such that each element is either an axiom or follows from earlier formulas by the rule of inference. A proof of a derivation from a set S of formulas is a finite sequence of formulas such that each term is either an axiom, or is a member of S, or follows from earlier formulas by the rule of inference.

If there is a proof for A, then A is a *theorem* and we denote that by $\vdash$ A. For example, it can be proved that A $\Rightarrow$ A is a theorem, as follows:

1. $(A \Rightarrow ((A \Rightarrow A) \Rightarrow A)) \Rightarrow ((A \Rightarrow (A \Rightarrow A)) \Rightarrow (A \Rightarrow A))$ (instance of A2)

2. $A \Rightarrow ((A \Rightarrow A) \Rightarrow A)$ (instance of A1)

3. $(A \Rightarrow (A \Rightarrow A)) \Rightarrow (A \Rightarrow A)$ (from 1 and 2, by MP)

4. $A \Rightarrow (A \Rightarrow A)$ (instance of A1)

5. $A \Rightarrow A$ (from 3 and 4, by MP)

This may seem like a lot of work to prove that "A implies A", but that's the nature of formal logic systems! Derivations are broken down into extremely small steps that are rigorously mathematically justified. In human commonsense inference we tend to proceed in large leaps instead, at least on the conscious level – but unconsciously, our brains are carrying out multitudes of small steps, though the analogy between these small steps and the small steps in logical proofs is a subject of debate in the AI and cognitive science community.

There is a link between the semantics of propositional logic and the above Hilbert-style system stating that the system is *sound* and *complete:* every theorem is tautology, and every tautology is theorem, i.e., $\models$ A if and only if $\vdash$ A.

While the above is a standard and workable, approach, there are also other inference systems for propositional logic, including the one obtained as restrictions of Gentzen natural deduction and sequent calculus (see the section on first-order logic). There are also variants for classical and for intuitionistic propositional logic: in the former A$\vee\neg$A is a theorem, and in the latter it is not (the above Hilbert-style system is classical).

2.3 Review of Predicate Logic

Standard, first-order predicate logic builds on propositional logic as defined above. We will review it using the same categories of syntax, semantics and deduction.

Firstly, syntax. Let Σ be a finite or a countable set, its elements will be called function symbols. Let Π be a finite or a countable set, its elements will be called predicate symbols. Let *arity* be a function that maps elements of Σ and Π to natural numbers. The triple

$(\Sigma, \Pi, arity)$ is called a *signature*. The set of *terms* over a signature $(\Sigma, \Pi, arity)$ and a countable set of variables V is defined in the following way:

- all elements of V are terms;
- if f is a function symbol and arity(f)$=0$, then f is a term;
- if f is a function symbol and arity(f)$=n$, and if $t_1, \ldots, t_n$ are terms, then $f(t_1, \ldots, t_n)$ is a term.
- each term is obtained by a finite number of applications of the above rules.

The set of atomic formulas over a signature $(\Sigma, \Pi, arity)$ and a countable set of variables V is defined in the following way:

- $\perp$ and $\top$ are atomic formulas;
- if p is a predicate symbol and arity(p)$=n$, and if $t_1, \ldots, t_n$ are terms, then $p(t_1, \ldots, t_n)$ is an atomic formula.
- each atomic formula is obtained by a finite number of applications of the above rules.

The set of formulas over a signature $(\Sigma, \Pi, arity)$ and a countable set of variables V is defined in the following way:

- each atomic formulas is a formula;
- if A is a formula, then so is $\neg A$;
- if A and B are formulas, then so are $A \wedge B$, $A \vee B$, $A \Rightarrow B$, $A \Leftrightarrow B$;
- if A is a formula and v is a variable, then $(\forall x)A$ and $(\exists x)A$ are formulas;
- each formula is obtained by a finite number of applications of the above rules.

Next, semantics. The *meaning* of a formula is defined with respect to a pair (D,I), where D is a non-empty set, called the *domain*, and I is a mapping such that:

- To each function symbol of arity 0, I associates an element c from D;
- To each function symbol of arity $n > 0$, I associates a total function f^I from D^n to D;
- To each predicate symbol of arity $n > 0$, I associates a total function p^I from D^n to $\{0, 1\}$.

A valuation v, in this context, is defined as a mapping from the set of variable V to the set D. An *interpretation* I_v of terms, with respect to a pair (D,I) and a valuation v is defined in the following way:

- $I_v(t) = v(t)$, if t is an element V;
- $I_v(t) = I(t)$, if t is a function symbol and arity$(t) = 0$;

- $I_v(f(t_1,\ldots,t_n)) = f^I(I_v(t_1),\ldots,I_v(t_n)))$ where $f^I = I(f)$.

An interpretation I_v of formulas, with respect to a pair (D,I) and a valuation v is defined in the following way:

- $I_v(\bot)=0$ and $I_v(\top)=1$
- $I_v(p(t_1, \ldots, t_n))= p^I (I(t_1), \ldots, I(t_n)))$ where $p^I=I(p)$.
- $I_v (\neg A)=1- I_v (A)$;
- $I_v (A \wedge B)=\min(I_v (A), I_v (B))$;
- $I_v (A \vee B)=\max(I_v (A), I_v (B))$;
- $I_v (A{\Rightarrow}B)=\max(1-I_v (A), I_v (B))$;
- $I_v (A{\Leftrightarrow}B)=1$, If $I_v (A)= I_v(B)$ and $I_v (A{\Leftrightarrow}B)=0$ otherwise.
- $I_v((\forall x)A)=1$, if for every valuation w that is identical to v, with a possible exception of x, it holds $I_w(A)=1$. Otherwise, $I_v((\forall x)A)=0$;
- $I_v((\exists x)A)=1$, if there is a valuation w that is identical to v, with a possible exception of x, such that it holds $I_w(A)=1$. Otherwise, $I_v((\exists x)A)=0$.

If there is a pair (D,I) and a valuation v, such that $I_v(A)=1$, then A is *satisfiable*, otherwise it is unsatisfiable, or inconsistent. If for a fixed pair (D,I) it holds that $I_v(A)=1$ for arbitrary valuation v, then A is *valid with respect to* (D,I). If it holds that $I_v(A)=1$ for arbitrary pair (D,I) and for arbitrary valuation v, then A is *valid* and we denote that by $\models$ A.

For instance, if the domain D is the set of natural numbers and if I maps p to the relation $\leqslant$, then $I_v((\forall x)p(x,x))=1$ in every valuation v, hence the formula $(\forall x)p(x,x)$ is valid with respect to (D,I).

2.3.1 *Deduction in First-Order Logic*

Deduction in first-order logic is similar conceptually to its analogue in propositional logic, but more complex in detail due to the presence of quantified variables. There are several different deductive systems available; one of the first was developed by Hilbert in the early 20th century and we will describe it now. In Hilbert's systems, formulas are built using only the connectives $\Rightarrow$ and $\neg$, and the quantifiers $\forall$ ("for all") and $\exists$ ("there exists"). The system consists of the following axiom schemes:

(A1) $A \Rightarrow (B \Rightarrow A)$

(A2) $(A \Rightarrow (B \Rightarrow C)) \Rightarrow ((A \Rightarrow B) \Rightarrow (A \Rightarrow C))$

(A3) $(\neg B \Rightarrow \neg A) \Rightarrow ((\neg B \Rightarrow A) \Rightarrow B)$

(A4) $(\forall x)A \Rightarrow A[x \rightarrow t]$, while the term t is free for x in A

(A5) $(\forall x)(A \Rightarrow B) \Rightarrow (A \Rightarrow (\forall x)B)$, while A does not involve free occurrences of x

and the following inference rules:

Modus ponens: $A, A \Rightarrow B \vdash B$

Gen: $A \vdash (\forall x)A$

A proof or a derivation in a Hilbert system is a finite sequence of formulas such that each element is either an axiom or follows from earlier formulas by one of the rules of inference. A proof of a derivation from a set S of formulas is a finite sequence of formulas such that each formula is either an axiom, or is a member of S, or follows from earlier formulas by one of the rules of inference. If there is a proof for A, then A is a theorem and we denote that by $\vdash$ A.

There is a link between the semantics of first order logic and the above Hilbert-style system stating that the system is *sound* and *complete:* every theorem is valid formula, and every valid formula is theorem, i.e., $\models$ A if and only if $\vdash$ A.

In Hilbert-style systems, even for trivial statements, proofs can be non-trivial and rather unintuitive. However, although this kind of system is very demanding for practical use, it is very suitable for formal analyses of formal logic (since it has just a few axioms and inference rules). On the other hand, Gentzen constructed (in the 1930's) a "natural deduction" system, that better reflects usual mathematical reasoning. The price for this increased naturalness is a larger set of inference rules – one for eliminating and one for introducing each logical connective ($\neg$, $\wedge$, $\vee$, $\Rightarrow$, $\Leftrightarrow$) and quantifier ($\forall$, $\exists$), and one for eliminating the logical constant $\bot$ (13 rules altogether). On the other hand, there is just one axiom scheme ($A \vee \neg A$), which is not even needed if one adopts the intuitionistic version of Gentzen's logic.

Some of the rules in Gentzen's deductive system are:

$$\frac{A}{A \vee B} \text{ (introducing } \vee)$$

$$\frac{A \quad \neg A}{\bot} \text{ (eliminating } \neg)$$

$$\frac{A \quad A \Rightarrow B}{B} \text{ (eliminating } \Rightarrow)$$

and so forth.

Proofs in Gentzen's natural deduction are usually represented as trees with the statement to be proved in the root (at the bottom), and with axioms or assumptions in leaves (all these assumptions have to be *eliminated* along the proof). Somewhat different in nature from usual mathematical proofs, is the Gentzen's sequent calculus, suitable for formal analyses and for automation. The elementary object in this system is a *sequent*, a construct of the form $A_1, A_2, ..., A_n \vdash B_1, B_2, ..., B_m$. The calculus itself consists of the inference rules for introducing logical connectives and quantifiers on both sides of sequents, for instance:

$$\frac{\Gamma \vdash \Theta, A}{\neg A, \Gamma \vdash \Theta} \text{ (introducing } \neg \text{ left)}$$

There are also structural rules for dealing with formulas within one side of a sequent, for instance:

$$\frac{\Gamma \vdash \Theta}{D, \Gamma \vdash \Theta} \text{ (weakening)}$$

There are many variations of the above inference systems, both for first order logic and for other theories. The above systems can also be used as inference systems for propositional logic – it suffices to omit all axioms and rules involving quantifiers.

Finally, it is worth noting that first-order logic is semi-decidable, which means that there can be an algorithm that can always confirm a valid formula is indeed valid (i.e, is a theorem), but cannot always detect that a non-valid formula is not valid. Things are simpler in propositional logic which is decidable, meaning that there is an algorithm which can always decide whether a given propositional formula is valid or not.

2.3.2   *First-order Theories*

Next, one can extend basic predicate logic by defining "theories" within it, which extend the basic axioms by adding other specialized axioms. We will be doing a lot of this in the present book, in the context of specialized theories about time and space.

Mathematically, we say that each such theory has a certain "signature," consisting of specific sets Σ and Π of function and predicate symbol (with certain arities) extending the basic ones used in predicate logic. Beside the new symbols, to create a theory one has to provide a list of axioms (in the described language). These axioms are then used within a selected deductive framework (e.g., Hilbert's system, Gentzen's natural deduction, etc.) as additional axioms of the system.

If a theory T is defined by a signature $(\Sigma, \Pi, arity)$, and within a deductive system, then we often write $T \vdash F$ or $\vdash_T F$ to denote that the formula F can be derived in the theory T (i.e., F is a theorem of T).

As an example within mathematics, the branch of math called "group theory" can be constructed easily as an extension of "pure" predicate logic. In this formalization, the signature of theory of group consists of:

- Functional symbol 0 (of arity 0);
- Functional symbol $+$ (of arity 2);
- Functional symbol $-$ (of arity 1);
- Predicate symbol $=$ (of arity 2),

And, the axioms of the theory of groups are:

$$(\forall x)(x = x)$$
$$(\forall x)(\forall y)(x = y \Rightarrow -x = -y)$$
$$(\forall x_1)(\forall x_2)(\forall y_1)(\forall y_2)(x_1 = y_1 \wedge x_2 = y_2 \Rightarrow x_1 + x_2 = y_1 + y_2)$$
$$(\forall x_1)(\forall x_2)(\forall y_1)(\forall y_2)(x_1 = y_1 \wedge x_2 = y_2 \Rightarrow (x_1 = x_2 \Rightarrow y_1 = y_2))$$
$$(\forall x)(\forall y)(\forall z)(x + (y + z) = (x + y) + z)$$
$$(\forall x)(x + 0 = 0 + x = x)$$
$$(\forall x)(x + (-x) = (-x) + x = 0)$$

These axioms, added on to the regular axioms of predicate logic, tell you how to use the entities $\{0, +, -, =\}$ in the manner required in group theory. For instance, it can be proved that the following formula is theorem of the theory of groups:

$$(\forall x)(\forall y)(\forall z)(x + z = y + z \Rightarrow x = y)$$

What we'll see later on in this book are similar theories that involve, not $\{0, +, -, =\}$ but rather entities such as time intervals, spatial regions, and relationships between them.

Finally, although we won't make use of this here, it's worth noting that, apart from the axiomatic approach to defining theories, theories can be also defined semantically. For a given signature L and a corresponding pair (D,I), a theory of a structure is the set of all sentences over L that are true in (D,I).

2.3.3   *Forward and Backward Chaining*

There are two basic search strategies for using inference rules in theorem-proving, and other related AI areas:

- Forward chaining

- Backward chaining

Both strategies are applied to tasks of the same sort: given a set of facts (axioms) and a set of inference rules, the task is to check whether some given fact (formula) F can be derived. The difference between the two strategies is the direction of their search. Namely, forward chaining (also known as *data-driven search*) starts with the available facts and derive all facts that can be derived, until the given fact F is reached. On the other hand, backward chaining (also known as *goal-driven search*) starts with the given goal F and apply inference rules in opposite direction, producing new subgoals and trying to reach the facts already available.

Let us consider the following example. Let there be given facts:

1) Derek will go out for lunch.
2) If Alison goes out for lunch, then Bob will go out for lunch as well.
3) If Bob goes out for lunch, then Clark will go out for lunch as well.
4) If Derek goes out for lunch, then Ellen will go out for lunch as well.
5) If Ellen goes out for lunch, then Clark will go out for lunch as well.

and assume the (only) inference rule is *modus ponens*: if X and X $\Rightarrow$ Y, then Y. The goal to be proved is "Clark will go out for lunch".

Forward chaining will try to match any two facts with X and X $\Rightarrow$ Y in order to apply modus ponens and to derive new facts. One (and the only at this step) option is to use the facts 1 and 4 and derive the fact "Ellen will go out for lunch". Then, in next step, this new fact and the fact 5 yield "Clark will go out for lunch", which was required.

Backward chaining starts from the goal – from the fact "Clark will go out for lunch". If it is matched with Y in modus ponens, then the new subgoals will be X and X $\Rightarrow$ Y, where X can be *anything*. The subgoal X $\Rightarrow$ Y matches the fact 3, so X is matched with "Bob will go out for lunch". When proving this subgoal, the fact 2 is used and a new subgoal "Alison will go for lunch" should be proved. However, this leads to failure. Another option is the following: the subgoal X $\Rightarrow$ Y matches also the fact 5, so X is matched with "Ellen will go out for lunch". When proving this subgoal, the fact 4 is used and a new subgoal "Derek will go out for lunch" should be proved. This is trivially true, by the fact 1. So, it was proved that "Clark will go out for lunch", as required.

The above description of forward and backward chaining is simplified. Typical applications of forward and backward chaining involve different methods of directing the search. Namely, the main problem that both strategies face is search expense, due to typically huge numbers of combinatorial options that have to be considered. Neither of these approaches is superior to the other one, and there are domains in which one if more appropriate than another. There are also hybrid approaches that combine forward and backward search.

2.3.4 *Decidability and Decision Procedures*

In this section we briefly introduce a distinction that may be important in practical large-scale logic-based systems: the distinction between proof procedures and decision procedures. Put simply:

- a proof procedure finds a specific series of steps for getting to a certain conclusion from the axioms of a logical theory
- a decision procedure checks whether a certain conclusion can be obtained from the axioms of a logical theory, without necessarily directly supplying the proof (the series of steps)

In practical cases, given the outcome of a decision procedure, plus knowledge of the algorithm used to carry out the decision procedure, it is in principle possible to construct a proof. But this may be quite laborious. In some situations, if one just needs to know whether something is true or not in a certain formal theory, it may be easier to use a decision procedure than to find a specific proof.

In the formal lingo of logic, one says a theory T is *decidable* if there is an algorithm that for any sentence F of T it can decide whether F is theorem of T or not. Such an algorithm is called a *decision procedure*. An example of a decision procedure for propositional logic is the DPLL (Davis-Putnam-Logemann-Loveland) procedure, which lies at the core of all modern SAT solvers. A SAT solver is a program that checks if a large propositional-logic formula can possibly be satisfied by any assignment of values to variables or not; and doing this via a decision procedure rather than a proof procedure is vastly more computationally efficient. SAT solvers are used in a huge variety of practical applications nowadays, including circuit analysis, natural language parsing, and all manner of large-scale discrete optimization problems. If one had to approach these problems using direct theorem proving in propositional logic, then one would run into terrible combinatorial explosions and quite possibly formal logic would need to be set aside in favor of some different analytical approach.

There are many widely applied decision procedures for first-order theories, including decision procedures for linear arithmetic over reals (involving only addition, not multiplication), multiplicative arithmetic over reals (involving only multiplication, not addition), theory of lists, theory of arrays, etc. (Barrett *et al.*, 2009). There is a family of modern decision procedures for first-order theories, heavily using propositional reasoning and SMT (satisfiability modulo theory) techniques. Decision procedures and SMT solvers are widely applied in software and hardware verification.

Mathematically speaking, there are many important theories that are not decidable, such as arithmetic over natural numbers, the theory of groups, etc. Hence, for these theories there can be no decision procedures, only heuristics that can prove/disprove certain classes of formulas. However, undecidability always involves infinity in some form; if one restricts attention to a finite set of data items (as is always the case in practical applications), then it is not an issue.

In practical applications, the use of decision procedures is sometimes unavoidable. However, developing an efficient decision procedure is not an easy task – it requires specific knowledge about the theory. There is no generic (decidable) method for constructing efficient decision procedures. In the case of temporal and spatial logics such as we will discuss here, scientists have not yet created appropriate specialized decision procedures, but this seems a highly worthy area of investigation.

2.4 Simple Examples of Formal Logical Inference

We've been discussing logic in an extremely abstract and mathematical way – but our main goal here is *real-world* reasoning, not mathematical reasoning. So before progressing further in the direction of elaborating abstract logic systems, we will digress a bit to clarify the relationship between logic and commonsense inference. This is after all where logic started: formal logic originated, not as a branch of math, but from the motivation of formalizing everyday human thinking. Many real world problems can be formulated in terms of propositional or first order logic. It is only during the last century and a half that logic has become a sophisticated branch of mathematics.

2.4.1 *Example of Kings and Queens*

Consider the following example, from (Hayes, 1997). The king and his family want to make a party for some ambassadors in their kingdom. The king, the queen, and the prince give their orders to the head of protocol and he has to make a final list of guests. The king said that either the ambassador of Peru, or the ambassador of Qatar, or the ambassador of

Romania should be invited. The queen said that if the ambassadors of Qatar and Romania are invited, then the ambassador of Peru should be invited too. The prince said that if the ambassador of Romania is invited, then the ambassadors of Peru or the ambassador of Qatar should be invited. The question is whether the head of protocol can obey all orders. The problem can be formulated in terms of propositional logic in the following way. Let us denote by p, q, r the fact that the ambassador of Peru, Qatar, Romania will be invited.

Then the orders can be formulated as follows:

- King's order: $p \lor q \lor r$
- Queen's order: $(q \land r) \Rightarrow p$
- Prince's order: $r \Rightarrow p \lor q$

Or, equivalently:

- King's order: $p \lor q \lor r$
- Queen's order: $\neg q \lor \neg r \lor p$
- Prince's order: $\neg r \lor p \lor q$

To solve a problem, the head of protocol has to check whether the formula

$$(p \lor q \lor r) \land (\neg q \lor \neg r \lor p) \land (\neg r \lor p \lor q)$$

is satisfiable. He can use a SAT solver for that (and he can find that he can meet all orders by inviting only the ambassador of Peru). Or, as this is a simple case, using any reasonable propositional logic theorem prover would also work fine.

2.4.2 Example of Minesweeper

Or consider, as an another example, the popular computer game of Minesweeper, as depicted in Figure 2.1:

There is a board of $n \times m$ places. When a player selects one position on the board, the game is over if it contains a mine. Otherwise, the player gets the number of mines in the adjacent positions. Let us denote by p, q, r, s, t, u six positions in the left upper corner of the board: Let us suppose that we open the position p, and there is no mine. Let us also suppose that we got the number 1 for the position p. If we open a position q and we get the answer 1 again, we can safely open the positions r and u. The explanation is as follows. We associate a propositional variable to each position – the variable is true if there is a mine on the position, and the variable is false otherwise. Since there is no mine on the position p, it

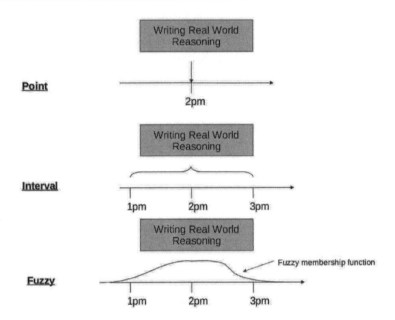

Fig. 2.1   A screenshot of a Minesweeper GUI

follows that:

$$\neg p$$

Since the position p has the associated value 1, there is one mine on either q, s, or t. We can encode this as follows:

$$q \vee s \vee t$$

$$q \Rightarrow \neg s \wedge \neg t$$

$$s \Rightarrow \neg q \wedge \neg t$$

$$t \Rightarrow \neg q \wedge \neg s$$

Since there is no mine on the position q, it follows that:

$$\neg q$$

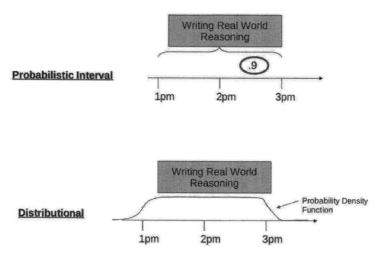

Fig. 2.2

Since the position q has the value 1, it means that there is one mine on either p, s, t, r, or u. We can encode this as follows:

$$p \lor s \lor t \lor r \lor u$$

$$p \Rightarrow \neg s \land \neg t \land \neg r \land \neg u$$

$$s \Rightarrow \neg p \land \neg t \land \neg r \land \neg u$$

$$t \Rightarrow \neg p \land \neg s \land \neg r \land \neg u$$

$$r \Rightarrow \neg p \land \neg s \land \neg t \land \neg u$$

$$u \Rightarrow \neg p \land \neg s \land \neg t \land \neg r$$

The question is whether one can safely open the position r, i.e., whether r is consistent with the above formulas (i.e., is it possible that there is a mine on r). A SAT solver (applied to the above formulas) would easily find that such a set of formulas is not consistent, so there cannot be a mine on the position r (and, similarly, there cannot be a mine on the position u).

2.4.3 *Example of Socrates*

The above examples all involve propositional rather than predicate logic. Concerning first-order logic, consider the following classical example. One is given the following two facts:

- Socrates is a man.

- All men are mortal.

We can encode this in first-order logic as follows:

- man(Socrates)
- $(\forall x)(\mathrm{man}(x) \Rightarrow \mathrm{mortal}(x))$

Applying deduction allows us to conclude that, since Socrates is a man, he must be mortal. For instance, a very simple proof procedure can verify that mortal(Socrates) is a consequence of the above facts by verifying that $\neg$mortal(Socrates) is inconsistent with the above formulas.

2.5 Modal logic

Propositional logic and first-order logic are sometimes not expressive enough for some sorts of common-sense reasoning. For instance, one may wish to extend them using so-called modal statements including qualifiers like necessary, possibly, future, past, etc. For such cases, specific logics are used, such as modal and temporal logics. These logics are not contradictory to first-order logic, and in fact could be viewed as specialized theories constructed within first-order logic; but this is not always the most useful way to look at them. It is often more helpful to think about them as alternative formalizations of logic.

Modal logic describes logical relations of modal notions. These notions may include metaphysical modalities (necessities, possibilities, etc.), epistemic modalities (knowledge, belief, etc.), temporal modalities (future, past, etc.), and deontic modalities (obligation, permission, etc.). Modal logics are widely used in philosophy, artificial intelligence, database theory, and game theory. Modern work on modal logics started in 1918. with the monograph *A Survey of Symbolic Logic* by C. I. Lewis.

The main metaphysical modal notions are *necessity* and *possibility*; and the modal logic that describe logical relations over them is called *alethic modal logic*. In alethic modal logic, one can express a statement like "It is possible that Bob quit his job". The modailities are represented by modal operators. Formulas are built using propositional connectives and these modal operators. The basic unary modal operators are usually written $\square$ (or L) for necessarily and $\lozenge$ (or M) for possibly. These two operators are linked in the following way:

$$\lozenge p \Leftrightarrow \neg \square \neg p$$
$$\square p \Leftrightarrow \neg \lozenge \neg p.$$

There is a number of modal extensions of some underlying logics, including the extension of first-order logic, called *modal predicate logic*.

The standard semantics of modal logics is Kripke semantics. The concept of the Kripke semantics of propositional modal logic includes:

- A non-empty set W – a set of possible worlds;
- A two-place relation R on elements from W – the *accessibility relation* between worlds, which represents the possible worlds that are considered in a given world, i.e., if we consider a world w_0, every world v such that it is in relation R with w_0 represents a possibility that is considered at a world w_0;
- A *frame* – a tuple (W, R);

Given a frame (W, R), a *model M* is a tuple (W, R, V) where V is a map that assigns to a world a valuation on propositional variables, i.e. for a given world w, $V(w)$ is a function from the set of propositional variables to $\{0, 1\}$. Interpretation of a formula F with respect to M *is* defined in the following way (the fact that F is true at a world w in a model M) is denoted by $M, w \models F$:

$M, w \models p$ iff $V(w)(p) = 1$ (where p is a propositional variable)

$M, w \models F \wedge F'$ iff $M, w \models F$ and $M, w \models F'$.

$M, w \models \neg F$ iff *not* $M, w \models F$

$M, w \models \Box F$ iff, for every world w' such that it is in relation R with w it holds that, $M, w' \models F$

The semantics of other propositional connectives and the operator $\Diamond$ are implied by the above definition. A formula is then defined to be *valid* in a model M if it is true at every possible world in M. A formula is *valid* if it is valid in all frames (or every model).

For the given semantics, there is a sound and complete inference system for propositional modal logic – the system **K**. In addition to underlying propositional axioms and inference rules, there is the axiom

$$\Box(F \Rightarrow F') \Rightarrow (\Box F \Rightarrow \Box F')$$

and the rule

$$\text{if } \vdash F, \text{ then } \vdash \Box F$$

There are various inference systems for propositonal modal logic obtained by adding extra axioms to **K**.

There are also fuzzy versions of modal logics (Thiele, 1993; Ying, 1988).

2.6 Deontic logic

An interesting specialization of modal logic, which is potentially useful for doing logical inference about human behaviors and motivations, is deontic logic – which is concerned with the ideal and actual behavior of social agents, and involves notions like permissible, impermissible, obligatory, gratuitous, optional, etc. Deontic logic has many analogies with alethic modal logic. In addition to theoretical interest, deontic logics are used for formalizing different real-world concepts and problems such as morality, normative law, legal analysis, social and business organizations and security systems, computer security, electronic commerce, or legal expert systems.

A survey of applications of deontic logic in computer science can be found in (Wieringa & Meyer, 1993), which supplies the following systematization of applications of deontic logic in computer science:

1. Fault-tolerant computer systems.
2. Normative user behavior.
3. Normative behavior in or of the organization.

    (a) Policy specification.
    (b) Normative organization behavior (e.g. contracting).

4. Normative behavior of the object system.

    (a) The specification of law.
    (b) The specification of legal thinking.
    (c) The specification of normative rules as deontic integrity constraints.
    (d) Other applications, not discussed above.

The first formalization of deontic logic was given by E. Mally in 1926. More details on deontic logic can be found in (McNamara & Prakken, 1999).

In the "Traditional scheme" for deontic logic, there are five normative statuses considered:

- it is obligatory that (OB)
- it is permissible that (PE)
- it is impermissible that (IM)
- it is gratuitous that (GR)
- it is optional that (OP)

The first one of the above can be used as a basis, while the remaining ones can be defined in the following way:

$$PEp \Leftrightarrow \neg OB\neg p$$

$$IMp \Leftrightarrow OB\neg p$$

$$GRp \Leftrightarrow \neg OBp$$

$$OPp \Leftrightarrow (\neg OBp \wedge \neg OB\neg p)$$

Standard Deontic Logic (SDL) is the most studied deontic logic. It extends propositional logic by the (one-place) **OB** deontic operator. Formulas are built in the standard modal-logic way. The semantics of SDL is usually given in Kripke-style. The inference system for SDL consists of axioms for (classical) propositional calculus and inference rules, the additional inference rule "if $\vdash p$ then $\vdash OBp$" *and the following axioms:*

$$OB(p \Rightarrow q) \Rightarrow (OBp \Rightarrow OBq)$$

$$OBp \Rightarrow \neg OB\neg p$$

Consider the following simple example. Let us assume that the hypotheses are:

It ought to be the case that Alison does the paperwork.
If Alison does the paperwork, then Alison leaves the office late.

Let us denote Alison does the paperwork by p and Alison leaves the office late by q:

*Then, we can prove It ought to be the case that Alison leaves the office late (i.e., **OB**q) as follows:*

(C1) **OB**p *(hypothesis)*

(C2) p⇒q *(hypothesis)*

(C3) **OB**(p⇒q) *(deontic inference rule, from (C2))*

(C4) **OB**(p⇒q) ⇒ (**OB**p ⇒ **OB**q) *(deontic axiom)*

(C5) **OB**p ⇒ **OB**q *(Modus ponens, from (C3) and (C4))*

(C6) **OB**q *(Modus ponens, from (C1) and (C5))*

There is a number of variants of the SDL inference system and there are interesting *logical and philosophical considerations for each of them.*

2.6.1   *Fuzzy deontic logic*

While there is a number of approaches to fuzzy modal logic (see the next chapter for a recall of fuzzy logic), there is a very limited literature on fuzzy deontic logic. One version of fuzzy deontic logic was introduced and discussed by (Gounder & Esterline, 1998). In their framework, given the statements

p = Person p receives a driver's license.

q = Person p is 18 or older.

r = Person p is an employee of company c.

s = Person p is over 80 years old.

t = Person p is under 20 years old.

u = Company c gives its employees a bonus.

v = The employees of company c arrive at work not more than ten minutes late.

one can consider the following interesting deontic statements:

$$\mathbf{OB}(p \Rightarrow q)$$
$$\mathbf{OB}p \Rightarrow \mathbf{OB}q$$
$$r \Rightarrow \mathbf{OB}(\neg s \wedge \neg t)$$
$$u \Rightarrow \mathbf{OB}v$$

These statements need not be crisp, but can be in a permissible range which is given in the fuzzy truth value in the interval [0, 1] and one obligation may lead to another obligation.

Concerning reasoning in this theory, as said in (Gounder & Esterline, 1998), since fuzzy logics work with numerical measures, axiomatic systems are not appropriate. Instead, fuzzy versions of the semantic properties exist and can be shown to correspond to some of the axioms for the crisp systems in special ways that support dependency among assertions in a modal domain.

2.7   The frame problem

A final issue that must be discussed, in the context of knowledge representation using formal logic, is the "frame problem," as originally recognized and named in (McCarthy & Hayes, 1969). Put most simply, this is the problem of representing the effects of action without having to represent explicitly a large number of intuitively obvious non-effects (i.e., properties that are not affected by the action). The frame problem also has a wider epistemological importance and it considers whether it is possible, in principle, to limit the scope of the reasoning required to derive the consequences of an action. The name "frame problem" was derived from a common technique used in producing animated cartoons where the currently moving parts of the cartoon are superimposed on the "frame", which depicts the non changing background of the scene.

While the frame problem is a major issue for certain approaches to logic-based AI, we don't see it as an objection to scalably deploying logic-based technology to draw inferences based on large spatiotemporal knowledge bases (nor to other scalable real-world inference applications). Rather, we see it as an objection to embedding logical inference engines in overly simplistic cognitive architectures. We believe the frame problem can be bypassed via judicious inference control heuristics, including some that are implicit in the ideas discussed in the previous section, and some others that will be discussed here.

2.7.1 Review of the Frame Problem

To elaborate the frame problem a little more fully, suppose we have the following knowledge:

- Alison is in her office and she wears a blue suit.
- If Alison moves from her office, then she is in the loby.

If we represent the above in classical first-order logic, using some suitable formalism for representing time and action (e.g., CTL logic, or an appropriate subset of PLN, both discussed below), we can derive that after Alison moves from her office she will be in the lobby. However, we will not be able to derive that Alison's suit is still blue. Namely, the knowledge given above does not rule out the possibility that the color of Alison's suit changes when she moves out of her office. A straightforward solution for this is to add rules that explicitly describe the non-effects of each action (e.g., "when Alison moves from her office, the color of her suit does not change"). Such formulae are called *frame axioms*. However, this is not a satisfactory solution. Namely, since *most* actions do not affect *most* properties of a situation, in a domain comprising M actions and N properties we will, in general, have to write out MN frame axioms which would make any reasoning process impractical.

In (Shanahan & Baars, 2005) there is a more detailed account on the frame problem, including a brief description of Dennett' memorable example:

... consider the challenge facing the designers of an imaginary robot whose task is to retrieve an object resting on a wagon in a nearby room. But the room also contains a bomb, which is timed to explode soon. The first version of the robot successfully works out that it must pull the wagon out of the room. Unfortunately, the bomb is on the wagon. And although the robot knows the bomb is on the wagon, it fails to notice that pulling the wagon out brings the bomb along too. So the designers produce a second version of the robot. This model works out all the consequences of its actions before doing anything. But the new robot gets blown up too, because

it spends too long in the room working out what will happen when it moves the wagon. It had just finished deducing that pulling the wagon out of the room would not change to color of the room's walls, and was embarking on a proof of the further implication that pulling the wagon out would cause its wheels to turn more revolutions than there were wheels on the wagon— when the bomb exploded. So the robot builders come up with a third design. This robot is programmed to tell the difference between relevant and irrelevant implications. When working out the consequences of its actions, it considers only the relevant ones. But to the surprise of its designers, this version of the robot fares no better. Like its predecessor, it sits in the room "thinking" rather than acting. "Do something!" they yelled at it. "I am," it retorted. "I'm busily ignoring some thousands of implications I have determined to be irrelevant. Just as soon as I find an irrelevant implication, I put it on the list of those I must ignore, and." the bomb went off.

It is obvious that the human brain incorporates a solution to the frame problem and does not suffer from overwhelming information when deriving new conclusions. When we say that Alison left her office, we don't need to state explicitly that her suit hasn't change its color, that Bob's cat hasn't changed its sex, that the Sun continues to shine, etc. Such information is taken for granted by common sense. In mathematical logic, however, nothing is taken for granted and in classical logic it is necessary to represent explicitly all the things that change and all the things that do not change by some action.

2.7.2 *Working around the Frame Problem*

Perhaps the best-known attempt to work around the frame problem, within the scope of logic-based AI, begins from the observation that the inference process in classical logic is *monotonic*, meaning that the set of conclusion can only grow when we add new premises (we do not retract some conclusions if we are presented with some new premise). But, it would be nicer if one could infer that Alison's suit is, generally, of the same color when she leaves her office and, in addition, it would be suitable, to add some exceptions, stating otherwise ("If Alison spilled coffee on her suit, then she has to change her suit before she leave her office"). In other words, one would like to be able to declare the general rule that an action can be assumed not to change a given property of a situation *unless* there is evidence to the contrary. Such reasoning is possible within non-monotonic logics. Despite the fact that there is also a number of problems with the frame problem when addressed by non-monotonic logics, it can be considered that they provide a satisfactory solution. In artificial intelligence, there are also some other approaches, that handle different incarnations of the frame problem with more or less success. The frame problem is still making an influence on issues in cognitive sciences, philosophy, psychology, etc.

Propositional and first-order logic as defined are monotonic. This means that the set of facts that can be derived from S increases when S increases. However, again, this is not appropriate for some sorts of common-sense reasoning. For example, if we are given a fact that Tweety is a bird, we by default derive the fact that Tweety flies. But, if we are given an additional fact that Tweety is a penguin, then we retract our conclusion and derive the new one – that Tweety does not fly. There is a family of logics following this motivation and trying to model common-sense reasoning, summarized for instance in (Reiter, 1980; Delgrande & Schaub, 2003)

However, nonmonotonic logic is not the only route for circumventing the frame problem; for instance in our own work with PLN, we have taken a significantly different approach, to which we will return in the final chapter of this book.

Chapter 3

Quantifying and Managing Uncertainty

Another major issue in formal logic systems is the quantification and incorporation of uncertainty. It is of course possible to represent uncertainty using theories within first-order logic, but many have argued that uncertainty is sufficiently basic to commonsense inference that it should be introduced into formal logic at a foundational level.

With this in mind, there are many different ways of representing uncertainty within logical formalisms. Some of the leading approaches may be summarized as:

- Fuzzy
- Traditional Probabilistic
- Imprecise / Indefinite Probabilistic

We have touched some of these briefly above, but we will now review them slightly more systematically.

3.1 Fuzzy logic

Fuzzy logic (Zadeh, 1965) extends the notion of boolean truth (true vs. false), to encompass degrees of truth varying between 0 and 1; and generalizes the standard boolean operators $\{\neg, \wedge, \vee\}$ by "fuzzified" counterparts. These generalized operators are usually (but not always) defined as follows:

$$\neg x = 1 - x$$
$$x \wedge y = \min(x, y)$$
$$x \vee y = \max(x, y)$$

It appears that for various instances of commonsense reasoning, fuzzy logic is more immediately appropriate than boolean crisp logic; for instance the fuzzy predicate:

$$(\text{strong}(x) \wedge \text{healthy}(x)) \vee \text{intelligent}(x)$$

allows one to characterize the degree to which a person is both strong and healthy, or
intelligent; while its boolean interpretation can only draw two crude categories for each
predicate, which does not fit how one would think about the proposition with our common
interpretation of the concepts strong, healthy and intelligent.

3.2   Possibility theory

In fuzzy logic, values associated to facts or propositions range from 0 to 1 but represent
truth values. In possibility theory (Zadeh, 1978), on the other hand, a proposition may be
boolean but what is considered instead is its degree of belief by an agent. That degree of
belief is represented by two values, the necessity denoted $\text{nec}(p)$ and the possibility denoted
$\text{pos}(p)$ representing the extent to which an agent considers p to be necessary and possible.
For instance $\text{pos}(\text{earth\_flat})=0.9$ and $\text{nec}(\text{earth\_flat})=0.2$ represent respectively how much
an agent believes the earth is possibly and necessarily flat.

The possibilities $\text{pos}(p)=1$ and $\text{pos}(\neg p)=1$ represent a total state of ignorance about
p, or equivalently $\text{nec}(p)=0$ and $\text{nec}(\neg p)=0$. Having $\text{pos}(p)=\text{pos}(\neg p)$ does not contradict
the principle of bivalence because this is the degree of belief of p which is considered not
its truth. Thus possibility and necessity are not self-dual, that is it is not the case that
$\text{pos}(p)=1\text{-pos}(\neg p)$, however there are mutually-dual as formalized by the following axiom:

$$\text{nec}(p)=1\text{-pos}(\neg p)$$

Other axioms permit one to determine the possibility and necessity of a formula based on
the possibilities and necessities of its components – but not always. For instance $\text{nec}(p \wedge q)$ equals to $\min(\text{nec}(p), \text{nec}(q))$ like in fuzzy logic, but $\text{pos}(p \wedge q)$ is not generally equal
to $\min(\text{pos}(p), \text{pos}(q))$; however one can always bound the latter value using necessity and
possibility measures combined:

$$\min(\text{nec}(p), \text{nec}(q)) \leqslant \text{pos}(p \wedge q) \leqslant \min(\text{pos}(p), \text{pos}(q))$$

Finally, although fuzzy logic and possibility theory are built around two different semantics,
if nec=pos then possibility theory amounts axiomatically to fuzzy logic (with the min/max
interpretation for $\wedge/\vee$); and for that reason possibility logic is sometimes referred as an
extension of fuzzy logic.

3.3 Inference using Traditional Probabilities

As probabilistic methods have become very popular in the AI field lately, there now exists a wide range of methods and theories regarding probabilistic inference and logic; we will only describe a handful of the most relevant ones here. To understand the following sections the reader needs to be familiar with probability theory.

3.3.1 *Bayesian Inference*

Methods to reason about probabilities include Bayesian inference and Bayesian networks, both called so because they mainly rely on Bayes' theorem, a formula from elementary probability theory recalled below:

$$P(Y \mid X) = P(X \mid Y)P(Y)/P(X)$$

Bayesian inference is a mean to infer or revise the probability of an hypothesis knowing a set of observations (for instance determining the probability of a disease in the presence of symptoms). Bayesian networks are graphical models, formally DAGs (directed acyclic graphs), representing dependencies and independencies between random variables. We will describe Bayesian networks in some detail here, as they will arise in later chapters when we discuss their applicability to mining causal relationships from large knowledge stores.

3.3.2 *Bayesian Networks*

A Bayesian network is a graphical model that represents a probabilistic joint distribution over a set of variables represented as nodes and direct dependences represented by arcs between nodes. More formally a Bayesian network is a DAG (directed acyclic graph), where each node contains a variable and a function representing a conditional probability of that variable knowing its parents, which are all variables that have an arc pointing to that given node. If the node has no parent then the function represents a marginal probability. See Figure 3.1 for an example of a Bayesian network with 4 variables.

Usually the probabilities, conditional and marginal, are coded into matrices. Figure 3.2 represents possible probabilities coded in matrices of the Bayesian network of Figure 3.1. They also can be coded in any other appropriate structures, like decision trees, decision graphs and such.

As mentioned above, direct dependences are represented with arcs between variables; additionally it is possible to assess the conditional dependence and independence of any

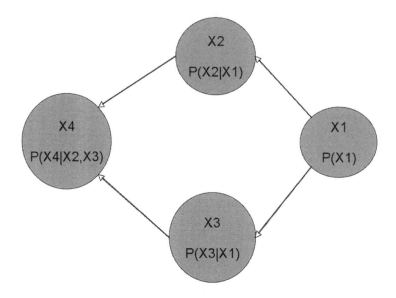

Fig. 3.1   A small Bayesian network

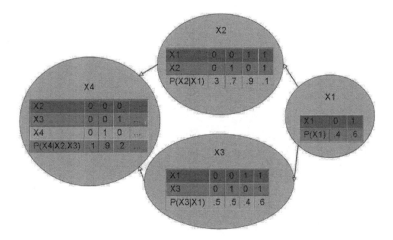

Fig. 3.2   Probability matrices associated with the network nodes

group of variables by applying the notion of d-separation introduced by Pearl [Pearl85]. When a triplet of variables **X, Y, Z** are d-separated then we can conclude that **X** and **Y** are independent conditionally to **Z**; and conversely if there are independent then they are d-separated (actually that equivalence between d-separation and independence does not always hold, only when the distribution is DAG-faithful; we won't recall what DAG-faithful is here, however one should note that most of practical real life distributions are DAG-faithful or close to it). We also won't recall the detailed definition of d-separation here, but what is most important to note here is that the d-separation criterion is a graphical one. This means that one can assess the dependences of variables solely based on the topology of the network, which in itself is a useful thing. Figure 3.3 and 3.4 display two examples of d-separated variables.

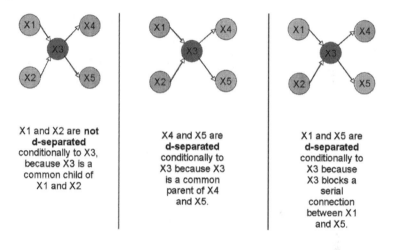

Fig. 3.3   *d*-separation in sets of variables

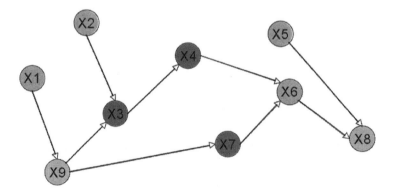

Fig. 3.4   *X*8 and *X*9 are d-separated conditionally to {*X*3, *X*4, *X*7} in this example

Given a Bayesian network one can compute the joint distribution of a set of variables $X_1, \ldots, X_n$ by applying the following formula:

$$P(X_1, \ldots, X_n) = \prod_{i=1}^{n} P(X_i \mid parents(X_i))$$

where *parent* (X_i) is the set of variables with outgoing arcs pointing to X_i.

It is worth noting that any distribution can be represented by a Bayesian network (see Figure 3.5 for an example of how that can be done). And there are usually many possible Bayesian networks to represent a given distribution, see Figure 3.6 for an example.

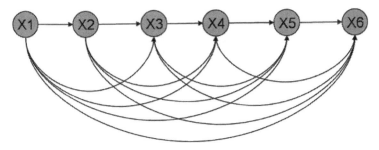

Fig. 3.5   Bayesian network so that parent $(Xi) = XI, \ldots, Xi - 1$

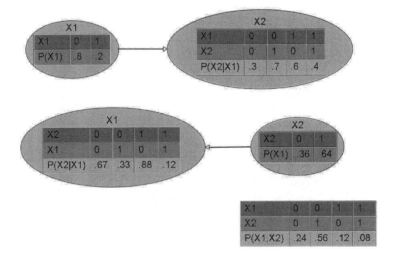

Fig. 3.6   Two Bayesian networks representing the same distribution (bottom)

3.3.3   *Bayesian Causal Networks*

Next, a Bayesian causal network is a Bayesian network where the arcs represent causal relationships. A probability distribution alone is usually not enough to determine causality, for reasons we reviewed earlier. And one needs additional knowledge either given by an expert (stating for instance that weather may influence ice cream sales but not the opposite), or coming from additional assumption, for instance the knowledge that if event A occurs before event B then A can be a cause of B but B cannot be a cause of A. Note however that this sort of assumption involving time must be used cautiously because when A occurs before B, both A and B may actually be the result of a common cause C; in this case, C is called a confounding variable. Real life is full of confounding variables!

Many techniques available for Bayesian networks apply with little or no modification to Bayesian causal networks. For instance Bayesian inference, described in the next section, works exactly the same for a causal or non causal Bayesian network. On the other hand, network learning techniques may diverge more significantly because they need to take into account additional background knowledge in order to decide whether or not a given causal relationship is authorized.

3.3.4   *Bayesian Inference*

Given a Bayesian network one can use it to perform various probabilistic inferences. In this context, inference means calculating joint marginal and conditional probabilities.

For instance, let us consider the Bayesian causal network of Figure 3.7.

Let I, P, O and R be binary random variables respectively representing Internet connection working, Pay-check arrived, On-line purchases and Router overloaded.

One may want for instance to know the probability that a particular individual is going to make on-line purchases knowing that his router is overloaded and he hasn't received his pay-check yet. That is, we want to compute the conditional probability:

$$P(O = 1 \mid R = 1, P = 0)$$

The basic method to compute the above is called variable elimination. That is, one eliminates by summation the variables which are absent of the conditional probability of interest, in this example the variable I. This permits one to compute any partial joint marginal probability and the conditional probability is obtained by normalization.

So, in the example, one needs to compute the joint marginal probabilities:

$$P(O = 1, R = 1, P = 0)$$

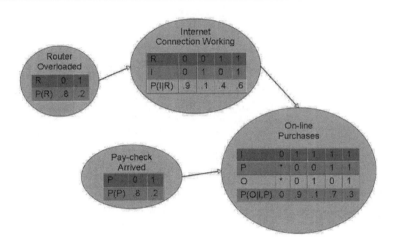

Fig. 3.7   Bayesian causal network

And the conditional probability is obtained by normalization:

$$P(O=1 \mid R=1, P=0) = P(O=1, R=1, P=0)/P(R=1, P=0)$$

Let's first compute

$$
\begin{aligned}
&P(O=1, R=1, P=0) \\
&= \sum_{i=0,1} P(I=i, O=1, P=0) \\
&= \sum_{i=0,1} P(R=1)P(I=i \mid R=1)P(P=0)P(O=1 \mid P=0, I=i) \\
&= P(R=1)P(P=0) \sum_{i=0,1} P(I=i \mid R=1)P(O=1 \mid P=0, I=i) \\
&= .2 \times .8 \times (.4 \times 0 + .6 \times .1) \\
&= .0096
\end{aligned}
$$

Then we compute $P(R=1, P=0)$, but since R and P are independent, according to the d-separation criteria, we can directly get $P(R=1) \times P(P=0) = .2 \times .8 = .16$

So the conditional probability of making on-line purchases is:

$$P(O=1 \mid R=1, P=0) = .0096/.16 = .06$$

There exists a variety of algorithms to perform these sorts of inferences, which include various optimizations, like caching and reusing intermediate results and using d-separation criteria (as we have done in the example above) to skip unnecessary summations.

3.3.5 *Markov Logic Networks*

Next, Markov Logic Networks (Richardson & Domingos, 2006) involve a combination of First Order Logic (FOL) and Markov Network. This constitutes an elegant way to define probability distributions over valuations (defined earlier in Section 2.2). Markov Networks are very similar to Bayesian Network but are represented by an undirected graph – instead of a DAG like in Bayesian Networks. As a Bayesian Network, a Markov Network can model any joint distribution; but it gives more compact models for certain classes of distributions. The notion of conditional independence has a simpler representation with Markov Networks. However traditional Bayesian Networks can explicitly represent causality while Markov Networks cannot.

In probability theory terms, the full joint distribution of a Markov Network is defined by composing together a set of partial joint distributions over a group of variables that are all directly dependent on each other (i.e., a clique in the usual graph-theoretic terminology). Logic-wise, what this means is that one can define a probability distribution over the set of valuations (or possible worlds) given a set of first order logic axioms by building its corresponding Markov network. An valuation is a truth table of all atoms defined in the logic (like for instance follows(Jill, Joel)=true, online(Joel, 11pm)=false, etc), and each atom has a corresponding random variable in the Markov network. Each axiom is associated with a clique (containing the atoms of the formula). Or if the axiom contains variables, as many cliques as instantiated formulas (called *ground formulas*) of that axiom. Which means that the larger the number of constants in the domain of interpretation is, the bigger the resulting Markov network will be. Informally, the probability of a valuation is proportional to the exponential of the sum of the ground formulas that this valuation satisfies. It is also possible to weight the axioms, so the higher an axiom is weighted the stronger is the constraint of its satisfaction. All ground formulas are weighted identically to their corresponding axioms. Formally

$$P(V = v) = \frac{1}{Z} \exp\left(\sum_j w_j \times f_j(v) \right)$$

where Z is a normalizing factor so that the probabilities over all valuations sum up to 1, w_j is the weight of ground formula j and f_j is the evaluation of formula j over the valuation v.

Once the Markov network has been built it can be used to determine the probability of any given valuation, and of course the conditional or marginal probabilities of any combination of atoms, like

$$P(online(Joel, 11pm) = false)$$

or

$$P\left(online\left(Jill, 11\text{:}20\text{pm}\right) \mid online\left(Joel, 11\text{pm}\right), follows\left(Jill, Joel\right)\right)$$

Valuations that do not actually satisfy all the axioms can have a non null probability as well – but they'll usually have a lesser strength, due to the fact that they fulfill less axioms than a satisfying valuation (although that actually depends on the weights of the axioms).

Interestingly, one can define any Markov network by listing the right set of axioms in first order logic. And most importantly one can perform probabilistic inferences about formulas using that Markov network, like computing the probability that a formula F2 is satisfiable knowing that F1 is satisfiable.

Let us conclude this section with a small example based on the following axioms

1) $\forall X \neg follows\left(X, X\right) < 5 >$
2) $\forall X, Y \left(follows\left(X, Y\right) \wedge online\left(Y, 11\text{pm}\right)\right) \Rightarrow online\left(X, 11\text{:}20\text{pm}\right) < 1 >$

with their respective weights between brackets. What it says is that it is quite true that someone does not follow itself (weight $= 5$). And it is relatively less true that someone following someone else who is online would be online 20 minutes later (weight $= 1$). The constants are Jill and Joel. 11pm and 11:20pm can be seen as constants of a different sort, but since they are not relevant for this example they are ignored by the universal quantifier (this would be easily formalized with a typed FOL).

The ground formulas of Axiom 1 are

1) $\neg follows\left(Jill, Jill\right) < 5 >$
2) $\neg follows\left(Joel, Joel\right) < 5 >$

The ground formulas of Axiom 2 are

3) $\left(follows\left(Jill, Jill\right) \wedge online\left(Jill, 11\text{pm}\right)\right) \Rightarrow online\left(Jill, 11\text{:}20\text{pm}\right) < 1 >$
4) $\left(follows\left(Jill, Joel\right) \wedge online\left(Joel, 11\text{pm}\right)\right) \Rightarrow online\left(Jill, 11\text{:}20\text{pm}\right) < 1 >$
5) $\left(follows\left(Joel, Jill\right) \wedge online\left(Jill, 11\text{pm}\right)\right) \Rightarrow online\left(Joel, 11\text{:}20\text{pm}\right) < 1 >$
6) $\left(follows\left(Joel, Joel\right) \wedge online\left(Joel, 11\text{pm}\right)\right) \Rightarrow online\left(Joel, 11\text{:}20\text{pm}\right) < 1 >$

with their respective weights between brackets. The corresponding Markov network is given in Figure 3.8

There are 8 variables and therefore 2^8=256 valuations. Let's give an example of the calculation of the probability of two valuations, the one where all variables are false and the one where all variables are true. In the case where all variables are false we can see that

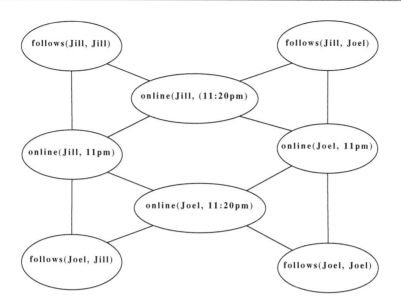

Fig. 3.8 Markov network corresponding to the axioms given above. A link between two atoms are build whenever the two atoms are both present in a ground formula as they then obviously depends on each other with respect to the probability distribution of valuations.

all axioms are satisfied (neither Jill nor Joel follows itself, and the premise of Axiom 2 is never fulfilled therefore true). The calculation goes as follows

$$P\left(v_{false}\right) = \frac{1}{Z}\left(2 \times \exp\left(5\right) + 4 \times \exp\left(1\right)\right)$$

In the case where all variables are true we can see that only the first axiom is not fulfilled, so the calculation goes as follows

$$P\left(v_{true}\right) = \frac{1}{Z}\left(4 \times \exp\left(1\right)\right)$$

We still need to calculate the normalizing factor

$$Z = \sum\sum\exp\left(w_j \times f_j(v)\right)$$

There are 7^2 valuations satisfying ground formulas 1 and 2, and there are 5^2 valuations that do not satisfy ground formula 3 to 6 (when the conclusion is false but the premise is true), therefore Z is

$$Z = 2 \times 7^2 \times \exp\left(5\right) + 4 \times \left(256 - 5^2\right) \times \exp\left(1\right) = 17056$$

which lets us with

$$P\left(v_{false}\right) = 0.018$$
$$P\left(v_{true}\right) = 0.0006$$

3.4   Imprecise and indefinite probability

Imprecise probability is a generic term referring to a variety of theories that extend probability theory when the probability measure is partially known or inadequate. The most common class of imprecise probabilities uses upper and lower probabilities (Walley, 1991). That is, an event may be characterized by two values, its upper and lower probabilities, instead of one probability; and this interval is interpreted to delimit the means the probability distributions lying in a certain envelope, and constructed according to certain distributional assumptions.

Other theories for dealing with imprecise probability use the notion of meta-probabilities (that is probability distributions over probabilities). There are debates amongst statisticians whether or not to allow meta-probabilities because that meta-level often cannot be subject to repetitive experiments. Therefore some prefer to consider a subjective interpretation of probability (as opposed to a frequentist interpretation), which may affect the choice of the assumptions regarding how to model imprecise probability.

One well developed imprecise probability theory using meta-probabilities is called Indefinite Probability (Goertzel *et al.*, 2006c); it uses lower and upper probabilities plus a degree of confidence, more formally any event w has an indefinite truth value consisting of a quadruplet $<[L, U], b, k>$ which roughly means that after k more observations there is a meta-probability b that the probability of w lies within $[L, U]$. This method of quantifying probabilities is used in the Probabilistic Logic Networks approach to inference, which is detailed in Chapter 12.

Chapter 4

Representing Temporal Knowledge

We've discussed the basics of logical reasoning and logical knowledge representation, in a general way. It's now time to get more specific and talk about one of the applications of logic that's most central to our topic: logical representation of time.

The natural way to present this material is to start with temporal representation and then move to temporal reasoning. However, we will first make a few brief comments about temporal reasoning, with the goal of motivating our choices in temporal representations. This should be expectable, because in large part it's the requirements of reasoning that determine what kinds of knowledge representation are appropriate.

Temporal reasoning, broadly construed, is the process of inferring new relations between events localized in time based on known facts and relations about those events. As such, temporal reasoning can be divided in two main branches, depending on how time is represented:

- **Quantitative:** in this variant, information regarding absolute, numeric temporal labels – or time stamps, using a computational jargon – is important for reaching conclusions about events, and therefore it is used as part of the modeling. Quantitative temporal reasoning will work with events specified in a temporally hard way, such as "event A begins at 01:31 and ends at 02:03".
- **Qualitative:** this variant is not concerned at all with absolute time stamps; instead, only relative relations between events - such as event A happens before event B, event C happens during event B, and so on - are relevant for producing inferences on the known temporal facts.

The quantitative approach is mainly applicable (and relevant) in applications where both accurate timing data is available and extreme time precision is necessary, such as reasoning about the functioning and performance of real-time systems. On the other hand, the qualitative approach is more appropriate to the analysis of data arising from human systems, or from noisy sensors as possessed by biological organisms or robots), and therefore we will concentrate here mainly on the qualitative approach.

Within the qualitative approach, there are two main issues to be confronted:

- how to represent basic units of time (how to "quantify time")
- how to represent relationships between basic units of time

A number of different approaches exists to both of these problems, and we will now review these.

4.1   Approaches to Quantifying Time

Figure 4.1 presents a simple ontology of the different approaches that have been taken to the representation of basic time-units.

As depicted in Figure 4.1, the essential aspect of time is its ordered nature: for any given two temporal units, we can judge whether one is before or after the other, or whether the two are simultaneous. All methods of quantifying time incorporate this ordering aspect. The simplest mean of ordering time, the point, has basically no qualitative aspects other than ordering. Two time-points can be compared as to their ordering, and there's nothing else to do with them, except to get quantitative and measure the distance between two time-points.

On the other hand, we can also consider models of the time-unit that have a richer set of relationships amongst them, such as intersection, adjacency and so forth. We call models like these "topological," and the most common approach here is to represent time using intervals. There is an argument that this is a more psychologically natural approach than time-points – a single, indivisible, instantaneous point being a kind of mathematical abstraction. The topological relationships between time-intervals are most commonly treated using Allen's interval algebra, to be discussed shortly below.

In addition to simple time intervals, there are other related approaches such as

- **fuzzy intervals** (the areas near the edge of the interval have less membership in the time-unit than the ones near the center, as determined by some fuzzy membership function)
- **probabilistic intervals** (with the meaning that each subinterval either does or does not belong to the event associated with the time-unit, but the subintervals near the edge of the interval have a smaller chance of belonging to it), which may take the form of treat-

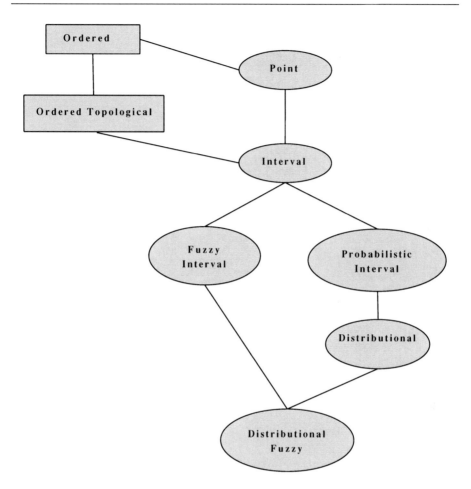

Fig. 4.1   Qualitative relations between approaches for temporal representation

ing an interval as a confidence interval, or of utilizing a whole probability distribution instead of an interval

- **distributional fuzzy intervals**, which use a probability distribution of fuzzy sets (meaning that each subinterval has a certain probability distribution of membership degrees in the event associated with the time-unit)

These various possibilities are depicted in Figure 4.2 and 4.3.

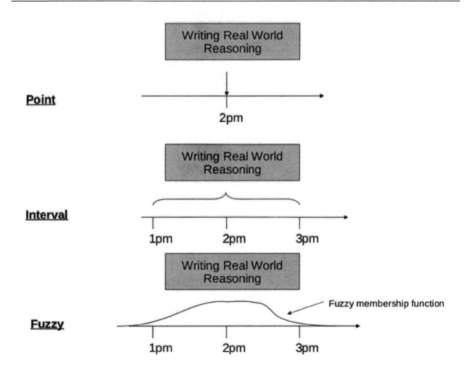

Fig. 4.2   Point-like, interval and fuzzy representations of an event

4.2   Allen's Interval Algebra

The most traditional and well-developed theoretical framework for systematizing the qualitative relationships between time-intervals is Allen's Interval Algebra, or simply Interval Algebra (IA), formalized for the first time in (Allen, 1983). IA, in its original and simplest form, models temporal events as intervals, that is, processes that have a beginning and an end in time. Based on that, thirteen temporal relations may exist between any given pair of events. Figure 4.4 illustrates those relations with a simple bar representation for intervals:

There is a calculus that defines possible relations between time intervals and provides a composition table (see the next chapter for an example of composition table) that can be used as a basis for reasoning about temporal descriptions of events. Time intervals are not necessarily represented by precise endpoints, but rather by their relationships. So, in this framework without metric one can express that a time interval is contained by another time interval etc.

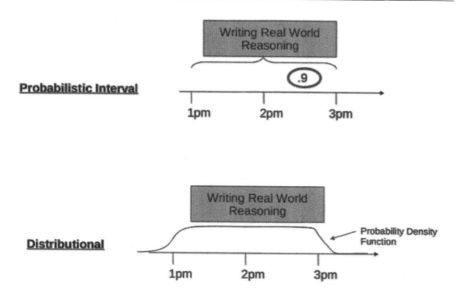

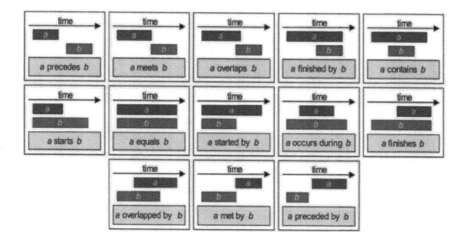

Fig. 4.3   Probabilistic and distributional representations of the same event

Fig. 4.4   Possible logic relations between two intervals according to Allen's Algebra

The following table shows many of the base relations in a different notation, explicitly typing them in with logical constraints (X- denotes the left end of the time interval X and X+ denotes the right end of X):

Relation	Name	Constraint
<	X Before Y	$X+ < Y-$
>	Y After X	
m	X Meets Y	$X+ = Y-$
mi	Y Met by X	
o	X Overlaps Y	$X- < Y- \wedge X+ < Y+ \wedge Y-$
oi	Y Overlaps by X	$< X+$
s	X Starts Y	$X- = Y- \wedge$
si	Y Started by X	$X+ < Y+$
d	X During Y	$Y- < X- \wedge$
di	Y Contains X	$X+ < Y+$
f	X Finishes Y	$X- > Y- \wedge$
fi	Y Finished by X	$X+ = Y+$
=	X Equals Y	$X- = Y- \wedge X+ = Y+$

Constraints in Allen's algebra are of the form

$$I_1(rel_1, \ldots, rel_i)I_2,$$

where I_1 and I_2 are time intervals, and rel_1,..., rel_i are some of the above 13 relations, with the meaning that at least one of them holds.

Consider the example, "John was not in the room when I touched the switch to turn on the light". Let

A be the time John was in the room,
B be the time I touched the light switch, and
C be the time the light was on.

Then we can say

$$A\{p, m, mi, pi, \}B,$$

that is, A precedes, meets, is met by, or is preceded by B; and B{m, o}C, that is, B meets or overlaps C.

Similarly, the sentences

During lunch, Alison reads newspaper. Afterwards, she goes to her office.

may be formalized in Allen's Interval Algebra as follows:

AlisonReadsNewspaper { d, s, f } AlisonIsHavingLunch

AlisonIsHavingLunch { <, m } AlisonGoesToOffice

For instance, the notation {d,s,f} refers to three relations in the above table, and indicates their disjunction; so it means "during or starts or finishes."

It is clear that all of the above relations can be defined from the three binary relations <, =, and > applied to the bounds of two intervals to be located w.r.t each other. For instance, the assertion X overlaps Y corresponds to

$$X- < Y- \land X+ < Y+ \land Y- < X+$$

as shown in the above table.

The basic relations describe relations between definite, certainly known intervals. Uncertainly known intervals may be described by a set of all the basic relations that may apply. We call such a set of basic relations a general Allen relation, or just an Allen relation.

There is a general relation for every combination of the thirteen basic relations: 2^{13} or 8192 of them. Each of the basic relations is a relation, of course, as are all their combinations. The full relation holds between two intervals about whom nothing is known. The empty relation {} has no meaning in terms of relations between actual intervals, but is the result of some operations on interval relations.

The "satisfaction problem" for Allen's interval algebra is determining, for a particular collection of relations on indefinite intervals, whether there is any set of specific time values for the intervals such that all the relations in the collection are true. For example, a collection of relations and intervals that is not satisfiable is three intervals A, B, and C such that A { p } B, B { p } C, and C { p } A (each precedes the next, and the last precedes the first). There are no definite intervals for which all these relations can hold. The satisfaction problem is shown to be NP-complete (Vilain *et al.*, 1989). However, there are subclasses of the problem that are tractable and that permit polynomial-time decision procedures.

4.2.1 *Allen Algebra in the Twitter Domain*

In order to better understand the practical uses of IA, we will now explain how to apply logical formalism to a specific domain, consisting of messages in the Twitter microblogging service. We will make use of this same example domain in some other examples in the following, and so take this opportunity to briefly summarize the domain before using it to exemplify interval algebra.

Twitter is a free web service allowing individuals to post brief public or private messages ("tweets"). Each "tweet" deals with specific concepts, entities and sentiments, and has a specific author. Further, there is a social network of tweet authors; tweets may be geographically localized via IP address; and information about tweets is publicly available via the Twitter software API. See Figure 4.5 for a screenshot of the Twitter interface.

Fig. 4.5   Screenshot of the Twitter.com web service

In order to develop some of our future examples using this domain, we will need to introduce some special "primitive" logical term and relationship types (i.e. a "signature" for our theory relating Twitter entities). The primitive terms and relationships we introduce are depicted in Figure 4.6 and 4.7.

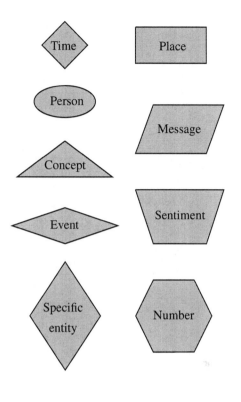

Fig. 4.6   Primitive terms for a logical formalism targeting

The commonsense semantics of these concepts and relationships should be fairly obvious; however, the right way to rigorously formalize some of these relationships (such as the spatial and temporal ones) is a complex issue, and will occupy a considerable percentage of this book!

Returning to interval algebra, Figure 4.8 shows schematically an example sequence of Twitter entries and the events that can be inferred from them.

Referring to Figure 4.8, note that many relations between the assigned events can be inferred. For instance:

"Peter watches debate" occurs during "Jane plays game".

"Jane plays game" overlaps "Bill writes report".

"Bill makes coffee" occurs during "Bill writes report".

"Peter watches debate" precedes "Bill writes report".

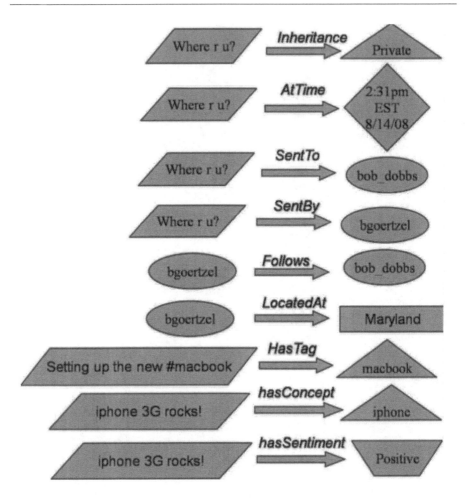

Fig. 4.7   Logical relationships in the Twitter formalism

Temporal relations such as those listed above can be represented in the form of a graph, forming a type of graph that we call a Temporal Interval Network. Those are methodologically interesting in the sense that they transform many problems of IA into graph problems. Figure 4.9 shows the equivalent TI network for many of the relations between the events in Figure 4.8:

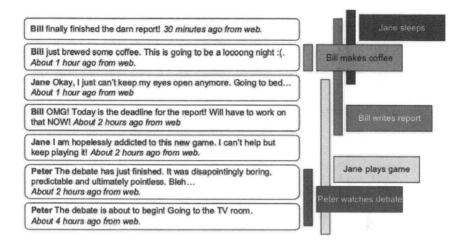

Fig. 4.8   Tweets as temporal events, associated with time intervals. Note that in the

4.3   Uncertain Interval Algebra

As noted above, IA in its original form presumes the existence of hard instants in time where events start and begin. However, in the real world, the actual start and end times of many events may be hard to define; and furthermore, in the specific case of the Twitter interface the imprecision of events in personal lives is taken into account by the use of a time scale of varying discretization (jumping from half an hour to hourly marks, for instance) as well as the use of words denoting imprecision ("about").

In the fuzzy version of IA, relations between events are defined in terms of degrees of truth. Putting it simply, the truth value of a relation is the degree of "existence" of that relation, varying from 0 to 1. For instance, one may estimate that event A precedes event B with a degree of truth of 0.7 . From now on, we will denote such assignments with a functional notation - for instance A precedes B with a truth value becomes precedes(A,B,0.7).

Interestingly, the use of fuzzy logic allows the existence of multiple relations that are mutually exclusive in the original, rigid IA. For instance one can say that at the relations precedes(A,B,0.7) and overlaps(A,B,0.3) are both valid under a fuzzy modeling. (The previous numeric also illustrates that the sum of the truth values of all relations between two events has to be 1.0, "full existence" so to speak.) Figure 4.10 shows another TI, this time fuzzy (with truth values attached to edges), showing some of those "ambiguously" modeled

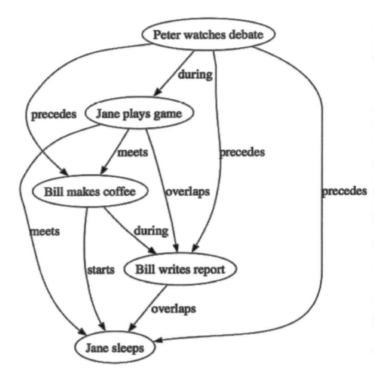

Fig. 4.9   Time interval network for the events of Figure 4.8

relations for the events of Figure 4.8. As one can see, now an edge between any two events is defined by a tuple that may be composed of multiple truth values for different relations.

Finally, in the probabilistic version of IA, a value represents the probability that a given relation between two events is assigned. Multiple probabilistic relations between two events that would have only one relation in the classic version of IA are also possible. At first, that may sound very similar to the fuzzy version, specially under the numerical viewpoint. However, conceptually they are completely different. Speaking in terms of TI networks, in the fuzzy case a given edge can be multiple types of relations at the same time, in different degrees. In the probabilistic case, a given edge can have the possibility of being multiple relations, with different probabilities, but that is a modelling of uncertainty on the nature of an edge that in the real world fits into just one of the options.

One aspect of probabilistic IA that may clarify its conceptual difference relative to the fuzzy version is the problem of determining the most likely subnetwork. An example of that is illustrated in Figure 4.11, where a very small subset of events from the example Twitter

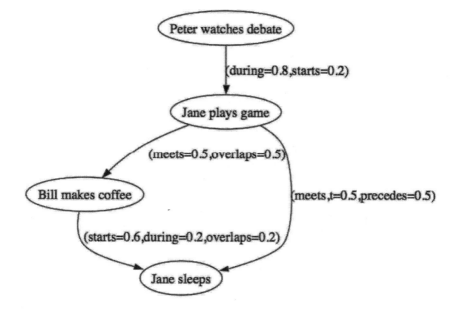

Fig. 4.10   Yet another variation of a TI network modeling imprecision

flow is used to compose a probabilistic IA network. For sake of clarity, different relations (with assigned probabilities) between two events are represented by different edges. The dotted edges form the less likely subnetwork, while the solid edges represent the most likely network. In the example, that hints at the sequence of events that most likely happened in reality.

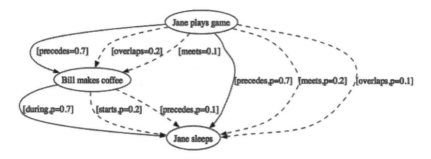

Fig. 4.11   Finally, a probabilistic TI network modeling the same events

While the possibility has not been explored in the literature, one may also conceive fuzzy probabilistic IA, involving intervals interpreted as confidence intervals of centers of fuzzy membership functions. Various other related options also exist, offering a great deal of modeling flexibility.

The problem of finding the most likely subnetwork brings to mind computational considerations on dealing with IA, which will be briefly examined here. As already mentioned (and as the most likely network example already illustrates) most if not all IA problems can be modelled in terms of graph problems, and finding the optimal solutions for many of them is combinatorially explosive, and not viable for realistically large IA networks. However, the theoretical work on IA has found subsets of it that are computationally tractable, as well as heuristics that significantly reduce computational time at the cost of finding a solution that is not guaranteed to be optimal (van Beek & Manchak, 1997). And much of that is just applied graph theory, since many of the relevant problems in IA are reducible to classical graph problems. That is, IA networks (classic or otherwise) are in principle manageable by an extremely diverse plethora of optimization methods, as in the case of any graph problem.

Chapter 5

Temporal Reasoning

In principle, logical inference about propositions involving events embedded in time and space could be treated the same as any other kind of logical inference, but experience shows that this is not an optimal approach, mainly because such an approach leads to extreme inefficiencies of inference control. Thus, in this section and the following ones we will consider specific logical formalisms recently proposed for reasoning about time and space.

A variety of logical formalisms have been proposed for reasoning about time, including

- Standard first-order logic with temporal arguments
- Reified temporal logic
- Modal temporal logic

(all of which we will review in detail below) and others. A large percentage of work in the area of temporal logic appears to fall prey to one of the pitfalls of

- Unrealistic simplicity
- Excessive complexity
- Computational intractability

The creation of a *scalable, reasonably general temporal logic* remains a difficult research problem, and one of our tasks here is to characterize this research problem and explain exactly which of its aspects are most pertinent and most worth attacking at this juncture.

In order to apply temporal logics such as the above to reasoning on large, complex real-world problems, several issues have to be addressed:

- **the logic should be simple** – if a logic is overcomplicated, crafting a workable, scal-able inference control strategy is very unlikely to be feasible; and integrating the logic

79

with other system components like query languages and knowledge bases will likely be infeasible

- **the logic should not be too simple** – for instance, for most serious real-world applications simple Prior's logic is too simple and inadequate for applications such as reasoning about real-time behaviour of software. Also, a logic that achieves simplicity at the expense of needed expressiveness will be impractical because the formulas describing real algorithms will be too long and complicated to understand.

- **the corresponding deduction procedures should be efficient**

It seems feasible to construct many different approaches satisfying these criteria (including perhaps a PLN based approach as will be exemplified in Part III below); but there is not yet any approach that has been convincingly validated by practical applications to satisfy them.

5.1 The Challenge Time Presents to Classical Logic

The essential challenge temporality poses to classical logic is that, in the latter, formulas are evaluated within a single fixed world and have fixed truth value, that does not change over time. However, most real-world systems are dynamic.

Temporal statements, statements involving temporal information, may have truth value that changes over time. For instance, the statements "it is Monday" or "I am at a meeting" have constant meaning, but their truth value can vary in time (but, of course, neither statement is ever true and false simultaneously; unless one is dealing with paraconsistent logic, which is beyond the scope of this book). Thus, "it is Monday" may be satisfied in some contexts, but not in others. Examples of temporal statements are also "I am *always* too busy", "I will *eventually* be at my office ", or "I will be at my office *until* John give me a phone call". In temporal logics, evaluation takes place within a temporal context.

Temporal relationships and reasoning deal with issues like *change, actions, causality, ontology of time*, underlying logic, temporal constraints used, reasoning algorithms employed, etc. A *change* describes moving from one state or condition to another one. This relation is temporal (either implicit or explicit) and requires an appropriate representation. Representing the temporal aspect of the knowledge adds the time dimension to the truth of the information. A formalism for representing temporal information has to provide a way for establishing a link between an *atemporal assertion* and a *temporal reference*. There is a number of approaches for representing temporal relationships, each of them requiring specific forms of reasoning. Most of them are influenced by studies by Aristotle and the Megarian and Stoic schools in ancient Greece.

Temporal systems can be classified according to different aspects (Emerson, 1991; Pani & Bhattacharjee, 2001):

- propositional versus first-order;
- global versus compositional;
- time points versus time intervals;
- discrete versus dense time;
- bounded versus unbounded time;
- branching versus linear versus paralel versus circular time;
- past versus future tense.

These aspects determine expressiveness, and also computational demands.

In the rest of this section we review three main families of modern approaches to temporal representation (more details can be found, for instance, in surveys (Pani & Bhattacharjee, 2001) and (Emerson, 1991). Approaches within these families may have different properties according to the list of aspect given above.

5.1.1 *First order logic: temporal arguments approach*

The simplest approach to handling time within logic is to represent time by numerical values. This representation can be applied within first order logic (FOL), with reals or integers as the intended domain for time variables and constants. There is a number of efficient methods for dealing with first order statements and reasoning with them, so this approach starts from a well established grounds. This approach is often referred as to *temporal arguments approach*. Within FOL, we can simply express temporal facts like "Alison is working on the same project as Bob at time t", for instance, in the following way:

$$work\_on\_same\_project(Alison, Bob, t)$$

Using sorted first order logic may be more suitable and, in this case, there is a distinguished sort for temporal arguments. For instance, the classical example "You can fool all the people some time and you can fool some people all the time, but you cannot fool all the people all the time" can be represented in sorted first order logic in the following way:

$$\forall x{:}H.\ \exists t{:}T.\ youcanfool(x,t)\ \wedge\ \exists x{:}H.\ \forall t{:}T.\ youcanfool(x,t)\ \wedge$$

$$\neg\forall x{:}H.\ \forall t{:}T.\ youcanfool(x,t),$$

with an intended semantics that links the sort H to the set of humans and the sort T to the set of all time values. By this, time is given a special syntactic and semantic status, but can still share much of the treatment of other sorts of values. If the theory is equiped with axioms on ordering, one can also reason (using general first-order reasoning frameworks) about statemets like the following one:

$$\exists t_0{:}T.\ \forall t{:}T.\ (t{>}t_0 \Rightarrow f(t)).$$

In a similar way, one can use arithmetic operators over time values.

Despite its simplicity, well-foundness, and developed proof theory and methods, this approach has severe limitations. For instance, without adding a host of specialized additional predicates, one cannot model *aspectual* distinctions between for example, states, events and processes, and cannot represent notions used in natural language like *now, then, since, while, until*, nor notions like *a bit later* and *similar*.

To get around these problems, there are different formalisms for representing temporal information within first order logic – a line of thinking that eventually leads back towards the more sophisticated approaches to time representation that we considered earlier.

For instance, Interval Temporal Logic (ITL) is a temporal logic for both propositional and first-order reasoning about periods of time found in descriptions of hardware and software systems, but also in artificial intelligence and linguistics. ITL can handle both sequential and parallel composition and offers powerful and extensible specification and proof techniques for reasoning about properties involving safety, liveness and projected time (Moszkowski, 1994). It is not identical to Allen's interval algebra, but has a great deal in common with the latter.

5.1.2 *Reified temporal logic*

Alternately, rather than the encoding of temporal information within FOL, there is a "reified" approach relating atemporal terms to temporal terms by specific temporal contexts. In the reification approach to temporal reasoning, the truth of temporal assertions is considered while keeping atemporal parts of assertions unchanged within a specific temporal context. A good overview of reified temporal logics can be found in (Ma & Knight,

2001). One of the most influential, formal approaches to reified logic was presented by Shoham in 1987 (Shoham, 1987).

Reifying a logic means moving into a meta-language where an assertion in an initial language (usually FOL, but a modal logic can also be used), becomes a term in a new language. In this new logic, one can reason about truth values of expressions in an object language through use of the truth values of expressions built with the operator like TRUE and with temporal object as arguments. Thus,

$$\text{TRUE(atemporal expression, temporal qualification)}$$

represents a statement whose intended meaning is that the first argument is true "during" the time denoted by the temporal qualification. TRUE is not a relation in the logic, nor it is a modal operator, rather it is a reifying context. For instance, the sentence "Alison is on a meeting with Bob between 11am and 12am" can be expressed as

$$\text{TRUE(MEETING(Alison, Bob), (11am, 12am))}.$$

The truth predicates are used to express not only the time when an expression is true but also the patterns of its temporal occurrence. So, in general, the pattern of temporal occurrence for the atemporal expression admits many interpretations other than *during*.

And this brings us back, finally to Allens's interval algebra as discussed above, which naturally leads to a form of reified temporal logic. In Allen's variant of reified temporal logic (Allen, 1984), temporal incidence is expressed using the operators HOLDS, OC-CURS, and OCCURING in order to express distinctions between states, events and processes.

Temporal reification has several advantages. On one hand, this logic gives a special status to time. On the other, it allows one to flexibly predicate and quantify over propositional terms. Therefore, it gives the expressive power to discuss relationships between propositional terms and temporal aspects with a high level of generality. Due to these qualities, the reified approach has enjoyed considerable popularity in AI. However, it has also been a subject of criticism and attacks. A number of authors have argued that reified temporal logics are unnecessarily complicated and imply a philosophically suspect ontology of time. However, it seems to us that these objections really pertain to specific, simple versions of reified temporal logic, rather than to reified temporal logic in general.

For instance, a major problem with simple reified logics is that there is no straightforward way of referring to one temporally referenced object within the context of another temporal interval, such as "The leader of the Konrad project in 2003 left our company in

2006". Rather, in simple reified logics, all non-temporal terms have to be evaluated with respect to the same temporal terms, i.e., those given in the TRUE context. So, in a simple reified logic, the given example could be expressed in the following inelegant way:

$$\forall x \; (\text{TRUE}(\text{project\_leader}(\text{Konrad})=x, \; (2003, 2004))$$

$$\Rightarrow \text{TRUE}(\text{left\_job}(x), \; (2006, 2007)))$$

In addition, in Shoham's reified temporal logic, there are no temporal predicates, except $\leq$ and $=$, which makes expression of some temporal phenomena awkward.

But in the BTK approach (named after the initials of its authors), presented by Bacchus et al in 1991 (Bacchus *et al.*, 1991), each predicate and function symbol can take any number of temporal arguments. For instance, the above example can be represented in a much simpler way:

$$\text{left\_job}(\text{project\_leader}(2003, \text{Konrad}), 2006)$$

This is also the approach adopted in PLN, as will be discussed a little later.

Alternatively, Galton proposed a method of unreification based on incorporating tokens (Galton, 1991). Galton's event token is basically the occurrence of some event at some point m in time Thus,"Alison is having a lunch at 3 00pm" is an event token. Event tokens act on the one hand as additional parameters to predicate and function symbols, while on the other they can be used in the temporal occurrence predicates.

5.1.3 *Modal temporal logic*

Modal logic, as discussed above, is a formal logic system that deals with modalities, like possibility and necessity. In modal logic, one can express a statement like "It is possible that Bob quit his job". The modalities are represented by modal operators. The basic unary modal operators are usually written $\Box$ (or L) for *necessarily* and $\Diamond$ (or M) for *possibly*. In a classical modal logic, these two operators are linked in the following way:

$$\Diamond p \Leftrightarrow \neg \Box \neg p$$

$$\Box p \Leftrightarrow \neg \Diamond \neg p.$$

Tense logic is a kind of modal logic-based system, introduced first by Prior in 1955 following the idea that tense is a sort of modality, to be set alongside the ordinary modes of *necessity* and *possibility*. Tense logic has two sets of modal operators, one for the past and one for the future (while ordinary modal logic has only one). In Prior's notation,

- Pp stands for "It has at some time been the case that p"

- Fp stands for "It will at some time be the case that p"
- Hp stands for "It has always been the case that p"
- Gp stands for "It will always be the case that p".

For instance, if p stands for "Alison's department moves to China" and if q stands for "Alison and Bob have communication problems", then G(p ⇒ Gq) stands for "It will be the case that if Alison's department moves to China, then Alison and Bob will always have communication problems." Tense operators can express standard modal operators □ and ◊:

$$\Diamond p \text{ can be expressed as } Pp \lor p \lor Fp$$

$$\Box p \text{ can be expressed as } Hp \land p \land Gp$$

Tense logic is obtained by adding the tense operators to an underlying logic, for instance propositional logic, or first-order logic. For instance, in tense logic built over first-order logic, the statement *"A woman will be a CTO"* can be represented as $\exists x(\text{woman}(x) \land F\ \text{cto}(x))$.

The standard model-theoretic semantics of tense logic is defined with respect to temporal frames. A *temporal frame* consists of a set of times together with an ordering relation $<$ on it. This defines the "flow of time" and the meaning of the tense operators. An interpretation of the tense-logical language assigns a truth value to each atomic formula at each time in the temporal frame. For instance, Pp is true at t if and only if p is true at some time t' such that $t' < t$ (the semantics of other tense operators is defined by analogy). A tense logic formula is valid if it is true at all times under all interpretations over all temporal frames. Prior developed several versions of a calculus of tenses in which one can derive, for instance, Gp ⇔ ¬F¬P, and also $(\neg p \land \neg Fp) \Rightarrow \neg \Diamond p$ *("what neither is true nor will be true is not possible")*, linking standard modal operators with Prior tense operators in an elegant way.

While in typical first order representation time is absolute, in modal temporal logic time is relative and statements refer to the present or to other events. There are variants of modal temporal logic for dealing with absolute precise times. Prior's system does not specify the nature of time (points or intervals), but in this approach understanding temporal elements as points of time is more natural.

Apart from tense logic, there is a whole family of other modal temporal logic systems. The modal μ calculus is a powerful class of temporal logics with a least fixpoint operator μ (Scott & De Bakker, 1969; Kozen, 1983). It is used for describing and reasoning about temporal properties of labelled transition systems. The modal μ calculus subsumes dynamic and temporal logics like CTL and LTL.

In linear temporal logic (LTL), time is not branching, and one can encode formulas about the future of paths, such as that a condition will eventually be true, that a condition will be true until another fact becomes true, etc. In linear temporal logic, there are operators for *next* (X), *globally* (G), *finally* (F), *until* (U), and *release* (R). For instance, if p stands for "There is electric power", and q is "I work on my computer", $G(\neg p \Rightarrow X \neg q)$ stands for "It always hold that if there is no electric power, in the next moment I will not work on my computer". In the simplest formulation of LTL, the U (until) operator is used to derive all the others.

On the other hand, computational tree logic (CTL) is a branching-time logic, meaning that its model of time is a tree-like structure in which the future is not determined; there are different paths in the future, any one of which might be an actual path that is realised. Some of the CTL operators are quantifiers over paths (for instance, Ap stands for "p has to hold on all paths starting from the current state") and path-specific quantifiers (for instance, Xp stands for "p has to hold at the next state", Gp stands for "p has to hold on the entire subsequent path"). For example, if p mean "I give a presentation", in CTL one encode "I will give a presentation, whatever happens" by AGp. There are also other variants of branching-time logic, such as Branching Temporal Logic which also generalizes LTL, and differs from CTL in subtle ways (Kontchakov, 2007).

Modal temporal logics are, in a sense, more expressive than FOL. They are also suitable for their modularity. They can directly and neatly be combined with other modal qualifications like belief, knowledge etc. For certain sorts of modal temporal logics there are efficient automated theorem provers.

Concerning applications, Prior used his tense logic to build theories about the structure and metaphysics of time, while now it has numerous other applications. The notational efficiency of modal temporal logics makes them very appealing for applications in natural language understanding, where they have been widely used. There are various areas of applications of temporal logic, such as, for example, controlling operation of a bank of identical elevators in a building (Wood, 1989). However, the area where modal temporal logics probably found the widest acceptance and success is in computing, including the theory of programming, database management, program verification, and commonsense reasoning in AI. In applications in program verification, following the influential work of Pnueli (Pnueli, 1977), the main idea is to formally specify a program and to apply deduction methods for proving properties of the program like correctness, termination, and possibility of a deadlock. In describing properties to be proved, one can use modal operators, for instance, to state that *whenever* a request is made, access to a resource is *eventually* granted, but it is *never* granted to two requestors simultaneously.

One of the very successful temporal logics used in verification is temporal logic of actions (TLA), developed by Leslie Lamport, which combines temporal logic with a logic of actions (Lamport, 1994). It is a logic for specifying and reasoning about concurrent systems. Systems and their properties are represented in the same logic. Syntax and semantics of TLA are very simple, yet it is very powerful, both in principle and in practice. It has been used to study and verify cache coherence protocols, memory models, network protocols, database protocols, and concurrent algorithms (Batson & Lamport, 2003).

5.1.4 *Integration of deontic and temporal logic*

There are several approaches for combining deontic and temporal logic. Some of them are based on expressing deontic constraints in terms of temporal logic, while in some deontic logic is extended by temporal operators. Some of the most important issues in combining deontic and temporal logic are:

- The temporal approaches considered are usually based on *tree-structures* representing branching time with the same past and open to the future.
- On top of these tree-structures, temporal deontic logics typically define one modal *necessity* operator, expressing some kind of *inevitability* or *historical* necessity, plus deontic *obligation* operators.

One family of those logics expresses the modal and deontic operators in temporal terms, while another family introduces temporal operators that can be combined with the modal and deontic operators.

In the approach described in (Dignum & Kuiper, 1997), deontic logic is extended by temporal operators. This approach is used for the specification of deadlines. It uses deontic constraints to specify what is the agent obliged to do and temporal constraints since the obligation is usually to be performed before a certain deadline. The following example from (Dignum & Kuiper, 1997) requires both deontic and temporal reasoning.

- Alison has to pay the mortgage for her house every month.
- Alison borrowed some money from Bob, which she has to repay as soon as she is able to do so.

- The roof of Alison's house started leaking. It has to be repaired before the October rains start (It is now September).
- Alison wants to go on a midweek holiday. She has an offer to rent a cottage for relatively little money which has to be paid within 30 days after the reservation has been made.

Formulas in the system introduced in (Dignum & Kuiper, 1997) are propositional formulas built in the standard way and, in addition, formulas involving *actions,* the *deontic operator OB,* and a preference relation over actions called **PREFER.** If α is an action and F is a formula, then $[\alpha]$F is also a formula, and its informal meaning is that "doing α neccessarily leads to a state where F holds". If F is a formula, then **OB**F is also a formula, and its informal meaning is "it has to be the case that F holds". If α_1 and α_2 are actions, then **PREFER**(α_1,α_2) is also a formula and its informal meaning is that the action α_1 is preferable to the action α_2. The formulas are built also using temporal operators X (unary, for next), U (binary, for until), P (unary, for held), S (binary, for held since), DO (unary, for an action to be performed next), DONE (unary, for an action that was performed last). The semantics of formulas is given in Kripke style.

For example, the statement *"If Alison borrowed some money from Bob, she has to repay as soon as she is able to do so."* is modeled by the formula:

DONE(borrow(Alison, Bob)) $\Rightarrow$

$\forall \beta$ OB(true $<$ repay(Alison, Bob)) $<$ DONE(β) $\wedge$ PREFER(repay(Alison, Bob), β)

where OB(x$<$y) states that y can not hold true before x is performed

In (Dignum & Kuiper, 1997) there is not a corresponding axiomatization and inference system, nor algorithms for automation of reasoning in the described logic.

Partly following and extending ideas from (Dignum & Kuiper, 1997), in (Broersen *et al.*, 2004), deontic logic SDL is combined with temporal logic CTL and deadline constraints are expressed in this new logic. Automation of reasoning in this logic is not discussed, but there is an expectation that it can be handled by CTL theorem provers.

The approach described in (Cheng, 2006) starts with linear temporal logic (LTL), extend it to state/event LTL (SE-LTL) which takes into account both events and propositions, and finally, extends it to the system SED-LTL with deontic modalities. The semantics of formulas is given in Kripke style, while there is no corresponding axiomatization or reasoning procedures. The system can be used in different computing scenarios involving both temporal and deontic notions. For instance, it can be used for expressing an access control policy in which the permissions depend on time or events. For instance, the following resource monitoring problem can be represented within the proposed logic:

- User$_i$ has the permission to use the resource r for 5 time units continuously, and he must be able to access it 15 time units after asking, at the latest;
- User$_i$ has always the permission to use the resource r, and he has to release it after 5 time units of utilization;
- If user$_i$ is asking for the resource and he has the permission to use it, then the system has the obligation to give it to him before 5 time units;
- If user$_i$ uses the resource without the permission, he must not ask for it during 10 time units.

Alternately, in the approach for combining temporal and deontic modalities proposed in (Åqvist, 2005), the "absolute" temporal operator R_t ("it holds at the time t that") is used, instead of the "relative" temporal operators X and U, which are more expressive. There is also a variant of the system with the temporal operator R_{th} ("it is realized at time t in history h that"). In semantics of deontic operators, frames that are used are considered as (finite) two-dimensional coordinate systems, where it is possible to distinguish between the *longitude* (i.e., x-value) and the *latitude* (i.e., y-value) of any point in such a coordinate system. *Times* are interpreted as longitudes, and *worlds*, or *histories*, as latitudes. There is a corresponding, sound and complete, axiomatization and inference system, but automation of reasoning is not considered.

Despite the fact that all combinations of deontic and temporal logic have been constructed with applications in mind, it seems that there are still no large-scale applications of these techniques for real-world problems. Hopefully this situation will change in the near future.

5.2   Inference systems for temporal logic

As noted above, there are three main approaches to temporal representation and reasoning. Here we continue the discussion and give some simple examples of inference in each of them.

We will focus here on inference systems for temporal logic, but wish to also note that there are decision procedures for some of the logics discussed here (Emerson, 1995). Recall that for a given formula F, a decision procedure only gives a yes or no answer whether F is valid/theorem, without providing deductive argument for that. Most decision procedures use model-theoretic, semantic arguments for obtaining the final result. In some cases, these arguments can be turned to deductive arguments, but that can be very expensive.

5.2.1 *Inference in the Simple First Order Logic Approach*

In the approach based on first order logic and expressing temporal information as first-order formulas, giving each predicate an extra argument place that corresponds to the temporal dimension. For instance,

$$work\_on\_same\_project(Alison, Bob, 2007)$$

If the first-order signature is extended with a binary infix predicate $<$ denoting the temporal ordering relation "earlier than", and a constant "now" denoting the present moment, then the tense operators can be simulated by means of first-order logic, in the following way ($p(t)$ denotes the result of introducing an extra temporal argument place to the predicate p):

Pp (informally: p held at some point in past):	$\exists t(t<now \wedge p(t))$
Fp (informally: p will hold at some point):	$\exists t(now<t \wedge p(t))$
Hp (informally: p always held):	$\forall t(t<now \Rightarrow p(t))$
Gp (informally: p will always hold):	$\forall t(now<t \Rightarrow p(t))$

In this framework, temporal information is completely expressed by means of first order logic, therefore standard classical first-order inference systems can be used as a reasoning vehicle. For instance, let us assume the following statements:

- Year 2007 was in the past.
- Alison and Bob worked together on the same project in 2007.
- If Alison and Bob worked together on the same project, they will always be friends.

One can represent these statements in the following way:

- $2007<now$
- work_on_same_project(Alison, Bob, 2007)
- Pwork_on_same_project(Alison, Bob) $\Rightarrow$ Gfriends(Alison, Bob)

According to the above definitions, this can be rewritten as:

- $2007<now$
- work_on_same_project(Alison, Bob, 2007)
- $\exists t(t<now \wedge work\_on\_same\_project(Alison,Bob,t)) \Rightarrow \forall t(now<t \Rightarrow friends(Alison,Bob,t))$

From $2007 <now$ and work_on_same_project(Alison, Bob, 2007), it follows that

$$2007<now \wedge work\_on\_same\_project(Alison, Bob, 2007)$$

and further,

$$\exists t\ (t<now \wedge work\_on\_same\_project(Alison, Bob, t)),$$

which, together with the implication from above, yields

$$\forall t(\text{now}<t \Rightarrow \text{friends(Alison, Bob, t)})$$

i.e., Alison and Bob will always be friends (all three inference steps in this derivation can be simply justified in any reasonable inference system for classical first order logic).

5.2.2 Reified temporal logic

In Allen's variant of reified temporal logic (Allen, 1984), discussed above, temporal incidence is expressed using relational predicates HOLDS, OCCURS, and OCCURING, as for example:

HOLDS(MEETING(Alison, Bob), (11am, 12am)).

OCCURS(DRIVES(Alison, Home, Office), (8am, 8.45pm))

where terms of the form (t,t') denote time intervals. These two predicates ensure distinctions between states and events.

Statements about states have *homogeneous* temporal incidence, i.e., they must hold over any subintervals of an interval over which they hold (e.g., the meaning of HOLDS(MEETING(Alison, Bob), (11am, 12am)) is that Alison and Bob are at a meeting at any time interval between 11am and 12am). On the other hand, statements about events have inhomogeneous temporal incidence, i.e., such a statement is not true at *any* subinterval of an interval of which it is true (e.g., if Alison drives from her home to her office from 8am to 8.45am, then in any subinterval of that interval, she does not drive from her home to her office, but between some other points).

These features of reified temporal logic (homogeneity of states and inhomogeneity of events) are ensured in inference systems by axioms such as

$$\forall s,i,i'(\text{HOLDS}(s,i) \land \text{In}(i',i) \Rightarrow \text{HOLDS}(s,i'))$$
$$\forall e,i,i'(\text{OCCURS}(e,i) \land \text{In}(i',i) \Rightarrow \neg\text{OCCURS}(e,i'))$$

where "In" denotes the proper subinterval relation.

Therefore, given HOLDS(MEETING(Alison, Bob), (11am, 12am)), the above axiom (along with the underlying first-order style inference system) enables deriving HOLDS(MEETING(Alison, Bob), (11.15am, 11.20am)). Indeed:

1. HOLDS(MEETING(Alison, Bob), (11am, 12am))
(assumption)

2. In((11.15am, 11.20am), (11am, 12am))

(by means of interval arithmetic)

3. HOLDS(MEETING(Alison, Bob), (11am, 12am)) $\wedge$

In((11.15am, 11.20am), (11am, 12am))

(by propositional calculus)

4. HOLDS(MEETING(Alison, Bob), (11am, 12am)) $\wedge$

In((11.15am, 11.20am), (11am, 12am)) $\Rightarrow$

HOLDS(MEETING(Alison, Bob), (11.15am, 11.20am))

(by homogeneity axiom and by Hilbert's axiom A4)

5. HOLDS(MEETING(Alison, Bob), (11.15am, 11.20am))

(from 3 and 4, by modus ponens)

5.2.3   *Modal temporal logic*

As discussed earlier, Prior's Tense Logic contains, in addition to the usual truth-functional operators, four modal operators P, F, H, G. P and F are known as the *weak tense operators*, while H and G are known as the *strong tense operators*. There is an intended correspondence between pair of these operators:

$$Pp \equiv \neg H \neg p$$

$$Fp \equiv \neg G \neg p$$

If this correspondence is ensured, then one pair of the operators is redundant.

Post worked on different variants of the inference systems for Tense Logic, trying to build an elegant system that has as theorems all formulas that are true following his intended semantics. Some of those formulas are:

Gp$\Rightarrow$Fp :   "What will always be, will be"

Fp$\Rightarrow$FFp :   "If it will be the case that p, it will be — in between —
                                          that it will be"

$\neg$Fp$\Rightarrow$F$\neg$Fp :   "If it will never be that p then it will be that it will never
                                          be that p"

$(\neg p \wedge \neg Fp) \Rightarrow \neg \Diamond p$:   "What neither is true nor will be true is not possible"

Fp$\rightarrow \Box$Fp :   "What will be, will necessarily be"

Of particular significance is the system of Minimal Tense Logic Kt for classical propositional tense logic which consists of Hillbert's axioms, the modus ponens inference rule, the following axioms:

(1) p$\Rightarrow$HFp ("What is, has always been going to be")

(2) p⇒GPp ("What is, will always have been")

(3) H(p⇒q) ⇒ (Hp⇒Hq) ("Whatever always follows from what always has been, always has been")

(4) G(p⇒q) ⇒ (Gp⇒Gq) ("Whatever always follows from what always will be, always will be")

(5) Gp⇒ GGp ("What will always be will always will always be")

and the following rules of inference:

(RH) p ⊢ Hp

(RG) p ⊢ Gp

(US) p ⊢ p[$\varphi \to \psi$]

The system K_t is sound and complete, i.e., its set of theorems is the set of all valid tense logic formulas. In addition, it is decidable whether a tense logic formula is theorem. The theorems of K_t are all the properties of the tense operators not relying on the temporal order.

Let us consider the following statements:

"If our company has small administrative overhead, then it has big profit"
"It will always be the case that our company has small administrative overhead".

From the above assumptions, one can derive the fact "It will always be the case that our company has big profit". Let us denote by p "our company has small administrative overhead" and by q "our company has big profit". The proof of Gq is as follows:

1. p⇒q   (assumption)
2. Gp   (assumption)
3. G(p⇒q)   (from 1, by RG)
4. G(p⇒q) ⇒ (Gp⇒Gq)   (instance of the axiom scheme (4)).
5. Gp⇒Gq   (from 3 and 4, by modus ponens)
6. Gq   (from 2 and 5, by modus ponens)

5.2.4 Computational Tree Logic

Computational tree logic (CTL), briefly described earlier, has many applications in describing and verifying computing processes. CTL uses the following temporal operators:

- Ap – stands for "all futures", i.e., "p has to hold on all paths starting from the current state"

- Ep – stands for "some future", i.e., "p has to hold on some path starting from the current state"

Temporal operators have to be followed by one of the following linear temporal operators:

- G –always
- F – sometime
- X – next time
- U – until

The semantics of p U q is that p is true in all states preceding the state where q holds and q will eventually hold. The semantics of other operators are intuitive. The syntax of CTL is given as follows. There are state formulas and path formulas defined in the following way:

- Each atomic proposition P is a state formula.
- If p, q are state formulas, then so are p∧q, ¬p.
- If p is a path formula, then Ep and Ap are state formulas.
- Each state formula is also a path formula.
- If p, q are path formulas, then so are p∧q, ¬p.
- If p, q are path formulas, then so are Gp, Fp, Xp, p U q.

The following system is a complete and sound deductive system for CTL (Emerson, 1991): Axiom schemes:

All propositional tautologies.

$EFp \Leftrightarrow E[\text{ true } U \text{ } p]$

$AGp \Leftrightarrow \neg EF\neg p$

$AFp \Leftrightarrow A[\text{ true } U \text{ } p]$

$EGp \Leftrightarrow \neg AF\neg p$

$EX(p \lor q) \Leftrightarrow EXp \lor EXq$

$AXp \Leftrightarrow \neg E\neg p$

$E(p \text{ U } q) \Leftrightarrow q \lor (p \land EXE(p \text{ U } q))$

$A(p \text{ U } q) \Leftrightarrow q \lor (p \land AXA(p \text{ U } q))$

$EXtrue \land AXtrue$

$AG(r \Rightarrow (\neg q \land (p \Rightarrow EXr))) \Rightarrow (r \Rightarrow \neg A(p \text{ U } q))$

$AG(r \Rightarrow (\neg q \land EXr)) \Rightarrow (r \Rightarrow \neg AFq)$

$AG(r \Rightarrow (\neg q \land (p \Rightarrow AXr))) \Rightarrow (r \Rightarrow \neg E(p \text{ U } q))$

$AG(r \Rightarrow (\neg q \land AXr)) \Rightarrow (r \Rightarrow \neg EFq)$

$AG(p \Rightarrow q) \Rightarrow (EXp \Rightarrow EXq)$

Inference rules:

If $\vdash$ p then $\vdash$ AGp (Generalization)

If $\vdash$ p and $\vdash$ p$\Rightarrow$q then $\vdash$ q (Modus ponens)

For example, it can be proved that $\vdash$ AGp yields $\vdash$ p, and if F_1 and F_2 are logically equivalent propositional formulas, then $\vdash$ AG F_1 $\Leftrightarrow$ AG F_2 (these statements will be used in the example in further text).

5.2.5 *Branching Temporal Logic*

An interesting variant of CTL is Branching Temporal Logic (Kontchakov, 2007), which also extends linear temporal logic.

In BTL, one defines a tree as a flow of time $F = (W, <)$ containing a root point r, for which $W = \{v | r < v\} \cup \{r\}$, and such that for every $w \in W$, the set $\{w | v < w\}$ is well-founded and (strictly) linearly ordered by $<$. A history in F is then defined as a maximal linearly $<$-ordered subset of W. Finally, an ω-tree is a tree of this sort in which every history is order isomorphic to $(N, <)$.

A "branching time model" is then defined as a structure $B = (F, H, pB0, pB1, \ldots)$, where $F = (W, <)$ is an ω-tree, H is a set of histories in F (conceived as the set of possible flows of time in the model), and $pBi \subseteq W$ for all i. A logical formula is then evaluated relative to a pairs (h, w) consisting of an actual history $h \in H$ and a time point $w \in h$ – i.e. formulas are evaluated at time-points in the context of their histories. In such a pair (h, w), the temporal operators are interpreted along the actual history h as in the linear time framework, while the operators E and A quantify over the set of all histories coming through w. We say that a BT L-formula φ is satisfiable if there exists a branching time model B such that (B,h,w) implies φ for some history $h \in H$ and some time point $w \in h$. The practical upshot is similar to CTL, but the formal properties are subtly different.

5.3   Examples of Temporal Inference in the Twitter Domain

In this section we give a concrete exampleof temporal inference in our target domain. Specifically, we illustrate the deductive system for CTL logic on one common-sense example. Let us suppose we have:

- Bob and Clark always have lunch together.
- If Alison is having lunch with Bob, and Bob is having lunch with Clark, then Alison is having lunch with Clark.
- In all circumstances, it is true that: if Alison has lunch with Clark, then he will not forget her name that day and potentially the next day Alison will have lunch with Clark again.

And let us assume that we want to derive:

If Alison has lunch with Bob, then potentially Clark will never forget her name.

Let us denote

Alison has lunch with Bob today by p

Bob has lunch with Clark today by q

Alison has lunch with Clark today by r

Clark forgets Alison's name today by s

Then, the assumptions can be represented as:

$$AGq$$

$$p \land q \Rightarrow r$$

$$AG(r \Rightarrow (\neg s \land EXr))$$

And the conjecture as:

$$p \Rightarrow EG\neg s$$

We will use the following metatheorem of propositional logic: if $\vdash a \Rightarrow b$ and $\vdash b \Rightarrow c$, then $\vdash a \Rightarrow c$.

One proof of $p \Rightarrow EG\neg s$ then looks like the following:

(1) $AG(r \Rightarrow (\neg s \wedge EXr))$ (hypothesis)

(2) $AG(r \Rightarrow (\neg s \wedge EXr)) \Rightarrow (r \Rightarrow \neg AFs)$ (axiom 12)

(3) $r \Rightarrow \neg AFs$ (1,2,modus ponens)

(4) $\neg AFs \Rightarrow \neg AF\neg\neg s$ (3, propositional logic)

(5) $r \Rightarrow \neg AF\neg\neg s$ (3,4, propositional logic)

(6) $\neg AF\neg\neg s \Rightarrow EG\neg s$ (axiom 5)

(7) $r \Rightarrow EG\neg s$ (5,6,propositional logic)

(8) AGq (hypothesis)

(9) q (8, theorem)

(10) $p \Rightarrow p \wedge q$ (9, propositional logic)

(11) $p \wedge q \Rightarrow r$ (hypothesis)

(12) $p \Rightarrow r$ (10,11,propositional logic)

(13) $p \Rightarrow EG\neg s$ (7,12,propositional logic)

Chapter 6

Representing and Reasoning On Spatial Knowledge

A large percentage of real-world knowledge pertains to space as well as time. Humans possess a great deal of evolved and learned common sense regarding representing and reasoning about space, but, this is not innate to software programs so we need to explicitly think about how to make our software systems space-friendly. From a logic point of view, space and time can in principle be treated just like any other sorts of relationships – but this turns out not to be an optimal point of view in terms of either human-friendliness or computational efficiency of logic systems. Rather, with space as with time, it is worthwhile to invest the effort to develop specialized techniques for handling spatial and spatiotemporal knowledge.

As in the case of time, we will not be able to entirely disentangle spatial representation from spatial reasoning; but we will endeavor to do so as much as possible, and in this chapter we will focus mainly on representation (introducing reasoning only when really needed for motivational purposes) and defer reasoning for later.

Most generally conceived, spatial reasoning (Cohn *et al.*, 2008) is the capacity to infer relations of direction, morphology, topology, distance, etc, about entities existing in a given space (typically 2D or 3D). There are many combinations of space representation/abstraction and inferential mechanics for dealing with spatial reasoning, usually focusing on different aspects of spatial representations: topology, morphology, direction, etc. In this chapter, we will describe in some detail the main representatives among them, and also discuss ways of extending and integrating those techniques.

6.1 An Example Scenario for Spatial Representation and Reasoning

In order to provide a common ground for explaining the different methodologies used for logically representing spatial knowledge, we will articulate an example scenario wherein various sorts of spatial reasoning can be performed.

In order to accommodate several types of spatial reasoning tasks, the example presented here is composed of layered data produced by multiple sources. The use of such multi-layered data portrays a situation possible and maybe even frequent in a real-world, large-scale, heterogeneous store of spatiotemporal knowledge.

The first layer of data is of linguistic nature - a stream of Twitter entries, from which semantic interpretation can extract many elements of spatial and temporal information, as we can see in Figure 6.1.

One of the spatial inferences that can be made from the Twitter stream is that the three characters involved - Pam, Sam and Tim - appear to be in the same city or same metro area, which is called simply "Metro City" by Pam. That brings the second layer of data, shown in Figure 6.2, which presents a more evident spatial nature: it is a simplified map of Metro City, showing many city features - neighborhoods, bridges, canals, rivers, islands - including those mentioned in the Twitter stream. Many of those features are of an imprecise nature - for instance often it is difficult to tell where a neighborhood ends and other one begins.

The stream also mentions a weather phenomenon - rain - that may affect the plans of the characters involved in the Twitter stream. That brings the third layer of data: a (admittedly simplistic) weather pattern map for Metro City, shown in Figure 6.3, portraying the conditions of the city at the time of the first message. Arrows in the picture show direction of the wind and therefore the overall tendency of the dislocation of the weather patterns. It is interesting to note that this third layer is intrinsically uncertain, as the arrows point to tendencies and weather forecast is essentially probabilistic.

Now that the common scenario is described and illustrated, the following sections will show how several approaches for representation oriented to spatial reasoning "see" that scenario, and how they may allow the inference of new information based on that scenario.

6.2 Topological Representation

The first mode of spatial representation we will discuss here is "topological" representation. To make a rather crude and concise definition, topology deals with connection and

Sam The guests are already arriving! Hope that the house does not look as messy as I think it is...
About 10 minutes ago from the web.

Pam I had this bright idea of choosing a hairdresser in Bridgetown, and Sam lives in the Island. Maybe I'll arrive unelegantly late at the party... :(
About 30 minutes ago from the web.

Tim I am leaving now. It is a bit early, but I heard that there is a traffic jam at the south Bridge. Hope to be at Sam's party in an hour or so, right on time.
About 1 hour ago from the web.

Sam Great, the bad news are that it is already raining down south. Maybe my plans of an outdoor party will be shatered. Still... There's nothing but blue sky here in Center Island, perhaps the rain will not get this far...
About 2 hours ago from the web.

Fig. 6.1   Twitter stream containing spatial and temporal assertions

inclusion of regions. For instance, telling if something is an island or a lake inside an island is a topological problem.

A spatial representation and reasoning technique that deals with both connection and inclusion at the same time is the *Region Connection Calculus* (RCC) (Cohn *et al.*, 1997). RCC may be interpreted as a possible extension of Allen's Interval Algebra into the spatial domain. The basic entities modeled by RCC are regions (as opposed to points), assumed to be embedded in the same space of some dimensionality. The basic relations in RCC are defined in terms of connection or inclusion between two regions of the analyzed space. The number of possible relations varies according to the "granularity" of the RCC variety being used. The "coarser" variety, RCC8, is thus called due to the set of just 8 primitive relations that define it. Those are illustrated in Figure 6.4.

A set of RCC relations stating spatial facts about a group of entities can be used to infer new spatial facts. For instance, if A is a non-tangential proper part of B and B is a non-tangential proper part of C, then A is a non-tangential proper part of C. If on the other

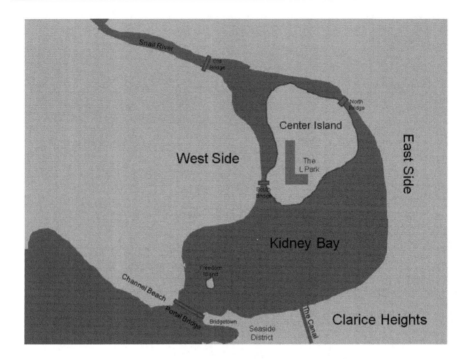

Fig. 6.2   High-level map of Metro City

hand A is a *tangential* proper part of B and B is a tangential proper part of C, then A can be either a non-tangential or a tangential proper part of C. Or, showing the same inferences predicate-wise:

nonTangentialProperPart(A, B) ∧ nonTangentialProperPart(B, C)

⇒

nonTangentialProperPart(A, C)

tangentialProperPart(A, B) ∧ tangentialProperPart(B, C)

⇒

tangentialProperPart(A, C) XOR nonTangentialProperPart(A, C)

(Please note that an exclusive or is used at the right side of the logical conditional in the last inference, for an entity cannot be at the same time a tangential and non-tangential proper part of another in the crisp formulation of RCC8.)

All such inferential combinations between three entities are summarized in the composition matrix for RCC8, shown in Table 6.1. For sake of space the usual abbreviations for

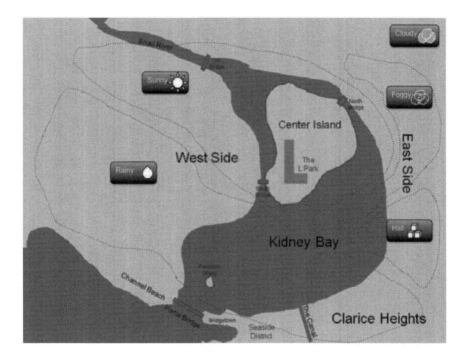

Fig. 6.3   Weather patterns over Metro City

RCC8 operations are used. A set of operations in a given cell means that if two entities
A and B are related by the operation corresponding to the row and B is related to a third
entity C by the operation in the column, then A and C are mapped by the operations in the
cell. For instance one can find the composition corresponding to the last inference above
by checking the cell at row TPP, column TPP. The symbol "*" in the table denotes the
"universal relation", meaning that any RCC8 relation between A and C is possible in the
corresponding case.

There are "finer-grained" versions of RCC like RCC15 and RCC23. Also, RCC can
receive extensions (for instance a primitive detecting concavity) that also deal with morphology to some extent. Those are extensively discussed in (Cohn *et al.*, 1997). With
RCC-8, though, it is already possible to see how space can be represented in terms of region connection in our example scenario. (And the relations in RCC15 and RCC23, as
well as their numerous compositions, are probably overcomplex for the didactic examples
intended here.)

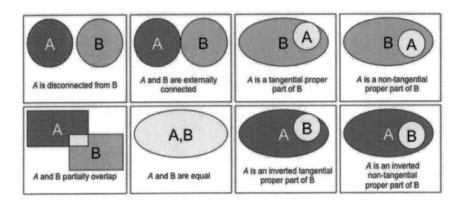

Fig. 6.4   Connection-inclusion relations in RCC8

Looking at the map in Figure 6.2, one can make the following assertions using the RCC8 predicates:

nonTangentialProperPart("Center Island", "Kidney Bay")
externallyConnected("Clarice Heights", "Seaside District")
tangentialProperPart("Bridge Town", "Seaside District")
overlaps("East Side", "Clarice Heights")
disconnected("West Side", "Center Island")
nonTangentialProperPart("L Park", "Center Island")
externallyConnected("East Side", "Snail River")
externallyConnected("West Side", "Snail River")
overlaps("Snail River", "Kidney Bay")

According to the rules of Region Connection Calculus, it is already possible to make some topological inferences about Metro City from the assertions above. For instance:

nonTangentialProperPart("Center Island", "Kidney Bay"),
nonTangentialProperPart("L Park", "Center Island") →
nonTangentialProperPart("L Park", "Kidney Bay")

Inferences like the one above can be seen as the construction of new links in a *RCC network*. As often happens in reasoning, problems represented through RCC can also be seen as a graph - the aforementioned RCC network -, and the reasoning problem is accordingly reduced to a graph problem with a plethora of methodologies and tools for dealing with it. In order to better illustrate that, Figure 6.5 shows the assertions in the list above in the form

Table 6.1 Composition matrix for RCC8 relations

o	DC	EC	PO	TPP	NTPP	TPPi	NTPPi	EQ
DC	*	DC EC PO TPP NTPP	DC EC PO TPP NTPP	DC EC PO TPP NTPP	DC EC PO TPP NTPP	DC	DC	DC
EC	DC EC PO TPPi NTPPi	DC EC PO TPP TPPi EQ	DC EC PO TPP NTPP	EC PO TPP NTPP	PO TPP NTPP	DC EC	DC	EC
PO	DC EC PO TPPi NTPPi	DC EC PO TPPi NTPPi	*	PO TPP NTPP	PO TPP NTPP	DC EC PO TPPi NTPPi	DC EC PO TPPi NTPPi	PO
TPP	DC	DC EC	DC EC PO TPP NTPP	TPP NTPP	NTPP	DC EC PO TPP TPPi EQ	DC EC PO TPPi NTPPi	TPP
NTPP	DC	DC	DC EC PO TPP NTPP	NTPP	NTPP	DC EC PO TPP NTPP	*	NTPP
TPPi	DC EC PO TPPi NTPPi	EC PO TPPi NTPPi	PO TPPi NTPPi	PO TPP TPPi EQ	PO TPP NTPP	TPPi NTPPi	NTPPi	TPPi
NTPPi	DC EC PO TPPi NTPPi	PO TPPi NTPPi	PO TPPi NTPPi	PO TPPi NTPPi	PO TPP NTPP TPPi NTPPi EQ	NTPPi	NTPPi	NTPPi
EQ	DC	EC	PO	TPP	NTPP	TPPi	NTPPi	EQ

of a RCC network, with the inferred relation *nonTangentialProperPart*("L Park", "Kidney Bay") represented as a dotted edge. (Due to space restrictions relation names are depicted in the figure as acronyms made from their initials, as traditionally done in RCC notation.)

Even in the reasonably crisp map of Metro City, it is possible to see that some of the classic RCC8 relations shown in Figure 6.5 are in fact ambiguous due to the intrinsically imprecise nature of many geographic concepts. For instance, is Bridge Town a tangential proper part of the Seaside District or are they externally connected or perhaps overlapping?

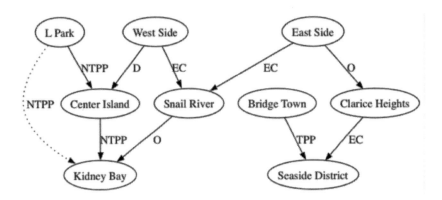

Fig. 6.5   RCC network representing some topological relations among Metro City regions

Are the East and West Side really disconnected or should the Old Bridge be considered a connection between them?

That imprecision and ambiguity of some geographical features in the RCC point of view can be better modeled by adding *fuzziness* to the representation (Schockaert *et al.*, 2008). In fuzzy logic, two entities can be related by multiple predicates, even ones that may sound mutually exclusive in classic logic. Those contradictions and ambiguities are conciliated by the use of *truth values* indicating the degree to which the relation applies between the two entities. In the notation used here, we define a new logic predicate *truthValue(R(A,B),v)*, indicating that the (fuzzy, in this case) truth value of relation *R(A,B)* between entities *A* and *B* is *v*. With that in mind, many fuzzy relations can be outlined among the entities shown in Metro City map, as exemplified below:

truthValue(overlaps("Bridge Town", "Sea Side District"),0.3)
truthValue(externallyConnected("Bridge Town", "Sea Side District"),0.3)
truthValue(tangentialProperPart("Bridge Town", "Sea Side District"),0.4)
truthValue(disconnected("East Side", "West Side"),0.9)
truthValue(externallyConnected("East Side", "West Side"),0.1)
truthValue(disconnected("Bridge Town", "Channel Beach"),0.9)
truthValue(externallyConnected("Bridge Town", "Channel Beach"),0.1)
truthValue(overlaps("Channel Beach", "West Side"),0.3)
truthValue(externallyConnected("Channel Beach", "West Side"),0.3)
truthValue(tangentialProperPart("Channel Beach", "West Side"),0.4)

As in the case of classic RCC, those relations can also be translated to a graph form. Figure 6.6 shows the fuzzy RCC8 network corresponding to the assertions above. The main difference visible between that graph and the one in Figure 6.5 is the presence of labels in the edges - each one is assigned to a tuple indicating the kind of relation and the truth value of it. (Due to space limitations, the unambiguous though highly verbose logic predication used in the list above is avoided.) Another difference is the presence of multiple edges (relations) between two nodes. As an example of a possible interesting subgraph that could be derived from that one, the most intense relations (those with higher truth values) between all connected pairs of nodes are shown as solid edges.

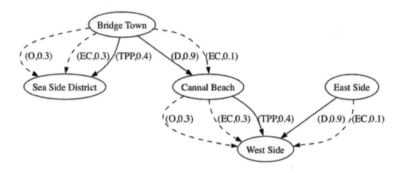

Fig. 6.6   A fuzzy RCC network representing some topological relations among Metro City regions

Finally, some types of spatial information are better modeled neither in crisp nor in fuzzy ways - they are better modeled in terms of *probability*. Probabilistic spatial relations are conceptually different from the fuzzy ones in the sense that they do not say that two entities have a set of relations at the same time in different degrees. Instead, a set of probabilistic relations between two entities assumes that the actual relation between the two entities is unknown/uncertain, but assigns different probabilities to the existing possibilities.

Weather forecast based on the map shown in Figure 6.3 is a perfect target for probabilistic modeling, as it represents intrinsically uncertain information. Here we will try to model through RCC an extrapolation of the weather situation on Center Island at the time of the last Twitter message, based on the patterns and tendencies shown in Figure 6.3. In order to accommodate the uncertainty inherent to such a "weather forecast", we introduce a new predicate *probability(R(A, B), p)*, indicating that a given spatial relation R between entities

A and *B* has a probability *p* of being real. The list below suggests some probabilities for relations extrapolated by the forecast:

probability(nonTangentialProperPart("Center Island", "Sunny"), 30%)

probability(overlaps("Center Island", "Sunny"), 30%)

probability(overlaps("Center Island", "Rain"), 30%)

probability(overlaps("Center Island", "Hail"), 20%)

probability(overlaps("Center Island", "Fog"), 10%)

probability(nonTangentialProperPart("L Park", "Center Island"), 100%)

probability(nonTangentialProperPart("L Park", "Sunny"), 40%)

probability(nonTangentialProperPart("L Park", "Rain"), 30%)

probability(nonTangentialProperPart("L Park", "Hail"), 20%)

probability(nonTangentialProperPart("L Park", "Fog"), 10%)

That list of assertions can also be represented as a RCC network, this time of probabilistic nature, as shown in Figure 6.7.

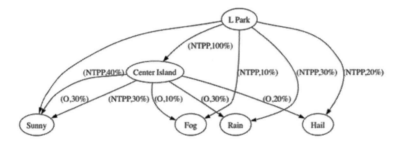

Fig. 6.7   A probabilistic RCC network representing some relations among Metro City regions and weather pattern zones

6.3   Directional Reasoning

Although qualitative topological reasoning such as that provided by RCC can encompass many spatial relations between entities of many kinds, as illustrated in the previous section, it is by no means without limitations. For instance, RCC is inadequate for representing *directional* assertions.

Directional spatial relations assume that the space is divided into a set of directions - or angular alignments - that are applicable to all entities. Directional relations are often used in everyday descriptions such as "Canada is north of the United States" or "the hurricane is heading Northwest" or "in order to get to the Main Plaza, turn right, follow two blocks and then turn left".

Qualitative directional reasoning is represented in a broader way by the STAR Calculus (Mitra, 2004), which by its turn can be considered a generalization of Frank's Cardinal Calculus (Frank, 1991). Cardinal Calculus used a system of four or eight directions (as in the conventional cardinal system used in geography, although they did not need a direct correspondence to those), while in the STAR calculus that is generalized to n directions forming n sectors of equal angular amplitude across the 360 degrees of the circle. (The mention of the circle bespeaks the fact that these forms of directional reasoning are primarily concerned with 2D spatial reasoning. However, it is not difficult to see that similar concepts can be produced in higher dimensional spaces with some work.) The two systems (hereinafter referenced collectively as "directional calculus") have still an additional special "Null" direction meaning no direction at all, or in other words meaning that the two entities directionally compared are "in the same place", that is, so close that any statement about directions is meaningless.

The basic operations of directional calculus are inversion and composition. Inversion allows commonsensical inferences such as

direction(A, B, North) $\rightarrow$ direction(B, A, South)

or "if B is North of A, then A is South of B", in natural language. Composition on the other hand combines known directional relations between entities in order to infer new ones, such as in

direction(A, B, North), direction(B, C, East) $\rightarrow$ direction(A, C, Northeast)

Indeed, similarly to the case of RCC, all possible compositions in directional calculus can also be mapped into a composition matrix. As an example, Table 6.2 shows a composition table for the classic subdivision of geographic 2D space into eight cardinal directions (plus the null direction), adapted from (Frank, 1991) (where other variations are also discussed). Indeed, the same case convention of that publication is used: upper case letters for "exact" directions and lower case for "Euclidean approximates". (The issue of "exact" and "approximate" directions is further discussed below as a prologue to fuzzy and probabilistic formulations of directional calculus.)

Using the directional predicates defined above, we can again describe the example scenario in terms of a symbolic spatial reasoning representation. Here is an example list of predicates taking into account directly information shown in Figure 6.1 and 6.2:

Table 6.2   Composition matrix for the operations corresponding to the eight cardinal directions

	N	NE	E	SE	S	SW	W	NW	Null
N	N	n	ne	Null	Null	Null	nw	n	N
NE	n	NE	ne	e	Null	Null	Null	N	NE
E	ne	ne	E	e	se	Null	Null	Null	E
SE	Null	e	e	SE	se	s	Null	Null	SE
S	Null	Null	se	se	S	s	sw	o	S
SW	Null	Null	Null	s	s	SW	sw	w	SW
W	nw	Null	Null	Null	sw	sw	W	w	W
NW	n	n	Null	Null	Null	w	w	NW	NW
Null	N	NE	E	SE	S	SW	W	NW	Null

direction("Sam", "Center Island", Null)

direction("Pam", "Bridgetown", Null)

direction("Center Island", "Bridgetown", South)

direction("Sam", "Pam", South)

In the case of Tim's Twitter entry, a human looking at Figure 6.2 can easily suspect that he is somewhere in the West Side, since he apparently has to cross the South Bridge to reach Sam, who lives in Center Island. An integrated spatial reasoning system taking into account both topological as well as directional reasoning could mount a graph of the connection relations in Metro City (like many of those exemplified here) and also reach the conclusion that Tim is likely on the West Side. (The system would of course have to reason on the assumption that people would choose the shortest path from one place to another, or make some related heuristic assumption, in order to rule out awkward possibilities like Tim being in the West Side, crossing Old Bridge, going South and then entering Center Island through South Bridge.) Therefore, we can also add the relations:

direction("Tim", "West Side", Null)

direction("West Side", "Center Island", East)

direction("Tim", "Sam", East)

Using composition on the assertions above, we can make the inference

direction("Tim", "Sam", East), direction("Sam", "Pam", South) $\rightarrow$

$\rightarrow$direction("Tim", "Pam", Southeast)

Again, all those facts can be represented (and reasoned upon) in the form of a graph, as shown in Figure 6.8.

Here again the question of imprecision and uncertainty comes into play. In the case of topological reasoning some relations are naturally crisp (for instance, an island is surely a

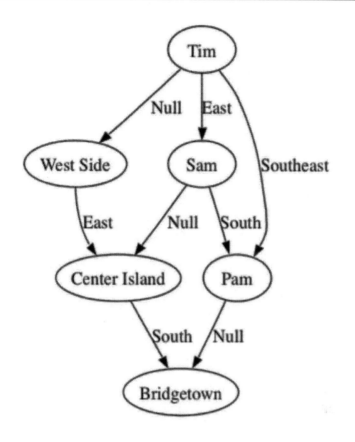

Fig. 6.8   A directional network showing spatial relations between the entities shown in Figure 6.1 and 6.2

non-tangential proper part of a body of water, by definition). In the case of directions, on the other hand, arguably there are no crisp relations in almost all practical cases. For instance in the crisp example, by the assertions above it is declared that Center Island is North of Bridgetown, although perhaps one could also say that it is northeast of Bridgetown. The very definition of directions in directional calculus states them in terms of broad sectors of the circle instead of sharp lines, hinting already at a non-crisp nature for directions.

Therefore, a fuzzy modeling for directional calculus comes naturally; it is basically a way of telling that entity A is more in this or that direction than others, relatively to entity B. Following the example case, the same geographical entities in the example above can have directional relations re-stated in fuzzy form as suggested below:

truthValue(direction("Center Island", "Bridgetown", Southwest), 0.5) truthValue(direction("Center Island", "Bridgetown", South), 0.5)

truthValue(direction("Center Island", "West Side", West), 0.8)

truthValue(direction("Center Island", "West Side", Southwest), 0.2)

The directional relations above, being between extensive regions, naturally look intrinsically fuzzy. In the case of the characters in the Twitter stream, though, we are talking about directional relations involving *point-like* entities. In that case, a probabilistic modeling seems to capture better the conceptual setting at play. For instance we can infer that Tim most likely is somewhere in the West Side, but since the West Side is rather extensive relative to Sam's location in Center Island Tim may be West, Southwest or Northwest of Sam. However, we cannot say that Tim is at the same time West and Southwest of Sam (as in a fuzzy statement), but we can say that Tim is West of Sam or Southwest of Sam with different probabilities for each alternative. The list below suggests a probabilistic reformulation of the directional relations between the Twitter characters.

probability(direction("Sam", "Tim", West), 70%)

probability(direction("Sam", "Tim", Southwest), 20%)

probability(direction("Sam", "Tim", Northwest), 10%)

probability(direction("Sam", "Pam", South), 60%)

probability(direction("Sam", "Pam", Southwest), 40%)

probability(direction("Pam", "Tim", Northwest), 40%)

probability(direction("Pam", "Tim", North), 60%)

As seen in previous approaches, fuzzy and probabilistic relations can also be represented as networks and thus be treated by many techniques for solving graph problems (analogously to the use of graph theory in analyzing biological networks, see e.g. (Przulj, 2005), (Grindrod & Kibble, 2004)). The graph in Figure 6.9 shows *at the same time* part of the crisp, fuzzy and probabilistic directional relations mentioned above. (This breakdown from the traditional approach of showing just "homogeneous" graphs used so far is in a way a preview of the following section, where we discuss a modeling tool that might allow the fusion of the approaches discussed so far.)

6.4   Occupancy Grids: Putting It All Together

The previous sections show that available representation models for spatial reasoning are somewhat compartmentalized. Region Connection Calculus is appropriate for reason-

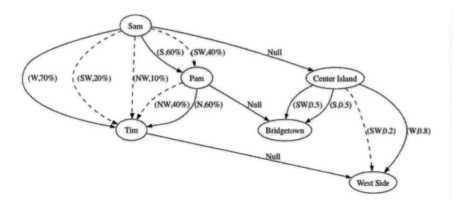

Fig. 6.9 A mixed network showing probabilistic, fuzzy and crisp directional relations between the example entities

ing in topological (and even morphological) terms on entities with non-negligible extension. STAR calculus is interesting for dealing with directional relations between entities treated as dimensionless points. Both approaches are qualitative and therefore they do not deal explicitly with distances and measurements (although it seems unproblematic to add these to the reasoning framework at least in the case of the directional models). A natural question is whether there is a third approach able to integrate most or all of the strong points of the previous approaches, perhaps with a few additional advantages?

A positive answer to this question is provided by a modeling construct originally developed not with reasoning explicitly in mind, but rather as a probabilistic spatial representation the distribution of entities in space. This is the formalism of so-called Occupancy Grids (Martin & Moravec, 1996).

Occupancy grids (also called Evidence Grids in their more complex and generic forms) were developed for Mobile Robotics and to date that remain their main field of practical application. The initial goal was simply to represent space and obstacles on it, in a probabilistic way that could accommodate noisy, incomplete or ambiguous sensor data gathered by a robot while navigating through an unknown terrain, thus providing an adequate data framework for typical tasks such as obstacle avoidance and path planning. However, it has been demonstrated that spatial data represented in the form of occupancy grids can be used to achieve topological, morphological and directional inferences about the work environment of a robot (Szabó, 2004). Moreover, the original purely probabilistic version can also incorporate fuzziness (Bloch & Saffiotti, 2003). Therefore, occupancy grids (and their variations) look like the most promising candidates for a common framework able to bridge and integrate all the aspects of spatial reasoning, even though (or perhaps because) they are a paradigm shift from the more symbolic, higher-level representations traditionally used in reasoning.

The original model of occupancy grids divides space into a regular lattice of cells, in which each cell has an associated probability of being occupied or not. Usually the grid is orthogonal and the space is 2D, although versions using other grid topologies (e.g., hexagonal) and higher-dimensional spaces are easy to devise. From the point of view of a conventional wheeled robot, "occupancy" is the presence of nondescript impassable solid obstacles. In order to accommodate versatile spatial reasoning about multiple entities, some complexity has to be added to that basic model. For instance the occupancy of a grid cell should not be nondescript. Rather, it should contain the probabilities of presence or fuzzy presences of the entities involved in the reasoning problem. In order to better illustrate that, Figure 6.10 and 6.11 show fuzzy and probabilistic occupancy grids representing data related to the example scenario.

Figure 6.10 shows a spatial discretization of Metro City land area in terms of an occupancy grid. Different regions of Metro City are shown in different shades. The representation is fuzzy in order to capture the imprecision inherent in dividing neighborhoods of a city. That fuzziness is coded in gray levels, and explains why for instance the East Side is light gray and Clarice Heights is darker, but the border zone between them is a gradation, representing the variation of pertinence to the two different neighborhoods as a given cell seems to be more part of Clarice Heights than the East Side, or the other way around. Shade mixtures observing the same convention can be observed along other neighborhood boundaries of the city.

Figure 6.11 on the other hand, is a probabilistic representation of the location of Tim, Sam and Pam. In terms of occupancy grids, those point-like individuals actually become clouds of probability. That can be an uniform cloud, as in the case of Sam - from the Twitter stream it is impossible to tell where exactly he is in Center Island, and so his probability cloud is homogeneous across the whole extension of the landmass. In the case of Tim, on the other hand, the grid cells of the West Side closer to the Old Bridge are less likely to contain him, since if Tim were in that location presumably he could opt to cross Old Bridge and then North Bridge instead of using South Bridge. (An option that would look particularly attractive if Sam lives on the North part of Center Island.) Finally Pam's probability cloud coincides with the fuzzy cloud from Figure 6.10 representing Bridgetown.

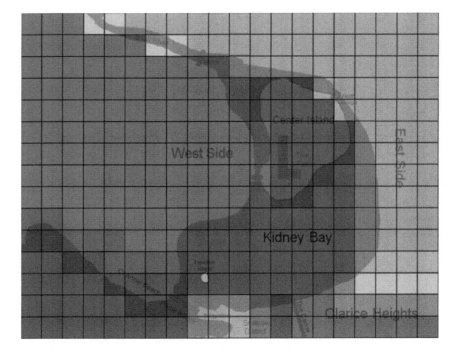

Fig. 6.10   A fuzzy occupancy grid representing different regions of Metro City

Both figures above point in an intuitive way to a set of methods – often borrowed from digital image processing and computer vision – that allow the "translation" of information in occupancy grids to more symbolic representation frameworks, such as RCC and directional calculus. For instance the shade gradations representing neighborhoods in Figure 6.10 can be segmented by a plethora of techniques in order to determine "crisp" neighborhoods, which would be suitable for classic RCC. And the probability clouds in Figure 6.11 could have their centroids determined and submitted to a crisp directional analysis or (perhaps more interestingly) directional probabilities could be computed by considering all the possible pairs of cells from two different clouds, supplying information in a very refined way for a probabilistic directional reasoning process.

Also, throughout this analysis of spatial reasoning we have tried to show the equivalence between many spatial reasoning representations and graph representations. In the case of occupancy grids, that equivalence comes with particular ease, as grids in general *are* graphs, in the sense that they are sets of cells (which can be viewed as nodes) connected

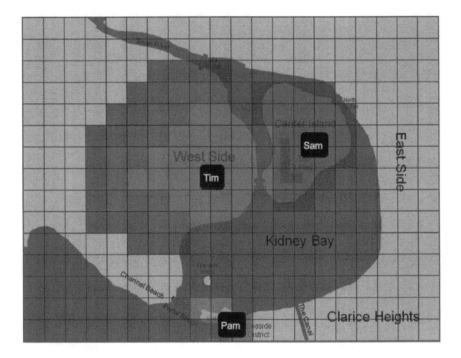

Fig. 6.11   a probabilistic occupancy grid showing the location clouds of Tim, Pam and Sam.

by a regular neighborhood topology (which can be represented by edges). Figure 6.12 illustrates that grid-graph equivalence

For the purposes of this text, more specifically we are talking about grid cells that can be related to spatial entities being reasoned upon by sets of logic predicates, often of probabilistic or fuzzy nature. Here we define the construct *occupies(A, cell(i, j))*, indicating that entity A occupies the cell assigned by coordinates i, j. (Many variations of an orthogonal coordinate system can be used, but throughout the examples in this section we will assume that i, j refer to row, column, with numbering starting at 1 for both dimensions.) The predicate *occupies* is different from the RCC predicates in the sense that it does not inform anything about the relative sizes and states of superposition of A and the cell. A may be a large entity and the cell contains just a tiny portion of it, or A may be a point-like entity that is somewhere in the space mapped by the cell. For instance, the following set of predicates could be related to the cell (20, 15), part of the blurred frontier between Bridgetown and the Seaside District in Figure 6.10:

truthValue(occupies("Bridgetown", cell(20, 15)), 0.63)

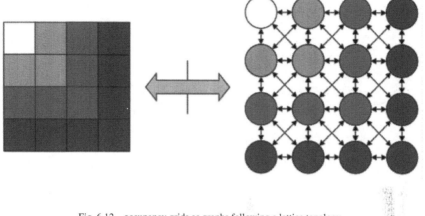

Fig. 6.12   occupancy grids as graphs following a lattice topology.

truthValue(occupies("Seaside District", cell(20, 15)), 0.37)

probability(occupies("Pam", cell(20, 15)), 63%)

Of course, an occupancy grid is in a sense a "fine-grained" and regular graph, while in the spatial reasoning representations shown here we have "coarse-grained" graphs (representing higher-level entities such as whole regions and people, instead of individual space cells). However, in principle, topological and directional information about higher-level entities *can* be extracted from occupancy grids. Indeed, the issue of low-level to high-level conversion raises the awareness that, in order to be used as a universal framework for spatial reasoning, the operation of occupancy grids has to involve translations from and to other forms of spatial representation. The diagram in Figure 6.13 outlines some possible input and output relations between several techniques (not restricted to spatial reasoning) that might play a role in an spatial reasoning engine centered on occupancy grids.

As one can see, a spatial reasoning engine created along these lines could potentially pass all the data flux through occupancy grids, which could be the main spatial data representation approach. External information sources (which can be anything, from raw sensory data to natural language extraction of spatial information) could write to the occupancy grids through the Visual Creation module. Interestingly, as one may note from the above discussion of mathematical morphology, many techniques for extracting information from occupancy grids can be borrowed from digital image processing and computer vision (grouped under Visual Interpretation), while techniques for adding information to occupancy grids can be borrowed from data visualization and computer graphics (grouped under Visual Creation). Data extracted from Occupancy Grids by Visual Representation may

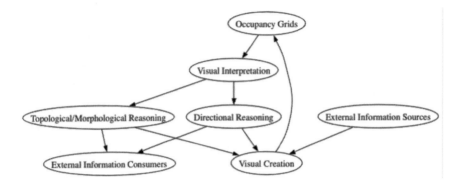

Fig. 6.13   A diagram showing inter-relationships between different kinds of processing that may exist in a comprehensive spatial reasoning engine

feed both Directional Reasoning and Topological/Morphological Reasoning processes, and those in turn may write their conclusions back to the occupancy grids through Visual Creation as well as output those conclusions to External Information Consumers.

6.5   Handling Change

The examples we've given using the grid-centered system proposed above, as well as higher-level graph representations, so far have involved *static* situations. (With the possible exception of the example involving weather, where uncertainty is implicit in the dynamics of the phenomena involved; but we did not focus on that aspect.) However, in the greater context of this work, the spatial reasoning approach described in the previous section would most likely work in a *dynamic* environment, where data from multiple sources and represented in many ways would constantly update the "world picture" maintained by the system. Those updates could be from higher-level entities and cascade down to the low level of occupancy grids. Conversely, change occurring on the lower levels could also cascade up and rearrange the relations between higher-level entities. This last aspect is specially interesting for detecting change between entities (usually high-level ones) important for the problem being handled by the system.

Such a bottom-up cascading event is illustrated by Figure 6.14 and 6.15. Indeed Figure 6.14 shows an updated weather map, representing the weather patterns over Metro city at the instant of the last message from Sam. (And here an occupancy grid representation is used instead of the "weather blobs" of Figure 6.3. Different shades are used to assign the prevalent weather pattern in the grid cell, and the lighter the shade the more intense the pattern represented.) We can see from that updated map that it is actually raining heavily over the whole of Center Island. Therefore, the probabilistic RCC network shown in Figure 6.7 must be updated with the new data. The result of such update is shown in Figure 6.15.

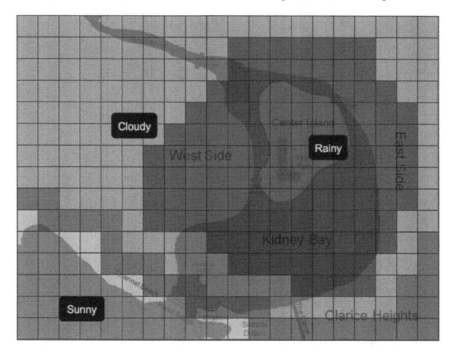

Fig. 6.14   an updated weather map of Metro City.

Instance (c) also adds one of the Twitter characters – Sam – to the picture, putting him in Center Island and therefore also under rain. The example network is kept small for didactic purposes, but considering the probabilities of Pam and Tim also being in the island, they could also be similarly related to present patterns. That kind of inference could be further used by a broader reasoning system (of which the proposed spatial reasoning engine would be just a component) to infer that perhaps the Twitter characters will make subsequent observations about rain at Sam's place in their tweets.

6.6   Spatial Logic

Temporal logic is a larger field than spatial logic, but the latter also has a long history and a flourishing body of contemporary work.

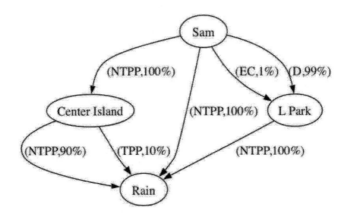

Fig. 6.15   An updated RCC network relating weather patterns to regions and individuals.

As an early example, consider Tarski's 1929 work in his *Geometry of Solids* (Tarski, 1956) – this is a second-order logic system, whose variables range not over points, but instead over the regular closed subsets of 3D Euclidean space (those subsets of R3 equal to the closure of their interior). Tarski's language features two non-logical predicates, corresponding to the binary relation of *parthood*, and the unary property of *being spherical*.

Much more recently, Aiello, Pratt-Hartmann and Benthem have reviewed the field of spatial logic in a masterful way in their lengthy book (Aiello *et al.*, 2007), which draws together research from a variety of different areas under a common spatial logic framework. They conceive spatial logic broadly as "the study of the relationship between geometrical structures and the spatial languages which describe them," and more precisely as follows:

> *By a spatial logic, we understand any formal language interpreted over a class of structures featuring geometrical entities and relations, broadly construed. The formal language in question may employ any logical syntax: that of first- order logic, or some fragment of first-order logic, or perhaps higher-order logic. The structures over which it is interpreted may inhabit any class of geometrical 'spaces': topological spaces, affine spaces, metric spaces, or perhaps a single space such as the projective plane or Euclidean 3-space. And the non-logical primitives of the language may be interpreted as any geometrical properties or relations defined over the relevant domains: topological connectedness of regions, parallelism of lines, or perhaps equidistance of two points from a third. What all these logics have in common is that the operative notion of validity depends on the underlying geometry of the structures over which their distinctively spatial primitives are interpreted. Spatial logic, then, is simply the study of the family of spatial logics, so conceived.*

As Aiello et al note, contemporary work in spatial logic emanates mainly from three application domains, the first two of which are highly relevant to the present work:

- AI, where attempts have recently been made to develop logics of *qualitative spatial reasoning*.
- The theory of spatial databases, related e.g. to geographical information systems
- Image processing, where it is convenient to describe objects as sets of vectors that can be 'added' (taking all linear sums) or 'subtracted' (taking all linear differences), and one may proceed to define logics involving these operations

6.6.1 *Extending RCC into a Topological Logic*

The spatial logic most relevant to our own work with PLN is the extension of RCC into a topological logic, an excellent example of which is presented in (Kontchakov, 2010).

To see how the RCC8 relations give rise to a spatial logic, let r1, r2 and r3 be regions in R2 that are homeomorphic to the disc, and suppose that r1, r2 stand in the relation TPP, while r1, r3 stand in the relation NTPP. It's easy to see (from the visual natural of these relationships) that r2, r3 must stand in one of the three relations PO, TPP or NTPP. In formal terms, what this means is that the RCC-8-formula

$$TPP(r1, r2) \wedge NTPP(r1, r3) \rightarrow PO(r2, r3) \vee TPP(r2, r3) \vee NTPP(r2, r3),$$

is valid over the spatial domain of disc-homeomorphs in the plane: all assignments of such regions to the variables r1, r2 and r3 make it true. Similar experimentation shows that, by contrast, the formula

$$TPP(r1, r2) \wedge NTPP(r1, r3) \wedge EC(r2, r3),$$

is unsatisfiable: no assignments of disc-homeomorphs to r1, r2 and r3 make this formula true.

A similar analysis may be done in Euclidean 3D space, and more generally. Suppose one has a formal language L, whose variables refer to spatial "regions" that are subsets of some geometric space. Given a subset K of regions, the notion of the satisfaction of an L-formula by a tuple of regions, and thus the notions of satisfiability and validity of an L-formula with respect to K, can be understood in the usual way. According to the approach of (Kontchakov, 2010), the pair (L,K) may then be called a *spatial logic*. If all the primitives of L are topological in character—as in the case of RCC8— then we have a topological logic. Otherwise one might have, say, a metric logic. For languages featuring negation, the notions of satisfiability and validity are dual in the usual sense.

Considering RCC8 as the foundation for a logic immediately makes the limitations of the RCC8 relationship-set apparent. For instance, constraints featuring RCC-8 predicates give us no means to combine regions into new ones. One way to remedy this deficiency is to turn the set of RCC regions into a Boolean algebra with binary operations $+$ and $\cdot$ and a unary operation $-$. Intuitively, we are to think of $r1 + r2$ as the agglomeration of $r1$ and $r2$, $r1 \cdot r2$ as the common part of $r1$ and $r2$, and $-r$ as the complement of r. Adding these operators to RCC8 yields what is known as BRCC8 (Boolean RCC8). For instance, in BRCC8, the formula

$$EC(r1 + r2, r3) \leftrightarrow EC(r1, r3) \vee EC(r2, r3),$$

is valid, whereas the formula

$$EC(r1, r2) \wedge EC(r1, -r2),$$

is unsatisfiable.

Taking things one step further, [Kontchakov, 2010a] explores the augmentation of BRCC8 with additional relationships representing connectedness: the unary predicates c and $c \leqslant k$ (for $k \geqslant 1$). Here one may interpret c(r) as "region r is connected" and $c \leqslant k(r)$ as "region r has at most k connected components."

These directions of research are highly relevant to the PLN approach that will be reviewed in Part III of this book, as PLN combines RCC relationships with Boolean and other operators in a fairly free way.

6.6.2 *Combining Spatial and Temporal Logic*

PLN also combines spatial and temporal logic freely, as we shall see in many of the examples presented in Part III. Further, it does so in a manner embracing rich time representations (such as intervals) and uncertainty. However, the full formalization of the combination of spatial and temporal logic is still a subject of current research. One classic paper in this area is titled "Spatial Logic + Temporal Logic = ?" (Kontchakov, 2007), and discusses several ways of combining the two, focusing on combinations of Branching Temporal Logic with spatial logics based on the RCC. This is a big step in the right direction, but doesn't handle interval representations of time or uncertainty.

Chapter 7

Representing and Reasoning on Contextual Knowledge

One of the critical issues confronted in doing logical inference on large spatiotemporal knowledge bases is the fact that most real-world logical relationships are *contextual* in nature. Contextuality must be explicitly taken into account to make real-world inference tractable. This is one of the issues with which formal-logic-based AI has traditionally had the most difficulty. In this chapter we briefly explore the notion of contextual inference and the key approaches that have been taken.

Generically speaking, cognitive processes are usually contextual in the sense that they depend on the environment, or context, inside which they are carried out. The notion of context, in different varieties, plays a crucial role in different disciplines including natural language semantics, linguistics, cognitive psychology, and artificial intelligence. Contextual information covers both knowledge representation and reasoning and their interaction.

A completely general representation of a particular piece of commonsense knowledge is impossible in practice, because "common sense" by its nature is not general but has to do with the properties of particular classes of situations. In this sense the only practical way to consider knowledge is as contextual. John McCarthy, one of the founders of the AI field, discussed this topic as follows (referring to axioms pertaining to real-world phenomena, rather than pure mathematics) (McCarthy, 1987):

"Whenever we write an axiom, a critic can say that the axiom is true only in a certain context. With a little ingenuity the critic can usually devise a more general context in which the precise form of the axiom doesn't hold. Looking at human reasoning as reflected in language emphasizes this point. Consider axiomatizing on so as to draw appropriate consequences from the information expressed in the sentence, 'The book is on the table'. The critic may propose to haggle about the precise meaning of on, inventing difficulties about what can be between the book and the table, or about how much gravity there has to be in a spacecraft in order to use the word on and whether centrifugal force counts. Thus we encounter Socratic puzzles over what the concept means in complete generality and encounter examples that never arise in life. There simply isn't a most general context. Conversely, if we axiomatize at a fairly high level of generality, the axioms are often longer than is convenient in special situations. Thus humans

find it useful to say, 'The book is on the table', omitting reference to time and precise identification of what book and what table. [...] A possible way out involves formalizing the notion of context [...]".

Another way to phrase this is to say that, generally, reasoning is local to a subset of all the known facts. One never consider all one knows, but rather a very small subset of it. This small subset, the subset that is used for reasoning about a given goal, determines the context of reasoning. A context encodes an individual's subjective view of some portion or aspect of the world. The individual's complete description of the world is given by the set of all the contexts. There can be different contexts for the same phenomenon and they can describe it at different levels of approximation. The same statement may have different truth values in different contexts. For instance, "Alison is my boss" can be true from John's point of view, but not from Mike's point of view.

As the above quote from McCarthy suggests, the topic of representing contextual information and contextual reasoning has its roots in the early years of artificial intelligence. Also, McCarthy's was probably the first proposal for rigorously modeling humans' common sense, the key feature for artificial intelligence. Another important early use of the concept of context in artificial intelligence was (Weyhrauch, 1980), who proposed a mechanized formal contextual reasoning system for *Advice taker,* a hypothetical computer program, proposed by John McCarthy (McCarthy, 1958) in the 1950's, that was the first proposal to use formal logic to represent information in a computer.

In the late 80's, interest in related issues grew, and context became a widely discussed issue, with a number of different formalizations and applications in knowledge representation and reasoning. Since the 90's the concept of *context-awareness* has increasingly gained importance in the area of computing and distributed systems, due to its promise as a solution for describing mobile computing in ever-changing environments. Most approaches in the literature have focused on addressing the modeling of context with respect to one application or an application class. While some models take the user's current situation (e.g., "in a meeting") into account, others model the physical environment (e.g., "in an office"); and some work in this area has taken steps towards a common understanding of context, with respect to location, identity, and time. The objective of this work overall is to develop uniform context models, representation and query languages, and accompanying reasoning algorithms.

In the remainder of this chapter, we give a brief account of some of the major context representation approaches discussed in the literature today, with an emphasis on logic-based approaches. More details and a survey of models of context can be found, for instance, in (Akman & Surav, 1996) and in (Strang & Linnhoff-Popien, 2004), while a survey of applications of context can be found in (Brezillon, 1999). A broad review of context modeling and reasoning can be found in (Bettini, 2010).

7.1 Logic-Based Context Models

Following (Bouquet *et al.*, 2001), logic based models of context can be divided into two groups: *divide-and-conquer* and *compose-and-conquer.*

7.1.1 *The Divide-and-conquer approach*

In this approach a context is a way of partitioning (and giving a more articulated internal structure to) a global theory of the world. This global theory has an internal structure, and this structure is articulated into a collection of contexts. Some of the main features of this approach are:

- the facts that are true in a given context c can be isolated and treated as a distinct collection of facts;
- there are hierarchical relations between contexts that allow reasoning to "climb" from a context to a more general context in which the dependence of a fact on a context is explicitly stated;
- there are non-hierarchical relations between facts of different contexts (for example, one would like to be able to represent the relation between facts of the form in_office(person;office_number) and facts of the form in_central_office(person) in a context that specializes the former context to one specific office).

The propositional logic of context (LoC) is one of the theories following this approach. It was first described by McCarthy, and then formalized by Buvac and Mason (Buvac & Mason, 1993). Some of the most important features of LoC are:

- Any formula can only be asserted in some context (there are no context independent formulae). The fact that a formula p is asserted in a context c is written as c: p.
- Context sequences are used to represent nested contexts. Context sequences allow distinctions, say, between the context of meeting in the context of one company team and the context of meeting in the context of a company.
- There is no outermost context. This means that one can always transcend a context c and move to a more general context in which facts about c can be asserted.

- Statements about a context c are made through the formula ist(c: p), meaning that the formula p is true in the context c.
- some relations between facts belonging to different contexts are stated through the *lifting axioms* with the general form ist(c: p) $\Rightarrow$ ist(c$_0$: p$_0$)

For example, if in the context of Alison's office, Alison's computer is close to her chair, then, in the context of their company, Alison's computer is close to her chair.

There is a Hilbert style axiomatization of validity for the logic of context (Buvac & Mason, 1993). It ensures that all propositional tautologies are valid in every context c.

Next, Dinsmore's theory of partitioned representations PR (Dinsmore, 1991) is similar to LoC, but in PR there is a special space, BASE, that cannot be transcended and can be considered as a sort of outermost context. In PR, a statement is always asserted in a space, while a space represents some potential reality. Each space has exactly one primary context. A primary context is defined as a function that maps the truth of a statement in one space onto the satisfaction of a (more complex) statement in another space. For example, the sentence "Bob is a project manager" can be asserted in a space S1 and "Alison believes that [S1]" can be the primary context of S1. This allows mapping the truth of "Bob is a project manager" onto the truth of the sentence "Alison believes that Bob is a project manager", which, in turn, is asserted in some other space. Of course, the semantics of "Bob is a project manager" would be very different in a space S2 whose primary context was, for instance, something like "John had a dream that [S2]". Dinsmore also introduces a notion of secondary context, which allows for lateral mappings. Intuitively, a mapping is a consequence of the semantics of the primary contexts involved. In other words, a secondary context opens a channel of communication between two spaces.

7.1.2 *Compose-and-conquer Approaches*

In these approaches, a context is a local theory, namely a (partial, approximate) representation of the world, in a network of relations with other local, domain specific theories. There is no global theory of the world, but only many local theories. Each local theory represents a viewpoint on the world and they are the building blocks of the individual's knowledge. The totality of his/her knowledge is given by composing such local theories through a collection of rules that connect them into a (still partial) representation of the world. A local theory is not a partition of some global theory, but it represents (partial) knowledge about some portion of the world, from a given perspective. For example, a local theory can be a representation of physical objects in an office.

In the compose-and-conquer approach, there are no a priori relations between contexts. This is a major difference from divide-and-conquer theories. Namely, in divide-and-conquer systems, global knowledge implies how contexts are related to each other. On the other hand, in compose-and-conquer theories, there is no predefined global knowledge and contexts are autonomous theories. This does not mean that there are no relations between contexts, but only that these relations are established on a peer-to-peer basis.

One example of a compose-and-conquer approach to contextual knowledge representation and reasoning is Ghidini and Giunchiglia's Local Models Semantics (Ghidini & Giunchiglia, 2001), together with its proof-theoretical counterpart (Giunchiglia & Serafini, 1994). It is based on the following two very general principles:

- principle of locality: reasoning always happens in a local theory (a context);
- principle of compatibility: there may be compatibility constraints between the reasoning processes that happen in different contexts.

7.1.3 Compatibility constraints

Compatibility constraints represent relations between different contexts. These may be formalized in many different ways.

For instance, in the logic based approach to contextual knowledge representation described in (Ghidini & Giunchiglia, 2001), one starts with a family of languages $L_1;\ldots,$ $L_n;\ldots$, where L_i is the representation language of a context c_i. Each language L_i has its set of models M_i. Every subset M_{Ti} of M_i satisfies a set of formulae, each corresponding to a different choice of the theory T_i associated with c_i. Once the theory T_i associated with c_i is fixed, a model belonging to M_{Ti} is called a local model of c_i. And then, relations between two contexts are represented by compatibility constraints, which state that the truth of a formula F in c_1 is related to the truth of the formula F' in c_2. This is achieved by imposing that: sets of local models c_1 and c_2 of the two contexts c_1 and c_2 are such that, if the set of local models of c_1 satisfies F, then the set of local models of c_2 satisfies F'.

Pairs $<c_1; c_2>$ satisfying the above relation are said to belong to a compatibility relation and define a model for the pair of contexts c_1 and c_2. Using the notion of compatibility, a wide range of relations between contexts can be formalized. For example, if a context c_1 represents Bob's beliefs at day d, and that it contains the statement "I have a board meeting" and if c_2 represents Bob's beliefs at day d+1, then there can be a relationship between the two contexts such that the sentence "Yesterday I had a board meeting" is true in c_2. The above relations are based on considering models, while there is also a deductive counterpart to imposing compatibility constraints.

7.2 Other Approaches to Contextual Knowledge Representation

Contextual knowledge representation is used in many different fields, including modeling psychological and cognitive processes. The most important real-world application of contextual knowledge representation at present is in distributed and mobile computing, an area that has to deal with computing devices working in changing contexts. More pertinently to the present book, context based frameworks have been also used in knowledge and data integration – for the integration of information (or knowledge) coming from different sources (see, for instance, (Farquhar *et al.*, 1995)).

Different information sources integrated in a unique system can be thought of as partial views (or contexts) on a world. Available information sources are often distributed, redundant, partial, and autonomous. Consequently, information sources may adopt different conceptual schemata (including domains, relations, naming conventions, etc). The relations between the different domains and between the interpretation domains of the different databases can be established.

For instance the different (but related) meanings of the predicate costs(x, y) in database 1 and database m can be represented by using the following formula:

$1 : costs(x, y) \Rightarrow m : \exists y' \, (costs(x, y') \wedge y' = 1.07 {}^*y)$

The meaning of the above relations is that if the models of database 1 satisfy the formula costs(x, y), then any models of the database m must satisfy the formula

$\exists y' (costs(x, y') \wedge y' = 1.07 {}^*y)$

which means that item x has price y' which is obtained by adding taxes to the price y.

One application of these ideas is to traditional relational databases. For instance, in one research project, a context-based knowledge was applied to the problem of specifying redundancy among different databases while maintaining a high degree of autonomy (Mylopoulos & Motschnig-Pitrik, 1995). In this work, there are mechanisms for change propagation: i.e., mechanisms that establish whether the effects of a change operation performed in one context are visible in other contexts.

In another sort of application, a rich contextual knowledge representation is required for the maintainance of a massive knowledge base such as CYC (Lenat & Sierra, 1999).

The (controversial) philosophy underlying the CYC AI project is that huge, hand-created knowledge bases covering a wide area of (human) knowledge are required in order to create generally intelligent programs (the authors give an example of a logic-based expert system with the rule that amphibians lay eggs in water; however, the system cannot answer the question whether amphibians lay eggs at all, because its rule base is not sufficiently rich to encompass such commonsense facts). However, maintaining and using a huge knowledge base, brings different challenges, one of which is the use of contexts, as the Cyc team has observed:

> "... as the CYC common sense knowledge base grew ever larger, it became increasingly difficult to shoehorn every fact and rule into the same flat world. Finally, in 1989, as CYC exceeded 100, 000 rules in size, we found it necessary to introduce an explicit context mechanism. That is, we divided the KB up into a lattice of hundreds of contexts, placing each CYC assertion in whichever context(s) it belonged."

Contexts in CYC have a fine internal structure with a dozen mostly-independent dimensions along which contexts vary. Each region of this 12-dimensional space implicitly defines a context. The capability of importing an assertion from one context into another is provided by lifting assertions. They have a general form:

$$\text{ist}(c: p) \Rightarrow \text{ist}(c_0 : p_0)$$

For instance, the fact that gold is more expensive than silver in the stock market, can be exported to the context of the black market by the assertion:

ist(StockMarket: MoreExpensive(gold, silver))

$\Rightarrow$

ist(BlackMarket: MoreExpensive(gold, silver))

7.3 Contextual Knowledge in Probabilistic Logic Networks

PLN has a special link to handle contextual knowledge called ContextLink (or simply Context). For instance one can express in the context of programming a method that is a class function by

```
Context
    Programming
    Similarity
        ClassFunction
        Method
```

The semantics of ContextLink is formally defined by the following equivalence:

```
Context
    C
    R A B
```

is equal to

```
R (A And C) (B And C)
```

So reasoning with context simply amounts to reasoning with non-contextual standard operators, in certain stereotypical patterns. However since contexts are often used it may be valuable to introduce some inference "macro rules" handling context, like the following, used in an inference example given later on:

```
Context C A
Implication A B
```

⊢

```
Context C B
```

Informally this rule says that if A is true in the context C and A implies B then B is true in the context C.

Also, one may note that the definition involving the Context link assumes that the context applies on a relationship (noted R in the definition given above), nevertheless a truth value over a concept A can be seen as the measure of how much the universe inherits A, that is:

```
A <w>
```

is equal to

```
Inheritance <w>
    U
    A
```

where U symbolizes the universe. Given this, we can define contextual versions of concepts as well as relationships.

7.4 User Models as Contexts

One area where contextual logic has not frequently been applied, but perhaps should be, is the modeling of the preferences, biases and other properties of individual users and user groups of information systems. (Bry and Jacquenet (Bry & Jacquenet, 2005) have laid out the logic for application of first-order logic to user modeling in the semantic web in some detail, but they do not consider contextual logic in specific.)

7.4.1 *User Modeling in Information Retrieval Systems*

A great deal of work has been done to date on user modeling in information retrieval (IR) systems. The relevance of the output of an IR system is not absolute, but relative to specific users; and because of this, the lack of user modeling is one of the main sources of weakness of most contemporary such systems. For example, a tourist and a programmer may use the same word "java" to search for different information, but many retrieval systems would return the same results. It was observed, already in late 70s and early 80s, that information retrieval systems can and should be personalized for users by means of profiles (Rich, 1979; Myaeng *et al.* , 1986). Since then, a lot of efforts have been invested in the area of individual user modelling and individual user profiles. The main objective of user modeling is to extract and store information about a user, and to adapt the retrieval tool to the user's needs and interests in order to improve the relevance of the results. Such, personalized search is still considered as one of the major challenges in modern information retrieval. For estimating the user-specific relevance of documents different computing methodologies are used, ranging from genetic algorithms, fuzzy logics, modal logic, to classical first-order logic approaches.

User profiles can model different users' preferences. For example, for some users it is preferable to have the list of all results to the query quickly, even with a number of bad results. On the other hand, some users prefer to have a short list of results, even if producing it takes more time. Some users prefer results only in some specific file formats, etc. These criteria and also criteria that define quality or relevance for a specific user define his/her *profile*. Generally, a (user) profile consists of a set of preferences with regard to behavior of a search engine as well constraints on the results it presents to the user (Van Gils & Schabell, 2003). For example, the following criteria may define a particular user-profile:

> I prefer a maximum of 25 results per page, and by selecting a relevant resource (clicking on the link) will open a new window. I prefer HTML and PDF formats and refuse the Microsoft DOC format. Furthermore, the size of the resource should not exceed 25Mb.

Profiles can be used for post-processing the results to the query (e.g., some resources can be converted into a prefered format), and most interestingly, can also be used for guiding search.

An important distinction in a user modeling context is between explicit and implicit preferences. Explicit preferences consist of information given by a user explicitly. On the other hand, implicit preferences refer to any context information available to the information retrieval system during a user's session. Relevance feedback (given by the user to the information retrieval system) is one way for providing more context explicitly and can be effective for improving retrieval accuracy. However, it is often unrealistic to motivate user to explicitly rate the results obtained. Therefore, implicit context information and implicit feedback is thus more interesting to exploit and it has been attracting more and more attention (see, for instance, (Kelly & Teevan, 2003) for a bibliography of implicit feedback). In addition, both user's explicit and implicit preferences may change over time.

There are different sources of implicit user preferences. For instance, the user often need to modify his query in a number of iterations until he is satisfied. In such scenario, the information to be used by the information retrieval system is not just the current query, but also the complete user's search history, information about which documents the user has chosen to view, and even for how long the user has read specific documents, etc. For instance, a simple user's profile can be based on keywords from his queries performed or documents that he read.

Many approaches use user's actions and navigation through data as implicit feedback. For instance, some web browsers record user actions and navigation, including dwelling times, mouse clicks, mouse movements, scrolling and elapsed times and user explicit ratings of web pages. Some experimental results show that implicit feedback, especially the dwelling time on a page, amount of scrolling on a page, the combination of time and scrolling, how a user exit a result or end a search session have all a strong correlation with explicit relevance ratings (Claypool et al., 2001; Fox et al., 2005). However, there are also some experimental results showing that there is no general direct relationship between display time and relevance (and that the display time depends on the specific tasks and specific users) (Kelly & Belkin, 2004).

There is a range of techniques for using user's query history in building his/her profile. Some web browsers use browsing history in past n days for personalized search. Some approaches store user's interests and can distinguish between long term interests and ad hoc queries. Thank to this, modification of queries that can not appropriately be supported by the user profile are not applied.

User modeling is widely used not only in Internet browsing, but also in *recommender systems* providing advice to users about items they might wish to purchase or examine. Recommendations made by such systems can help users navigate through large information spaces of product descriptions, news articles, social information, or other items (Burke, 2000).

A general survey covering many aspects of user modeling in information retrieval systems can be found in (Kobsa, 2007). Another survey of the field, including extensive discussion of different forms of communication with the user (querying, navigation through structures, and visualization) can be found in (Nurnberger & Detyniecki, 2005). A survey of the field of adaptive user interfaces can be found in (Dieterich *et al.*, 1993).

7.4.2 *User modeling from the cognitive perspective*

Beyond the specific domain of information retrieval, there are several types of computer related models considered by cognitive psychology. Apart from the *user models* – the computer's model of the user (as described above in the context of information retrieval systems), there are also

- *mental models* – user's model of the system;
- *conceptual models* – models presented to the user by the system designer.

User models can be split into two major categories: empirical quantitative models and analytical-cognitive models (Palermiti & Polity, 1995).

Empirical quantitative models are based on users' performances when using a given system. Empirically collected performance data are used for constructing abstract formalizations and for defining groups (e.g., skill groups such as "experts", "beginners"). These user models do not express beliefs, reasoning or cognitive processes, but rather external performances.

Analytical cognitive models attempt to construct a more qualitative behavioral modeling. The models aim to detect the purposes, strategies, plans or beliefs of the user, so that the system may issue predictions and draw conclusions. These models are not static but dynamic, able to evolve according to different tasks or categories of users, and adaptive, by using the cognitive features detected in the user behavior. Their role is to help the system cooperate, to indicate hypotheses, and to single out areas of interest.

User models can also be classified according to three main dimensions:

- models of a single "typical" user versus collections of individual models;
- explicit models defined by the designer versus models inferred by the computer on the basis of the user's behavior;
- long term user characteristics such as areas of interest and expertise versus short term characteristics such as the subject of the last sentence typed.

7.4.3 Logic-based user modeling

Instead of using approximate models and reasoning, logic based user modeling aim at employing formal reasoning for deducing facts about the user. This family of user modeling approaches is relatively small, but has a number of important ideas and techniques.

Some of the logic-based representations used in user modeling are (Kobsa, 1993):

- *PROLOG-based*, which offers a comparatively rich representation language with built-in backward reasoning and the possibility of a smooth migration from knowledge representation to programming;
- *Predicate logic*, which offers more expressiveness than PROLOG, as is needed in many application domains;
- *Languages with second-order predicates* and *modal logic*, which allow representing assumptions about beliefs and goals of different agents in the same representation language;
- *Connectionist networks*, which have been particularly employed for classification tasks.

An overview of different reasoning techniques used in logic-based user modeling systems can be also found in (Kobsa, 1993). Typically, most logic-based systems use simple forward or backward reasoning (using the knowledge from the knowledge base), or some their combinations.

7.4.4 Contextual Logic for User Modeling

One potentially promising avenue for applying logical methods to user recommendation involves deploying contextual logic, in such a fashion that each user connotes a distinct context for inference. As this approach seems not to have been touched in the literature yet, we explore it here via a "thought experiment" style example.

Our examples concerns book recommendation systems which, when a user locates one book, recommend to him/her other books of potential interest. In such systems today, models of individual users are not necessarily built at all; instead most recommendations are generic – the same for all users locating a certain book. Typically, relationships between books, as a basis for recommendations, are inferred from purchases of individual users, i.e., from the database of all purchases. For a certain book A, it is calculated how many users that bought the book A also purchased a book B, a book C, etc. Then the books (a fixed number of them – say 10) with the highest score are recommended to the user, as of potential interest. This simple and generic model, commonly used in practice, can be refined in many ways, for instance by applying a specific ordering among the 10 recommended books, derived with respect to the specific user. Let us consider one possible approach for this through a simple example.

Suppose there are the following books available:

(A) Katya Walter The Tao of Chaos
(B) Katya Walter: Dream Mail: Secret Letters for Your Soul
(C) Martin Schonberger: I Ching & the Genetic Code: The Hidden Key to Life

Suppose there is also stored the relevance of these books to two areas: spiritual literature and popular science. These relevance data (given by weight factors from 0 to 1) may then be taken to form two contexts:

Popular science context:

1. relevance(A, 0.5)
2. relevance(B, 0.2)
3. relevance(C, 0.7)

Spiritual literature context:

1. relevance(A, 0.6)
2. relevance(B, 0.8)
3. relevance(C, 0.3)

Let there also be models of two users, Alice and Bob, and their interests, again described by weighting factors. Assume these weighting factors are computed based on their past purchases.

Alice's model:

1. interested_in(popular science, 0.2)
2. interested_in(spiritual literature, 0.7)

Bob's model:

1. interested_in(popular science, 0.9)
2. interested_in(spiritual literature, 0.2)

Now, let us assume that Alice searches the book recommendation system and locates the book (A). The engine queries the database and finds that other users that purchased this book most often also purchased books (B) and (C). So, these two books should be recommended to Alice in some suitable ordering and the relevance of these books to Alice should be estimated.

Information from the contexts of certain areas apply to all specific users; so, in our example, all facts from all area contexts are also used in specific user's contexts by, so-called, *bridge* rules:

Inference rule in User N's model:

Context for the area X: relevance(Y, w1)

interested_in(X, w2)

relevance(Y, w3)

relevance(Y , max(w3, w1*w2))

The meaning of this rule is as follows: if, in the context of the area X, the relevance of the book Y is w1, and if w2 is the weight of the user N's interest in X, then the relevance of the book Y for the user N is w1*w2. Such relevance factors can be calculated for all available areas, and the final relevance factor for the book Y is the maximum over all areas (the initial relevance factor is 0). In our example, we should apply, within Alice's model, the above rule twice for each of the books (B) and (C):

Popular science context: relevance(B, 0.2)

interested_in(popular science, 0.2)

relevance(B, 0)

relevance(B, 0.04)

Spiritual literature context: relevance(B, 0.8)

interested_in(spiritual literature, 0.7)

relevance(B, 0.04)

relevance(B, 0.56)

Popular science context: relevance(C, 0.7)

interested_in(popular science, 0.2)

relevance(C, 0)

relevance(C, 0.14)

Spiritual literature context: relevance(C, 0.3)

interested_in(spiritual literature, 0.7)

relevance(C, 0.14)

relevance(C, 0.21)

Hence, the estimated relevance of the book (B) for Alice is 0.56, and the relevance for the book (C) is 0.21 and the ordering in recommendation is (B), (C). We can also apply, within Bob's model, the same rules:

Popular science context: relevance(B, 0.2)

interested_in(popular science, 0.9)

relevance(B, 0)

relevance(B, 0.18)

Spiritual literature context: relevance(B, 0.8)

interested_in(spiritual literature, 0.2)

relevance(B, 0.16)

relevance(B, 0.18)

Popular science context: relevance(C, 0.7)

interested_in(popular science, 0.9)

relevance(C, 0)

relevance(C, 0.63)

Spiritual literature context: relevance(C, 0.3)

interested_in(spiritual literature, 0.2)

relevance(C, 0.06)

relevance(C, 0.63)

Hence, the estimated relevance of the book (B) for Bob is 0.18, and the relevance for the book (C) is 0.63 and the ordering in recommendation is (C), (B).

It is not hard to see how the same form of contextualization could play a role in other sorts of user modeling besides product purchase investigations. For instance, suppose Bill and Betty are two criminal investigators, investigating a crime involving an individual named Giulio (A). Suppose Giulio has connections to

(B) Elias, a known drug dealer who is suspected to have sold drugs to Giulio's uncle
(C) Jonas, a banker convicted of fraud, who works at the bank where Giulio used to work

Suppose that Bill's expertise is in drug crimes, whereas Betty's expertise is in bank fraud. Then, in the context of Bill's investigation, the association between A and B should be more prominent; whereas in the context of Betty's investigation, the association between A and C should be more prominent. The structure is exactly the same as in the book purchasing example. (And of course there are many subtler examples of how contextual reasoning could be used to aid in user modeling; we have just presented a simple sort of example to make the conceptual connection clear.

7.5   General Considerations Regarding Contextual Inference

Now we turn to issues involving the combination of contextual representation with logical inference systems. The explicit incorporation of context into inference is a subtle matter; a number of approaches have been posited in the research literature, yet none have yet been battle-tested in real-world applications. Here we will review some general considerations regarding contextual inference, then go into more detail regarding PLN-based contextual inference, and give a fairly complex, realistic example of the latter.
Generally speaking, any deductive system (say, Hilbert style first-order logic, or temporal logic) can be used contextually, by restricting its rules to certain domains. But this is different than explicitly contextual reasoning, in which a notion of context is incorporated in both the knowledge representation and the inference rules. In practice, the way explicitly contextual reasoning systems tend to work is that inference rules are supplied for specific contexts, and then special rules are also applied for bridging pairs of contexts.

For example, the relationship "to be superior" can be described by the following (implicitly) universally quantified axioms:

team_leader$(x, z) \Rightarrow$ superior(x, z)
superior$(x, y) \wedge$ superior$(y, z) \Rightarrow$ superior(x, z)

The axioms can be associated by an additional parameter describing a context – for instance, a company or a sport club. They can then be exported, by *lifting rules*, to specific contexts:

team_leader(x, z, context) $\Rightarrow$ superior(x, z, context)

superior(x, y, context) $\wedge$ superior(y, z, context) $\Rightarrow$ superior(x, z, context)

or, to the following notational form:

context: team_leader(x, z) $\Rightarrow$ superior(x, z)

context: superior(x, y) $\wedge$ superior(y, z) $\Rightarrow$ superior(x, z)

The basic idea here, due originally to McCarthy, is to tackle the problem of generality by using more general axioms if the context is irrelevant, and less general axioms otherwise.

In addition to inference rules local to specific contexts, contextual inference systems also utilize rules that link different contexts. For instance, in the inference system described in (Ghidini & Giunchiglia, 2001), there are bridge rules. Bridge rules are rules whose premises and conclusion belong to different contexts. For instance, the bridge rule corresponding to the compatibility constraint

if the set of local models of c_1 satisfies F, then the set of local models of c_2 satisfies F'

would be the following:

$$\frac{c_1 : F}{c_2 : F'}$$

where c_1:F is the premise of the rule and c_2:F' is the conclusion. Obviously, bridge rules are conceptually different from local rules, rules used in individual contexts. Bridge rules can have different forms and can involve more than two contexts. A deduction is a tree of local deductions, obtained by applying only local rules, concatenated with one or more applications of bridge rules. In a special case when there is no relation between the two contexts, there are no constraints on what is true in the two contexts.

Using the machinery of compatibility, a wide range of relations between contexts can be formalized. For example, let c_1 represent the prices on the American market at the present moment and assume "Gold gets cheaper" is true in c_1. If c_2 represents the prices on the Asian market at the present moment, then the sentence "In America, gold gets cheaper" must be true in c_2. This conclusion is based on the inference rule of the form:

$$\frac{c_1 : F}{c_2 : F \text{ is true in } c_1}$$

7.5.1 *Uncertain Contextual Inference*

Although there is very little literature in this area, there is no reason contextual reasoning can't be applied in the context of uncertain logics.

For instance, to "uncertainize" the example given above, the fact "Gold gets cheaper" could have a degree of certainty of 0.9 in the context c_1 of the American market. Furthermore, the relevant bridge rules could also have degrees of certainty associated with them. So, for instance, there could be a bridge rule

$$\frac{c_1: \text{Gold gets cheaper}}{c_2: \text{Gold gets cheaper}}$$

where c_1 is the context of the American market, while c_2 is the context of the Asian market. This rule could have a degree of certainty, say, 0.8, indicating that it is likely that if gold gets cheaper on the American market, that it also gets cheaper on the Asian market. So, finally, the degree of certainty that gold gets cheaper on the Asian market could be calculated as the product of the degree of certainty that gold gets cheaper on the American market (0.9) and the degree of certainty of the bridge rule (0.8), giving 0.72.

On the other hand, there could be a bridge rule

$$\frac{c_1: \text{local currency gets stronger}}{c_2: \text{local currency gets stronger}}$$

where c_1 is the context of USA, while c_2 is the context of Japan. This rule could have a degree of certainty, say, 0.2, indicating that it is unlikely that if US dollar gets stronger, then yen also gets stronger. If the degree of certainty that US dollar gets stronger is, say, 0.95, then the degree of certainty that yen gets stronger is 0.95*0.2=0.19.

7.6 A Detailed Example Requiring Contextual Inference

In this section we present a simple, specific example of contextual inference, and explain how the ideas discussed above may be applied in this case. In working this example, we will use the approach close to (Ghidini & Giunchiglia, 2001) and first order logic as the underlying logic, but, for the sake of simplicity, instead of first-order notation, we will formulate the statements in natural language form. In a following section, we will run through this same example using PLN inference.

The basic assumptions of the inference, expressed in common informal English, are as follows:

Alison is an accountant who is also a musician. Alison is emotional in the context of music, but not in the context of accounting. She frequently mentions Canadian place names in the context of music (maybe she's a Canadian music fan), but not in the context of accounting. Bob is in a similar situation, but he frequently mentions Canadian related stuff in both the music and accounting contexts. Clark is also in a similar situation, but he frequently mentions Canadian related stuff only in the accounting context, not the music context. Trivially, Canadian places are associated with Canadian people. People who have a lot to do with Canadian people, and a lot to do with money, have a chance of being involved in suspicious log trafficking activities. Trivially, accounting has to do with money.

To formalize the above using contextual inference, we will consider the following contexts: music, accounting, to-be-involved, and Canada. We can encode all the above information as axioms in these contexts, while we also have to add some bridge rules (linking different contexts and corresponding to compatibility constraints). Each inference step is made in a specific context. If a person is an accountant, we can encode this information as being that the person is knowledgeable in the context of accounting. It is similar for the context of music.

More explicitly, the contexts under consideration are as follows:

Music context:

(1) Alison is knowledgeable.

(2) Alison is emotional.

(3) Alison frequently mentions Canadian place names.

(4) Bob is knowledgeable.

(5) Bob is emotional.

(6) Bob frequently mentions Canadian place names.

(7) Clark is knowledgeable.

(8) Clark is emotional.

(9) Clark does not frequently mention Canadian place names.

Accounting context:

(10) Alison is knowledgeable.

(11) Alison is not emotional.

(12) Alison does not frequently mention Canadian place names.

(13) Bob is knowledgeable.

(14) Bob is not emotional.

(15) Bob frequently mention Canadian place names.

(16) Clark is knowledgeable.

(17) Clark is not emotional.

(18) Clark frequently mention Canadian place names.

(19) Money is important.

To-be-involved context:

(20) If someone is knowledgeable and X is important, then he/she is highly involved with X.

(21) If someone frequently mentions place names from X, he/she is highly involved with these places.

(22) If someone is highly involved with places from X, he/she is highly involved with anything that is associated with these places.

Canada context:

(23) Canadian places are associated with Canadian people

(24) If someone is highly involved with Canadian people and with money, then he/she has a chance of being involved in log trafficking.

To keep things relatively comprehensible and informal, we won't explicitly specify the languages of the contexts, and we'll assume that all relevant information can be expressed in any of the contexts (for instance, we assume that in the music context it can be expressed that someone is involved with Canadian people). Also, we use the following bridge rules:

To be involved: F	Canada: F
Music: F	Music: F

To be involved: F	Canada: F
Accounting: F	Accounting: F

In the described system, for example, one can infer that Clark has a chance of being involved in log trafficking (in the context of accounting).

The inference in the accounting context goes as follows:

Step	Inferred information	Justification
(C1)	If someone is knowledgeable and X is important, then he/she is highly involved with X.	bridge from (20)
(C2)	If someone is knowledgeable and money is important, then he/she is highly involved with money.	instance of (C1)
(C3)	Clark is highly involved with money.	from (16), (19), and (C2)
(C4)	If someone frequently mentions place names from X, he/she is highly involved with these places.	bridge from (21)
(C5)	If someone frequently mentions place names from Canada, he/she is highly involved with these places.	instance of (C4)
(C6)	Clark is highly involved with places from Canada.	from (18) and (C5)
(C7)	If someone is highly involved with places from X, he/she is highly involved with anything that is associated with these places.	bridge from (22)
(C8)	If someone is highly involved with places from Canada, he/she is highly involved with anything that is associated with these places.	instance of (C7)
(C9)	Canadian places are associated with Canadian people.	bridge from (23)
(C10)	Clark is highly involved with Canadian people.	from (C6), (C9), and (C8)
(C11)	If someone is highly involved with Canadian people and with money, then he/she has a chance of being involved in log trafficking.	bridge from (24)
(C12)	Clark has a chance of being involved in log trafficking.	from (C3), (C10), and (C11)

Notice that one can prove that Alice is highly involved with Canadian people in the context of music, but cannot prove that Alice is highly involved with Canadian people in the context of accounting. Hence, it cannot be proved that Alison has a chance of being involved in log trafficking.

If one use a bridge rule connecting the two contexts:

$$\frac{\text{music: F}}{\text{accounting: F}}$$

for all sentences F that can be expressed in the two contexts, then one can infer that Alison is highly involved with Canadian people in the context of accounting, too (if all relevant properties can be expressed in that context). However, such a bridge rule would be unlikely used.

Notice also that, in the same manner as for Clark, one can prove that Bob is highly involved with Canadian people in the context of accounting, and further that Bob has a chance of being involved in log trafficking. One may wonder if there can be made a distinction between Bob and Clark. Namely, Bob is highly involved with Canadian people in both contexts music and accounting, while Clark is highly involved with Canadian people only in the context of accounting. In addressing this there are several issues. First, one might eliminate the axiom (24), and instead add the following bridge rule:

Accounting: X is involved with Canadian people and with with money

Music: X is not involved with Canadian people

Accounting: has a chance of being involved in log trafficking.

Intuitively, this would eliminate the conclusion that Bob has a chance of being involved in log trafficking and keep the conclusion for Clark. However, it is not necessarily the case. Namely, in the context of music, one cannot prove that Clark is involved with Canadian people, but it still does not mean that one can prove that Clark is not involved with Canadian people. Different default logics address this issue and hence can be used for reasoning of the above sort.

Using the variants of the systems described above one can infer crisp conclusions as to whether Alison, Bob, or Clark have a chance of being involved in log trafficking or other information. However, one cannot infer information on how likely it is that Alison/Bob/Clark is involved in log trafficking. For such information, one might use some fuzzy/probabilistic logic as the underlying logic and keep the rest of the inference system. In such a modified system, one could end up with a conclusion that Clark is the most likely to be involved in log trafficking, Bob is second most likely, and Alison is third most likely. Also, if one would replace "accounting" with "marketing" in the above examples, then these degrees of suspicion should decrease, while if "accounting" is replaced with "corruption", then the degrees of suspicion should increase. However, these specifics will depend on the inference system in question.

Chapter 8

Causal Reasoning

Many of the inferences one wants to draw about real-world, spatiotemporal, contextual knowledge involve cause and effect. But the relation between causation and logical inference is subtle and storied. As outlined above, deductive reasoning aims at deriving consequences (or effects, outcomes) from premises (or causes). Abductive reasoning aims at deriving possible causes from effects. Finally, inductive reasoning aims at deriving relationships between causes and effects, rules that lead from one to another. Causal reasoning is generally considered a form of inductive reasoning. More concretely, causal reasoning aims at an epistemological problem of establishing precise causal relationships between causes and effects, with focusing on detecting genuine, real causes for some effects, and genuine, real effects of some causes.

Although they share a lot in their background and inferential process, causal inference and statistical inference are different. Statistical inference is concerned with associational inference and used for finding associations between exposures (causes) and outcomes, rather then for inferring causation relationships from observations. Causal relationship implies correlation between two events, but the opposite does not hold.

The first attempts at dealing with causality date back to the old Greek philosophers, including Aristotle, but systematic approaches had to wait centuries to come [Danks2006]. In his *Novum Organum* (1620), Francis Bacon introduced the notions of:

- The table of presence (*tabula praesentiae*)
- The table of absence (*tabula absentiae*)
- The table of degrees (*tabula graduum*)

According to Bacon, the cause of a phenomenon is the set of properties that explains every case in each of the three tables. In the mid-nineteenth century, John Stuart Mill proposed an improved form of Bacon's method. But already by then, the limitations of such approaches

were understood – since in the eighteenth century, David Hume noticed that causal inference, often intuitive and natural, cannot be formally justified using deduction. This fact is
actually a general property of inductive reasoning. It is not possible to justify the pattern
"the future will continue the pattern of the past" via deductive reasoning based on observations, without falling into circular reasoning. One can reason "the sun will rise tomorrow
morning because it rose for the last 100 mornings", but this relies on the assumption "the
future will continue the pattern of the past", and it's circular to say "the future will continue
to obey the pattern 'the future will continue the pattern of the past' because it obeyed it in
the past."

From the twentieth century till the present, philosophers, statisticians, and computer
scientists have developed, often building on statistics, various approaches and methods for
representing causal structures and solving problems of causal inference. Some of them
follow the view of the philosopher Karl Popper in which falsification of a hypothesis is
more informative than corroboration of a hypothesis. There could be a number of cases
that are consistent with a false hypothesis, but a single counterexample requires modifying
the hypothesis. A hypothesis that has survived many attempts to refute it is more likely to
be true than one that has been corroborated many times.

Today as in the past, the problem of causal inference is a central challenge for most
of the empirical sciences. *Causal effect* may be the effect of a given drug or therapy for a
specific disease, the effect of education on employment and earnings, the effect of training
courses on the labor market, etc. If a causal relationship is discovered and established, it
may be possible to control future events to some extent by producing (or preventing) occurrence of certain outcomes. There are many real-world applications of causal reasoning,
including in economics, law, social sciences, and human-computer interactions, but most
important are perhaps those in various branches of medicine and health research.

In the following text, we will briefly discuss some of the central problems in causal
reasoning and some of the most significant approaches for modeling it. For a more detailed
survey, see, for instance, (Kluve, 2001).

8.1 Correlation does not imply causation

The assumption that correlation and causation are equivalent often leads to significant
flaws in reasoning. The phrase "correlation does not imply causation" stresses this fact,
meaning that if there is a correlation between two events, it still does not necesserily mean

that one causes the other (although it is possible that it is the case). A prototypical example of such flawed reasoning, employed in medicine, is discussed in (Lawlor, 2004). A number of studies showed that women who were taking combined hormone replacement therapy also had a lower-than-average incidence of coronary heart disease. This correlation led to a widespread idea that hormone therapy was protective against coronary diseases. However, carefully designed experiments demonstrated that this was not true. The explanation was that women taking hormone therapy were mostly from higher socio-economic groups, with better nutritive regimes and, hence, with lower incidence of heart disease. Thus, lower incidence of heart disease was not a consequence of taking hormone therapy, but both were effects of a common cause.

Coming to the conclusion that an event X is caused by an event Y if there is a correlation between the two is generally wrong, although this causation can be indeed present. Other potential explanations for correlation between X and Y are the following:

- Y is caused by X.
- It is both the case that X is caused by Y and Y is caused by X.
- There is a common cause for both X and Y.
- Correlation is present due to a pure chance, or due to reasons that are so complex and deep that they cannot be considered as causation between X and Y.

8.2 Other Challenges in Causal Reasoning

Causal relationships can be very complex and difficult to deal with. For instance, there are situations when there are several hypotheses about a causal relationship, and it is difficult to select the one that is most likely true. Also, one of the problems is recognizing irrelevant events or causes with small impact on the observed outcome. Let us consider the example, given in (Modern Epidemiology, 2008), that illustrates the process of understanding causality with a description of a child learning that moving a light switch causes the light to turn on. However, in wider contexts, the turning-on of the light was sometimes caused also by other subjects:

- The mother who replaced the burned-out light bulb.
- The electrician who replaced a defective circuit breaker.
- The lineman who repaired the transformer that was disabled by lightning.
- The social service agency that arranged to pay the electricity bill.

Table 8.1   Illustration of Simpson's Paradox

	A	B	%A
smokers	5	5	50%
non-smokers	2	3	40%
a: Proportion of students smokers and non-smokers who received A			
A	B		%A
smokers	5	4	56%
non-smokers	1	0	100%
b: Low-income students			
A	B		%A
smokers	0	1	0%
non-smokers	1	3	25%
c: High-income students			

- The power company, the political authority awarding the franchise, the investment bankers who raised the financing, the Federal Reserve that eased interest rates, the politician who cut taxes, and the health care providers who contributed to the child's safe birth and healthy development.

And there are other deep issues with causal reasoning. Consider an example from (Pearl, 2000), illustrating the problem known as Simpson's Paradox. Suppose that a teacher discover that a higher proportion of his students who smoke received a final grade of A than students who do not smoke, as shown in Table 8.1a. Confused by the hint that smoking has a positive impact on grades, the teacher tries to find a rational explanation and partition the same data differently, looking at students with low parental income (Table 8.1b) separately from those with high parental income (Table 8.1c). Then, surprisingly, he finds that the situation has been completely reversed: smoking has negative impact on grades in both groups.

According to Pearl, Simpson's Paradox comes from trying to understand causality solely through probability and statistics: *"It is an embarrassing yet inescapable fact that probability theory, the official language of many empirical sciences, does not permit us to express sentences such as 'Mud does not cause rain'; all we can say is that the two events are mutually correlated, or dependent—meaning that if we find one, we can expect to encounter the other"* (Pearl, 2000).

8.3   Mill's Methods

In his 1843 book *A System of Logic: Ratiocinative and Inductive*, John Stuart Mill described five methods for drawing conclusions about causal relationships. The account of the Mill's methods given here and the running example are based on (Kemerling, 2006). The running example is based on the following scenario: in a college, one day an unusual number of students are suffering from severe indigestion. The college nurse naturally suspects that this symptom results from something the students ate for lunch, and she wants to find evidence that will support a conclusion that eating a certain food caused indigestion. The Mill's methods are the following.

- **Method of Agreement:** this method applies to cases in which the effect that occurred reveals only one prior circumstance that all of them shared. It is based on the expectation that similar effects are likely to arise from a similar cause. As an example, suppose that out of the four students with indigestion, one had pizza, coleslaw, orange juice, and a cookie; the second had a hot dog and french fries, coleslaw, and iced tea; the third ate pizza and coleslaw and drank iced tea; and the fourth ate only french fries, coleslaw, and chocolate cake. The nurse, by the method of agreement can conclude that eating coleslaw caused the indigestion.

- **Method of Difference:** by this method, a comparison of a case in which the effect occurred and a case in which the effect did not occur, reveals that only one prior circumstance was present in the first case but not it the second. In such situations, it is supposed that, other things being equal, different effects are likely to arise from different causes. As an example, suppose that the two students with indigestion ate together, but one became ill while the other did not. The first had eaten a hot dog, french fries, coleslaw, chocolate cake, and iced tea, while the other had eaten a hot dog, french fries, chocolate cake, and iced tea. Again, the nurse concludes that the coleslaw is what made the first student ill.

- **Joint Method of Agreement and Difference:** This method is a combination of the first two methods, and it assumes that genuine causes are necessary and sufficient conditions for their effects. Consider the following example: eight students come to the nurse: four of them suffered from indigestion, and with each of these four there is another who did not. Each pair of students had exactly the same lunch, except that everyone in the first group ate coleslaw and no one in the second group did. The nurse arrives at the same conclusion as above.

Method of Concomitant Variation: this method applies when evidences appear to show that there is a correlation between the degree to which the cause occurred and the degree to which the effect occurred. This conforms to our exprectations that effects are typically proportional to their causes. This method does not only notice occurrence or non-occurrence of the causal terms, but also the extent to which each of them takes place. As an example, suppose that there are five students with indigestion: the first ate no coleslaw and feels fine; the second had one bite of coleslaw and felt a little queasy; the third had half a dish of coleslaw and is fairly ill; the fourth ate a whole dish of coleslaw and is violently ill; and the fifth ate two servings of coleslaw and had to be taken to the hospital. The conclusion is again that coleslaw caused the indigestion.

- **Method of Residues:** many elements of a complex effect are shown to result, by reliable causal beliefs, from several elements of a complex cause; whatever remains of the effect must then have been produced by whatever remains of the cause. As an example, suppose that the nurse, during prior investigations of student illness, has already established that pizza tends to produce a rash and iced tea tends to cause headaches. Today, a student arrives at the nurse's office complaining of headache, indigestion, and a rash; this student reports having eaten pizza, coleslaw, and iced tea for lunch. Since she can recognize most of the student's symptoms as the effects of known causes, the nurse concludes that the additional effect of indigestion must be caused by the additional circumstance of eating coleslaw.

Notice that in all of the above methods, the issue of relevance is crucial. The nurse began with the assumption that what students had eaten for lunch was relevant to their digestive health in the afternoon. That is a reasonable assumption, but the real cause could have been something completely different, something about which the nurse never thought to ask. Therefore, application of Mill's methods succeeds only if every relevant suspected cause is taken into account, but that is impossible to guarantee in advance. Indeed, the most difficult cases are those in which the real cause was excluded from the analysis as being unobserved or considered irrelevant. Thus, Mill's methods can't help to discover causes unless the list of all potential causes is already known. Problems with using Mill's methods for proving that one event is the cause of another, are even bigger (Kemerling, 2006). Because of their limitations, Mill's methods should rather be considered as a tool for confirming (and not for discovering) hypotheses. If there are several hypotheses about a causal relationship, then Mill's methods can be helpful, since they will often enable eliminating most of the considered causes and the last remaining hypotheses will likely be valid.

8.4 Hill's Criteria

Causal reasoning in different forms had been widely used in medicine in twentieth century. In 1965. Austin Bradford Hill made a seminal summary of criteria to be used in causal inference in epidemiology (Hill, 1965). The basic underlying questions in Hill's criteria for causal inference are: "is the association real or artifactual?" and "is the association secondary to a 'real' cause?". Hill's criteria are widely recognized as a basis for inferring causality in epidemiology, but not only in epidemiology:

1. **Strength of the association** – the stronger an association, the less it could reflect the influence of some other factor(s). This criterion includes consideration of the statistical precision and methodological rigor of the existing studies with respect to bias.

2. **Consistency** – replication of analysis by different investigators, at different times, in different places, in different populations, with different methods leads to identical or similar findings. Namely, identical or similar findings are not likely to be all due to error or artifact. In addition, there should be reasonable and convincing explanation for different findings.

3. **Specificity of the association** – the more accurately defined the disease and exposure, the stronger the observed relationship should be. But the fact that one agent contributes to multiple diseases is not evidence against its role in other diseases.

4. **Temporality** – the ability to establish that the putative cause preceded in time the presumed effect.

5. **Biological gradient (dose-response)** – strength of disease changes with changes in exposure. Still, there could be a "threshold effect".

6. **Plausibility (credibility)** –general knowledge and beliefs should be able to explain the observed causal relationship. Still, the observed relationship could be beyond the current knowledge.

7. **Coherence** – causal interpretation should not conflict with observations and with known facts about the natural history of the disease.

8. **Experiment** – not a guideline, but a method for testing a specific causal hypothesis. If available, well designed and conducted experimental studies (e.g., with controlled conditions and changing the exposure) provide strong evidence for or against causation.

9. **Analogy** – use analogies or similarities between the observed causalities and other causalities.

Hill himself did not intend his criteria to be used as a self-contained framework, but rather as guidelines: "Here there are nine different viewpoints from all of which we should study association before we cry causation ... None of my nine viewpoints can bring indisputable evidence for or against the case-and-effect hypothesis and none can be required as a *sine qua non*. What they can do, with greater or lesser strength, is to help us make up our minds on the fundamental question – is there any other way of explaining the set of facts before us, is there any other answer equally, or more, likely than cause and effect".

8.5   Graphical models

Next, in graphical models of causality, causal relationships are represented by *causal graphs* (Greenland, 1999; Robins, 2001). A directed acyclical graph (DAG) is *causal* if every directed edge represents the presence of an effect of the parent (causal) variable on the child (affected) variable. In a causal graph, a directed path represents a causal pathway, and an X-to-Y directed edge represents a direct effect of X on Y. Absence of a directed path from X to Y in the graph corresponds to the causal *null hypothesis* that no change of the distribution of X can change the distribution of Y. Causal graphs provide simple visual and graph theory methods to check for confounding factors (common cause for two event analyzed for causal relationship) and other relevant properties.

8.6   Potential-outcomes (counterfactual) models

In *counterfactual* (or *potential-outcomes*) approaches to causal reasoning, statements about causality are considered in forms of counterfactual statements (Lewis, 2000). Reasoning focuses on what would have happened if, contrary to fact, the exposure had been something other than what it really was. For instance, the statement that a coleslaw ate by a student caused his indigestion is equivalent to the statement that had not the student eaten the colesaw, he would not have suffered from indigestion. This approach is justified by the fact that there are sistematic ways for dealing with counterfactual statements. For instance, Pearl gave an axiomatic system with clear semantics and effective algorithms for computing counterfactuals (Pearl, 2000). In his framework, for instance, one can calculate a probability that the student would not have indigestion had he not eaten colesaw if it is the case that the student has eaten colesaw and is suffering from indigestion. The potential outcomes framework has applications in epidemiology and medical research, economics, education, psychology; and social science (Gong, 2008). Because of Donald Rubin's contributions this is sometimes referred to as the "Rubin Model".

In potential outcomes models, all possible outcomes, both observable and unobservable, are considered simultaneously, forming outcome vectors. The framework can briefly be describes as follows (Greenland, 2002). Suppose we have a population of individual units under study (e.g. mice, people, counties) indexed by $i = 1, \ldots, N$, a treatment or exposure with $M + 1$ levels (or actions) 0, 1, ..., M, and an outcome variable of interest Y. The standard potential-outcome model assumes that:

- Each individual could have received any of the treatment levels.
- For each individual i and treatment level j, the outcome for the individual i if the individual gets treatment level j is considered even if the individual does not in fact get j; this value is called the *potential outcome*.

The variable Y represents a generic variable for the actual outcome under the treatment actually given. Then, $Y_i(j)$ will be an indicator for the outcome for individual i if that individual is given treatment level j. The vector $[Y_i(0), Y_i(1), \ldots, Y_i(M)]$ is the *potential outcome vector* for the individual i. Notice that, in practice, for each individual only one of the potential outcomes $Y_i(j)$ is observable, since an individual receives only one possible treatment (and the other treatment states and associated potential outcomes are *counterfactuals*). Outcomes that are not observable can only be estimated. This problem, called *missing data problem*, is one of the fundamental problem of causal inference. The *causal effect* is defined as a quantity that contrasts the components of the potential outcomes vector. The choice of treatment is said to have had no effect on Y for individual i if $Y_i(j) = Y_i(k)$ for every possible pair of treatment levels j and k; otherwise, treatment choice could have had an effect. Treatment choice is said to have had no effect on the population if it had no effect on any individual in the population.

As an illustration, let us consider the simplest case when the treatment is binary, i.e., M = 1 (corresponding, for instance, to situations when there is and there is no treatment). Let T_i be a level of the actual treatment for the individual i. Then, the vector $[Y_i(0), Y_i(1)]$ is the potential outcome vector for the individual i. The outcome Y_i is equal $Y_i(0)$ if $T_i = 0$ and $Y_i(1)$ if $T_i = 1$. This can be written as:

$$Y_i = Y_i(0) + T_i(Y_i(1) - Y_i(0))$$

The difference of the outcomes with and without treatment is characterized by $Y_i(1)-Y_i(0)$, the benefit of treatment. The average treatment effect is equal to (where **E** denotes expected value):

$$\text{ATE} = \mathbf{E}[Y(1) - Y(0)]$$

The average treatment on the treated individuals is equal to:

$$\text{ATT} = \mathbf{E}[Y(1) - Y(0) \,|\, T = 1]$$

These quantities cannot be computer because of unobserved potential outcomes. For instance, let the available data are given in the table given below. The observed values $Y_i(j)$ are printed in bold. The quantities ATE and ATT can be computed only using estimated values for $Y_i(j)$ and this gives ATE=2, ATT=1. Different approaches for estimating these and other unobservable quantities by observable quantities are discussed in (Angrist, 1996).

Individual	Treatment	$Y_i(0)$	$Y_i(1)$	$Y_i(1) - Y_i(0)$
1	0	**3**	5	2
2	1	2	**5**	3
3	1	5	**4**	−1
4	0	**2**	7	5
5	1	1	**2**	1

One of the practical results of the potential-outcomes models is the identification of a sufficient set of variables could yield the correct causal effect between variables of interest. That characterization of variables, called "backdoor" criterion, helps in identifying sets of variables worthy of observing.

8.7   Structural-equation models

In structural equation approach, a network of causation is modeled by a system of equations and independence assumptions (see, for instance, (Greenland, 2002). Each equation shows how an individual response (outcome) variable changes as its direct (parent) causal variables change. The 'individual' may be any unit of interest, such as a person or aggregate. In the system, a variable may appear in no more than one equation as a response variable, but may appear in any other equation as a causal variable. A variable appearing as a response in the system is said to be *endogenous* (within the system); otherwise it is *exogenous*. Relationships between variables can be linear but can also be much more complex. Structural equations can be viewed as formulas for computing potential outcomes under various actions. For instance, equations can assert that one variable will not vary with another variable, if some other variables remain constant. Structural equations differ from ordinary regression equations (that represent only *associations* of actual outcomes with actual values of the covariates as one moves across individuals). Structural equations with unknown parameters specify the functional form of effects, but do not provide the exact values of effects; thus, they don't not fully quantify causal relations.

8.8 Probabilistic causation

If a causal relationship "A causes B" is interprered deterministically then it states that A must be always followed by B. "Drinking alchohol causes headache" is often true, but still not always, so this causal relationship could be considered invalid. Probabilistic causation tends to overcome simple yes or no causation and in this approach, cause only raises the probability of the effect (rather then implies effect), all else being equal. In other words, A probabilistically causes B if occurrence of A increases the probability of B (Hitchcock, 2002). In this approach, causal relationships are explored by using the apparatus of the probability theory. We will not elaborate on this approach here, but it will rise to significance in later chapters of the book. Standard Bayesian approaches to causal inference will be discussed in Chapter 11 in the context of pattern mining; and then the PLN approach to RWR, discussed in Part III of the book, will include a different variant of probabilistic causal inference in an essential role, tightly integrated with probabilistic approaches to other aspects of inference such as deduction, induction and abduction.

PART II

Acquiring, Storing and Mining Logical Knowledge

Chapter 9

Extracting Logical Knowledge from Raw Data

Logical methods are extremely powerful when supplied with appropriate data, but this begs the question of where the data comes from. How does data from the real world get into logical format in the first place?

So far we have discussed simple toy examples, involving a small number of relationships; or else relationships that come from an already-formalized domain such as the Minesweeper game. But the real world is large, messy and not pre-formalized. Our overall goal here is to discuss the application of logic-oriented methods to large, heterogeneous knowledge stores; so we cannot entirely bypass the critical question of how one would construct large, heterogeneous stores of *logical information*. Essentially the question is how to usefully translate raw data observed in the real world, into sets of logical expressions in appropriate formal languages. This is not an easy question and there is no single answer: the answer is roughly as heterogeneous as the data involved. This is not our main focus here, so in this brief chapter we will merely overview some of the issues involved, giving a few references into some relevant literatures where appropriate.

In some cases, the transformation process is completely obvious and straightforward. For instance, Figure 9.1 shows how Twitter metadata regarding a message can simply and immediately be transformed into formal relationships (which could easily be mapped from diagrammatic into logical form):

For instance, if one has a logical term T1 corresponding to the entity bob_dobbs, and a logical term M1 corresponding to the message "Where r u?", then one may create from this diagram a logical predicate-argument relationship such as

SentTo(M1, T1)

and interpret this within many of the formal-logic systems discussed in Part I above.

To take a different sort of example, in the project described in (Goertzel & de Garis, 2008; Goertzel, 2008) an architecture is described for controlling physical or virtual robots

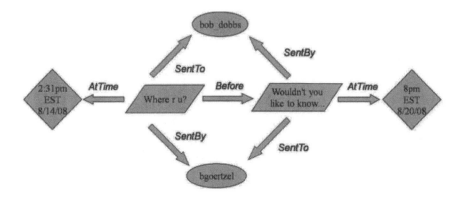

Fig. 9.1   Formal relationships extracted from Twitter metadata

using a logic-based cognitive engine. In this case the logical relationships come directly
from the outputs of sensors, and from the commands needed to be issued to actuators. Here
there are no major difficulties in representation, though there are significant difficulties in
reasoning! For instance, we may represent a certain perceptual relationship by stating that
there is a logical relationship of the form

$$\text{tangentialProperPart}(P1, P2)$$

between polygons P1 and P2, whose coordinates are then indexed in a special data structure
(tangentialProperPart is a spatial logical relationship to be discussed a little later on). And
we might represent a relationship regarding the movement of an actuator by

$$\text{moveJoint}(7, 1.3, 1.4, 2)$$

indicating the movement of joint 7 at speed 2 in the direction with $\theta = 1.3$ radians and
$\varphi = 1.4$ radians (referring to the standard spherical coordinates). Here, as in the Twitter
metadata example, the translation of life into logic is relatively straightforward.

However, in other cases – including many cases relevant to the topic of this book – the
transformation process involves much more difficult choices.

In general, transforming raw data into logic is a highly nontrivial matter, which requires
the best of current technologies; but it is certainly within the scope of the feasible rather
than the impossible. In practice subtle decisions must be made about how much intelligence
to put into the transformation process, versus how much to leave to the logical-inference
processes acting on the logical knowledge base.

For example, if a software system is given the text "Dogs eat bones," one simple approach
at logicizing this input would be to simply turn it into a sequence of propositions about

the individual characters of the text: essentially, propositions of the form "At time so-and-such, I received a text message with 'g' as the third character" and so forth. This kind of proposition can be represented easily in formal logic, but this is not necessarily the most useful thing to do.

In the remaining sections of this chapter, we will very briefly consider two cases of the extraction of logical information from nonlogical sources: tabular and relational data, and linguistic data. Other cases also exist, of course: for instance audio, video and so forth; but reviewing the literatures in all these areas would take us too far afield.

9.1 Extracting Logical Knowledge from Tabular and Relational Data

Conceptually, it seems straightforward enough to map tabular or relational data into logical format. Figure 9.2 shows a simple example of a spreadsheet mapped into formal semantic relations:

In real life, however, this sort of mapping is extremely difficult, because of the problem of figuring out the semantics of the rows and columns of spreadsheets and databases. The field of "table recognition" confronts this issue, and is summarized in (Zanibbi *et al.*, 2003).

9.2 Extracting Logical Knowledge from Graphs, Drawings, Maps and Tables

A yet more difficult issue is the extraction of formal relationships from graphs, engineering drawings, maps and tables that are encoded as bitmap images or vector drawings. The set of techniques in charge of extracting semantics out of graphical information is grouped under the term "Diagram Recognition" and has been given some attention for the past two decades. Several algorithms, techniques and toolkits have been developed and work well in many cases. However in general it remains a hard problem, probably much harder than one who is unfamiliar with the domain may realize at first. This is due to the variety of manners one can choose to convey information graphically. Sometimes to interpret correctly a diagram one even needs contextual information possibly scattered in the rest of the document or relying on common sense knowledge.

Various domain dependent algorithms have been formulated and applied. However recent work has focused on unifying these techniques into a single framework using formal grammars comparable in a way a compiler generates machine code out of a program written in some programming language [Blostein02]. Except that here the program is a 2D image and the machine code is a diagram model. A diagram model encodes the semantics

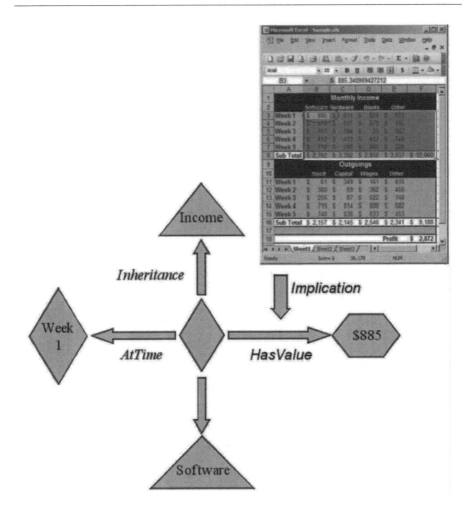

Fig. 9.2   Extracting formal semantic relations from tabular data

of the image, for instance if the diagram is a graph, the diagram model may be a list of relationships, and the "compiler", or rather called diagram recognizer, would produce an XML file containing the list of nodes and relationships represented by the graph. Following that approach a diagram recognizer may carry out several grammar parsing and data production passes, like:

1) a layout pass, that captures the spatial structure of the image and encodes it into a tree, like inside(circle, left_to_right("B", "o", "b"))

2) a lexical pass, that tries to group symbols into lexical tokens, for instance "B", "o", "b" becomes "Bob"

3) syntactic and semantic passes to finally generate the diagram model, for instance node("Bob") that expresses that the diagram is a graph with a single node called "Bob".

Similarly regarding table recognition there exists several techniques and recent work has been focused on unifying them (Zanibbi *et al.*, 2004, 2006; Blostein *et al.*, 2000).]. Again the process is divided in several passes, where each pass analyze a certain layer to produce more abstract knowledge for the upper layer and so on until the semantic model is built.

9.3 Extracting Logical Knowledge from Natural Language Text

Extracting logical relations from text requires multiple intermediate stages of Natural Language Processing, each of which is subtle and complex in itself.

For instance, using state-of-the-art natural language technology, one can transform a sentence such as "The dog ate the bone" into relationships such as

$$eat(dog, bone)$$

which is an abstract relationship embodying the semantic meaning of the sentence. Or, further, one can transform it into

$$eat\_2(dog\_1, bone\_1)$$

which indicates that the sense of "eat" used in the sentence is the second one in the system's reference dictionary, whereas the senses of "dog" and "bone" used are the first ones in the system's reference dictionary. But performing similar operations on more complex sentences pushes the boundaries of what today's technology can do.

One can frame this problem of "natural language information extraction" (Cowie & Wilks, 2000) in terms of three stages:

- mapping text into a syntactic representation
- mapping the syntactic representation into a semantic representation
- mapping the semantic representation into a more abstract logical representation

Figure 9.3 shows a relevant example of these stages, produced using the open-source RelEx software system created by Novamente LLC (Goertzel *et al.*, 2006), which incorporates as a major subsystem the link parser (Grinberg *et al.*, 1995) created at Carnegie-Mellon University. In the figure, the input sentence is first transformed into a set of low-level syntactic relations between words. Then these relations are translated into dependency relations such as "subj" and "obj" (representing subject and object relations). Finally these dependency relations are translated into formal relationships that can easily be given logical interpretation. The presence of these multiple stages illustrates the complexity of the natural language information extraction process.

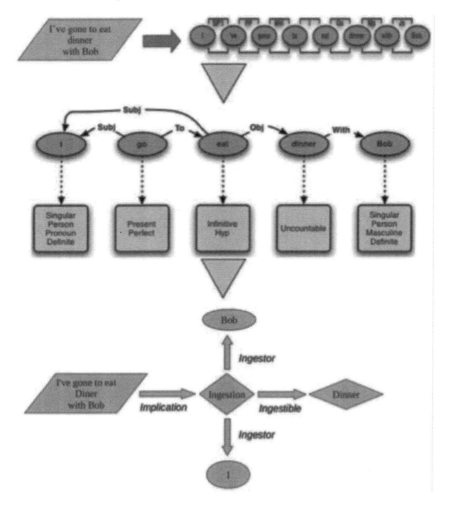

Fig. 9.3   Successive transformations of text into syntactic, grammatical and finally formal relationships (that are easily transformable to logical relationships)

The deepest problem in natural language information extraction has to do with the various sorts of ambiguity that exist in natural language. Words may have multiple meanings;

sentences may have multiple parses that all seem syntactically plausible but have varying semantic and pragmatic sensibleness; words may refer back to other words, and so forth. Computational linguistics provides only heuristic and approximative techniques for handling these methods (e.g. (Jurafsky & Martin, 2008); (Manning & Schuetze, 1999)), so, although one may currently make software systems that map natural language text into sets of logical relationships, such systems cannot be expected to work perfectly even for simple sentences, and can provide highly erratic results for complex sentences.

Chapter 10

Scalable Spatiotemporal Logical Knowledge Storage

Having dealt with the representation of logical knowledge of various sorts, and briefly discussed the problem of translating nonlogical knowledge into logical knowledge, we now turn to the question of how large amounts of logical knowledge can pragmatically be stored. This chapter presents a brief and relatively nonmathematical interlude before we plunge into the more technical topics of mining patterns in logical knowledge stores, and carrying out inferences regarding changes and other patterns in logical knowledge stores.

Suppose that we represent temporal and spatiotemporal knowledge, appropriately contextualized, in one of the multiple logical formalisms briefly discussed above. If we apply these formalisms to real-world situations we are going to obtain incredibly huge numbers of logical propositions, which presents various potential practical difficulties. The mathematics is the same whether one has a dozen logical propositions or a trillion, but the pragmatics of information-management differs significantly!

In this chapter we review the various available technologies for managing massive amounts of logical terms and relationships.

10.1 Comparison of Available Storage Technologies

The following table summarizes the strengths and weaknesses of available data storage technologies from the perspective of storing and managing large amounts of logical information.

Technology	Strengths	Weaknesses
Relational DBs	• Mature, enterprise grade solutions • Ease of integration with other systems	• Poor conceptual fit for logical information storage • Inadequate model for reasoning • Complex scalability
Object-Oriented DBs	• Better conceptual fit than relational DBs (still not perfect) • Mature solutions	• Single data model • Small ecosystem • Not designed for reasoning
Graph DBs	• Flexible, dynamic data model • Good performance and scalability • Designed with data analysis in mind	• Less mature than competing technologies
Hypergraph DBs	• Best data model fit • Designed with reasoning and data analysis in mind	• Alpha stage technology
RDF Triplestores	• Semantic web friendly • Adequate data model for some inferences	• Less mature technology • Rigid data model
Document-oriented DBs	• Flexible data model • Performance and scalability • Rapidly maturing solutions	• Not adequate for reasoning and analysis • More work is left for application layer

Continued on next page

continued from previous page

Technology	Strengths	Weaknesses
Column-oriented DBs	• Very flexible, dynamic data model • Performance and scalability • Rapidly maturing solutions	• More work is left for application layer • Not designed for reasoning
Key-value DBs	• Extremely good performance and scalability • Mature and rapidly maturing solutions	• No data model, leaving most work for application layer • Not designed for reasoning

Representing and querying large graph data stores using traditional relational databases is certainly possible, but it would lead to profound scalability and performance problems. Despite efforts from industry leaders in the RDBMS arena, relational databases and graph data are a poor conceptual and implementation fit.

Graph data typically has a flexible structure where connections among similar objects (representing people, entities, time points, spatial locations, and so forth) are numerous. And these connections are the whole point of graph data stores. The natural way to map these connections among similar objects to relational databases requires self-joins, since the connected objects are typically stored in the same table. Contemporary RDBMS technology is not optimized for these kinds of self-joins, which creates large bottlenecks both for querying at scale and writing to the database (Lightstone *et al.*, 2007).

Object-oriented databases (OODBMS) are mature technologies that provide a better fit for graph data, since object instances are naturally persisted as graphs. Distributed, highly scalable commercial products exist, although the whole OODBMS category remains a niche after decades of development efforts.

Despite those benefits, there is a major drawback for OODBMS in a graph dataset context, which is the implicit assumption of a single object model. While this is adequate for large-scale object-oriented applications, graph data mining and analysis sometimes requires that the stored data be interpreted in different ways, especially when spatial and temporal dimensions are added. There's always a 1-to-1 mapping between a OODBMS representation and some OO design – but for analyzing graph data we often want to switch the design without changing the stored data format (which is expensive for a large database), because we care more about the answers we can get than about retrieving the original data in a way that's fully consistent with how it was stored.

Technology that's explicitly oriented towards graph data (as opposed to using graphs to persist object instances) has been developed over the past few years. These tools emphasize the ability to traverse relations and discover new connections. This explicit focus makes such tools a better fit for data analysis and mining projects, especially ones involving probabilistic logic. Graph databases aren't as mature as their OOBDMS counterparts, however.

Among graph DBs, the Hypergraph DB (HGDB) open source project (kobrix.com/hgdb.jsp) was conceived with AI and data mining applications in mind. In fact HGDB goes beyond the graph database paradigm and constitutes a hypergraph DB, involving a basic representation that allows n-ary links and links pointing to links as well as nodes. This is convenient because sets of logical predicates are more naturally represented as hypergraphs than graphs.

Traditional graph DBs may be used as hypergraph DBs via transforming hypergraphs to and from graphs; but this introduces a performance penalty for the translation, and also has the drawback that, after the translation, some simple hypergraph queries become significantly more complex graph queries. But HGDB is still at the alpha stage of the development, and the potential advantages of hypergraph DBs over standard graph DBs are still relatively unexplored.

The growing interest in the semantic web has led to a number of commercial and open source products for storing knowledge encoded in the RDF data model. These storage solutions, known as Triplestores, can scale up to billions of RDF triples. The triple-based data model in RDF, however, is more limited than a free-form graph, which impacts scalability (as a more verbose knowledge representation is needed) and analysis (as algorithms have to be tailored to the more rigid RDF format, sometimes with a significant performance penalty).

Finally, the recent years have seen an explosion in alternative data storage technologies, which are often collectively referred to as "NoSQL", emphasizing their rejection of the dominant relational data model. However, the "NoSQL" umbrella actually contains a number of very diverse technologies, with different design goals and motivations.

At the simplest level, we have key-value data storage solutions, some of which are decades old, while others have been developed recently in order to answer the growing need for very fast, distributed (sometimes with complex dynamics for delayed consistency) datastores to support leading web sites, with a large number of concurrent read and write requests. These DBs have essentially no built-in data model, allowing for complete flexibility and excellent performance, at the cost of increased application level complexity.

More complex solutions exist in the form of column-oriented DBs, which store a flexible, dynamic data model that is adequate for representation of logical data. While these DBs are typically very fast and easily distributed, graph-based traversals and queries remain expensive unless great care is taken at the application level to organize data, which reduces analytical flexibility.

The third major kind of storage solution in the NoSQL umbrella is the document store, in which documents have a very flexible set of properties, although no structural consistency is necessary. This leads to excellent performance and scalability, along with an evolvable data model that is more adequate for logical information than the extreme simplicity of key-value stores. However, graph-specific analytical operations remain problematic.

Overall, our conclusion is that graph databases, whether commercial or open-source, are the current best alternative for storing and analyzing very large graph datasets, striking a good balance between the extreme flexibility of key and column oriented DBs and the convenience of built-in traversal and search operations.

10.2   Transforming Logical Relationship-Sets into Graphs

The discussion in the above section bypasses one issue: the effective representation of sets of logical relationships as graphs. This is not a problematic issue, but bears brief comment because, most literally interpreted, sets of logical relationships would better be represented as mathematical structures called "generalized hypergraphs" than as graphs per se. So one encounters the problem of translating generalized hypergraphs into traditional graphs, using appropriate, hopefully not too complex transformation rules.

Recall that a graph, mathematically, is a set of nodes together with a set of links, where each link is construed as an ordered or unordered pair of nodes. Links and nodes may be labeled and may have various numerical weights attached to them (such as fuzzy or probabilistic truth values). A hypergraph extends this model, in that links may join more than two targets. This is useful for representing logical relationships such as

$$\text{give(Jim, Bob, ball)}$$

which naturally relate three rather than two entities.

Of course, one can work around the need for hypergraph links via using labeled binary links, for example

$$subj(give, Jim)$$
$$obj(give, Bob)$$
$$obj2(give, ball)$$

which is how the RelEx NLP system (mentioned earlier) analyzes the sentence "Jim gives the ball to Bob" (and other dependency parsers would do it similarly). Similarly, the relation

$$eat(Ben, steak)$$

could be represented using a ternary link, or a labeled binary link; or, as RelEx would have it, as a set of labeled binary links

$$subj(eat, Ben)$$
$$obj(eat, steak)$$

However, attaching a broad variety of semantic labels to links is not always the desired strategy. In general it is desirable to support a broad variety of representational mechanisms, as different approaches to logical formalization of commonsense information are going to choose different ways to set up relationships.

In any case, it is straightforward to eliminate hypergraph links via introducing a "phantom node" corresponding to each hypergraph link, and having the phantom node link binarily to the targets of the hypergraph link. What's required is that the links emanating from the phantom node be indexed with numbers or some other distinct markers, if the targets of the hypergraph links were so marked. Figure 10.1 illustrates some examples of this, for the above examples.

Next, what we call a "generalized hypergraph" extends the hypergraph model further, via allowing links to point to links, which is the most natural way to represent statements like "Ben believes Bob likes Jim", e.g.

$$believes(Ben, likes(Bob, Jim))$$

Alternately, a RelEx-style representation of the above would be

$$subj(believes, Ben)$$
$$obj(believes, likes)$$

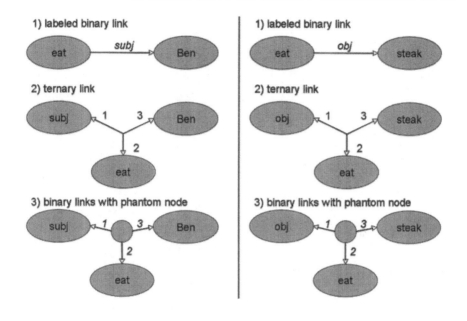

Fig. 10.1   Some hypergraph representations for the "Ben eats steak" example

subj(likes, Bob)

obj(likes, Jim)

Mapping generalized hypergraphs into graphs is also simply accomplished using phantom nodes, as illustrated in Figure 10.2

Just to make sure the point is clear, we next give some examples involving more complex logical constructs such as actually arise in using PLN for carrying out inferences involving changes in complex knowledge bases.

```
EvaluationLink
        believes
                Ben
                Inheritance
                        Bob
                        busy
```

and

```
Context  < .9 >
```

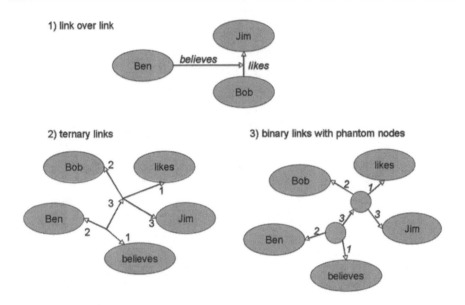

Fig. 10.2   Hypergraph to graph conversions for the "Ben believes Bob likes Jim" example

```
Accounting
Evaluation
      Mention
      List
            Bob
            CanadianPlaceNames
```

and finally one that is more complex and involves variables

```
AverageLink  < .9 >
      $X, $Y
      Implication
            Evaluation
                  Mention
                  List
                        $X
                        $Y
            IntensionalInheritance
```

```
$X
$Y
```

In summary, using this sort of mapping based on phantom nodes, one can straight-forwardly store logical relationships, interpreted as generalized hypergraphs, in graph databases. The transformation required is fairly simple and does not require the same sort of inefficient manipulations as mapping logical propositions into tabular structures as required to store them in standard relational databases.

However, the subtle question in mapping hypergraphs into graphs is: which graph operations will have the expected results when mapped back into hypergraph operations. For instance, if we map a hypergraph into a graph and then find the shortest path P between two nodes N and M in the graph ... is the hypergraph path corresponding to P the shortest path between the hypergraph nodes or links corresponding to N and M? Similarly, does a minimum-cost spanning tree in the graph derived from a hypergraph, correspond to a minimum-cost spanning hypertree in the original hypergraph? Is the set of nodes within radius R of graph node N, closely related to the set of hypergraph nodes/links within radius R of the hypergraph node/link corresponding to N? These issues go beyond the scope of the present book, and are in most cases not extremely difficult to resolve, but do require real care.

Chapter 11

Mining Patterns from Large Spatiotemporal Logical Knowledge Stores

Once one has stored a large knowledge base of logical relationships, then what? One can query the knowledge base – if one knows what one wants to ask for. One can carry out reasoning toward various goals. And another important question is how to find "unknown unknowns" – patterns in the knowledge base that are surprising and interesting yet unexpected. This quest goes by multiple names – data mining, pattern mining, information exploitation, and so forth. Whatever you call it, it's a difficult challenge because in any large dataset, the number of possible patterns to search through is mind-boggling.

Many different pattern mining algorithms exist, and a large subset of these are applicable to the case of mining patterns among logical relationships. Here we will review only two classes of algorithms: frequent subgraph mining, and causal network inference. These are important approaches, but are by no means the only approaches of interest.

Furthermore, as will be emphasized in later chapters, pattern mining algorithms in themselves are unlikely to be sufficient for the task of finding relevant and interesting relationships in large logical knowledge bases. The problem is that without significant background knowledge, and the capability to deploy this background knowledge intelligently for analogical inference, it's very hard to tell interesting patterns from uninteresting ones. So, in order to really do a good job of spotting interesting patterns in large logical knowledge bases, it's likely to be necessary to combine pattern mining algorithms with uncertain and causal inference algorithms.

That is, one will need to use pattern mining to produce a moderate-sized pool of potentially interesting patterns, and then use inference to filter this down into a smaller set of probably-interesting patterns. As many pattern mining algorithms (including the ones considered here) an be instructed to look for new patterns "in the neighborhood" of a set of target patterns, the patterns identified as interesting by inference may then be used to seed further pattern mining. This kind of hybridized approach has not been explored much if at all in the research literature, but there is little doubt it will be necessary as the sorts of applications envisioned in this book become realities.

To add to the challenges, pattern mining in extremely large bodies of knowledge poses particular difficulties in terms of scalability. For instance, algorithms must cope with the inability to store the whole knowledge base in the memory of any one machine. This is an area computer science is just beginning to explore. For instance, in the following section we will discuss algorithms for identifying "surprisingly frequent subgraphs" in large graph knowledge bases, following (Hsu *et al.*, 2008). The unique aspect of their approach is a clever mechanism for recursively decomposing a large graph into a large number of smaller subgraphs, recognizing patterns in the subgraphs, and then assembling overall graph patterns from the patterns recognized in the subgraphs. This general sort of idea likely has much more general applicability.

Furthermore, even within the scope of what can be stored within a single machine, there can be sufficient data to render standard pattern mining algorithms inapplicable. So as well as crafting distributed algorithms, one must devise special algorithms capable of handling large bodies of knowledge efficiently within a single machine. We will consider one example of this below: algorithms for finding "partial causal networks" in large bodies of knowledge, which essentially are simplifications and scalings-up of better-known algorithms for finding full causal networks in smaller datasets.

11.1   Mining Frequent Subgraphs of Very Large Graphs

The staple of standard "data mining" in relational databases is a technique called "frequent itemset mining" or FIM (Goethals & Zaki, 2004), which seeks to find the most frequent combinations of data items. There are variants of FIM which seek the most surprising combinations of data items; these are essentially algorithmically identical to FIM, with slightly different underlying mathematics (Chakrabarti *et al.*, 1998; Gallo *et al.*, 2007).

In the graph domain, the analogue of FIM is "frequent subgraph mining," an area in which there are numerous publications and a handful of open-source software toolkits. An overview of the field is given in (Ivancsy & Vajk, 2005). These algorithms are directly relevant to our problem of mining patterns in large stores of logical knowledge, because logical predicates may be mapped into graph structures as we discussed in the previous chapter.

Two simple examples of frequent subgraphs that might be found in large graphs in the Twitter domain are as follows:

- Women in East Anglia often send each other private messages about the band Coldplay
- Young Chinese in London often express positive sentiment about the Chinese government on the day after the Chinese soccer team wins a game

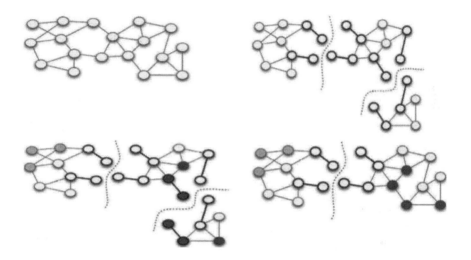

Fig. 11.1   Stages of distributed pattern mining in large graphs, in the HLW algoritm. Top, left: original graph. Top, right: partition into subgraphs fitting RAM of individual machines. Bottom, left: identification of frequent subgraphs. Bottom, right: merge of subgraphs embodying repeated patterns.

Datamining large graph bases is a challenging problem, because most of the highly scalable datamining algorithms available were designed to operate on tabular data, and perform poorly when adapted to graphs. These adaptations often require a fixed graph structure, which isn't practical. Spatiotemporal databases (Yeung & Hall, 2007) make the problem even harder due to their continuously changing nature. A datamining algorithm for a large spatiotemporal graph database must fullfil at least the following requirements:

- Ability to handle data too voluminous to fit in RAM without severe performance degradation.
- Ability to incrementally mine the database, including the ability to consider only new information

- Ability to find patterns that are frequent in space (occur often across different locations), time (occur frequently over time) and both. These patterns can be static or dynamic with regards to time and/or space.

One such algorithm, that we've explored in detail, is due to Hsu, Lee and Wang (hence we nickname it HLW) and it has three phases, loosely illustrated in Figure 11.1:

- Partition the graph database into units that fit into RAM.
- Apply a standard graph datamining algorithm to each unit, generating a set of patterns.
- Merge the obtained patterns from each unit, obtaining database-wide patterns.

Alternative algorithms exist and others can be developed. We don't think this particular algorithm is necessarily ideal, but we believe that any software system designed to identify patterns in a large spatiotemporal logic database needs to include an algorithm that fullfils the above requirements.

11.2 Learning Partial Causal Networks

Another important example of data analysis that must be performed on large spatiotemporal logical knowledge bases is the search for causal patterns. Note the key distinction between correlation and causation, as depicted in Figures 11.2–11.3: put roughly, causation may be characterized as the combination of correlation with the presence of a plausible causal mechanism... where the assessment of the plausibility of a causal mechanism always depends upon contextual understanding.

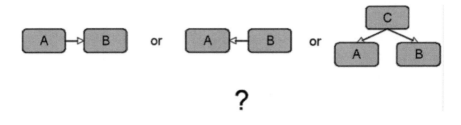

Fig. 11.2   Correlation is not causation

Techniques for inferring networks of causal relationships from databases of events are well known, and are mainly based on the interpretation of a causal network as a Bayesian belief network with causal links [Pearl94].

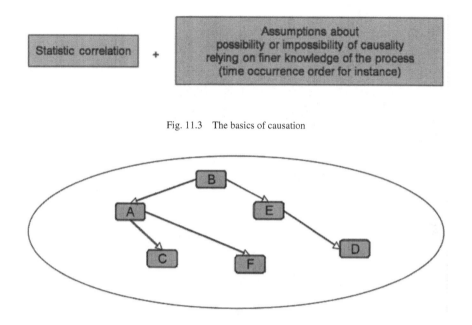

Fig. 11.3   The basics of causation

Fig. 11.4   A causal network

Figure 11.5 shows some causal relationships in the Twitter context that may be represented this way: a causal relation between message contents of a given person, and a causal relation between message content and follower subscription.

None of the standard Bayes net based methods scale up at all well. On the other hand, there are some modern variations of these methods that do deal with reasonably large datasets, via scaling down their ambition and searching for "partial causal networks" rather than complete ones. Building a partial causal network (still capturing most of the causal relations) is relatively tractable even for processes involving tens of thousands of variables. To apply these methods to really huge datasets, one would then combine them with the same sort of graph-partitioning scheme described in the previous section in the context of frequent itemset mining. However, articulating the details of this combination would go beyond the scope of this book.

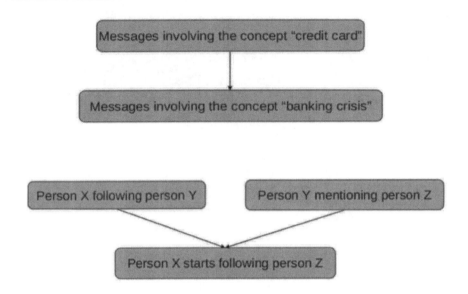

Fig. 11.5   Examples of a causal relation between message contents of a given person and a causal relation between message content and follower subscriptio.

11.3   Scalable Techniques for Causal Network Discovery

The leading algorithm for scalably discovering partial causal networks in massive datasets is Local Causal Discovery (LCD), a straightforward technique which has many specialized variants [Silverstein98, Mani01].

The basic idea underlying LCD is simple : testing Conditional Independence for two variables assuming one cause, instead of assuming a conjunction of causes. Recall that the notation X//Y|Z stands for X and Y are independent knowing Z, or more formally $P(X|Y,Z)=P(X|Z)$ and $P(Y|X,Z)=P(Y|Z)$. In these terms, the basic idea of LCD is assuming X//Y|Z instead of X//Y|C where C is a set of variables. This core principle underlies all variations of the algorithm.

This sort of algorithm can be reasonably efficient; but has the serious limitation that can only discover causal relations involving one cause at a time.

There are also global approaches that can handle events with multiple causes, via approaches such as

- making special causal assumptions [Cheng97]
- pre-processing dependence over the graph (that is computing a dependency measure for each pair of variables) [Cheng97]

- pre-processing the Markov Boundary (which is the minimal Markov Blanket) [Margaritis99]

The pre-processing approach allows one to reduce the number of conditional independence tests because many configurations of causes are ruled out after the pre-processing (or/and by causal assumptions).

A good example of a more scalable global method is [Margaritis99]. This approach operates by first estimating the "Markov boundary" (i.e. the minimal set of variables that isolates, that is makes independent, a given variable from the rest of the network) of each variables to limit the conditional independence search over the Markov boundary of a given variable. This works excellently when for instance a variable has a small number of direct causes. Another, related approach is [Nielsen08], which uses the algorithm of the previous paragraph but in an incremental way, based on the assumption that the joint probability distribution is changing over time.

PART III

Probabilistic Logic Networks for Real-World Reasoning

Chapter 12

Probabilistic Logic Networks

The preceding portion of this book has largely constituted "literature review"; this final part is a little different and presents original material, designed to cover important areas that seem omitted by the approaches reviewed above.

Above we have reviewed aspects of the representation of uncertain spatiotemporal knowledge, and also systems for reasoning on real-world knowledge; but there are major gaps between those two sets of ideas as we have presented them so far. Our discussion of representation focused heavily on fuzzy and probabilistic spatiotemporal knowledge, but the logical reasoning systems discussed don't handle these sorts of uncertainty in a sophisticated or integral way. We suggest that one prerequisite for effective, scalable RWR using a logic-based approach, is to have a logic system that incorporates fuzziness and probability into spatiotemporal, contextual and causal inference in a fundamental way.

In the chapters in this Part of the book, we aim to show how to do this via creating and manipulating special logical relationship types within the Probabilistic Logic Networks (PLN) formalism that we have introduced in prior publications (Goertzel *et al.*, 2008), and developed in the context of our work on the Novamente Cognition Engine (Goertzel *et al.*, 2004) and OpenCog (Hart & Goertzel, 2008) integrative AI architectures, and will use in some of the detailed examples in later chapters. A complete exposition of PLN would be out of place here; our goal will be to explain enough of the elements and the notation to make the examples given in later chapters comprehensible.

12.1 Motivations Underlying PLN

The guiding motivation behind the design of PLN was the desire to create an uncertain inference framework capable of encompassing all the sorts of inference that may confront a general intelligence operating in the everyday human world – including reasoning based on uncertain knowledge, and/or reasoning leading to uncertain conclusions (whether from certain or uncertain knowledge). Among the general high-level requirements underlying the development of PLN were the following:

- To enable uncertainty-savvy versions of all known varieties of logical reasoning, including for instance higher-order reasoning involving quantifiers, higher-order functions, and so forth
- To reduce to crisp "theorem prover" style behavior in the limiting case where uncertainty tends to zero
- To encompass inductive and abductive as well as deductive reasoning
- To agree with probability theory in those reasoning cases where probability theory, in its current state of development, provides solutions within reasonable calculational effort based on assumptions that are plausible in the context of real-world embodied software systems
- To gracefully incorporate heuristics not explicitly based on probability theory, in cases where probability theory, at its current state of development, does not provide adequate pragmatic solutions
- To provide "scalable" reasoning, in the sense of being able to carry out inferences involving billions of premises. Of course, when the number of premises is fewer, more intensive and accurate reasoning may be carried out.
- To easily accept input from, and send input to, natural language processing software systems

The practical application of PLN is still at an early stage. Based on our evidence so far, however, we have found PLN to fulfill the above requirements adequately well, and our intuition remains that it will be found to do so in general.

The overall structure of PLN theory may be described as follows. First, PLN involves some important choices regarding knowledge representation, which lead to specific "schematic forms" for logical inference rules. The knowledge representation may be thought of as a definition of a set of "logical term types" and "logical relationship types" (some of which we will elaborate below), leading to a novel way of graphically modeling bodies of knowledge. It is this graphical interpretation of PLN knowledge representation that led to the "network" part of the name "Probabilistic Logic Networks." It is worth noting that the networks used to represent knowledge in PLN are generalized weighted directed hypergraphs (Bollobás, 1998), much more general for example than the binary directed acyclic graphs used in Bayesian network theory. Later on we will review some methods for translating generalized hypergraphs into ordinary graphs, which can be useful for purposes of visualization, analysis and storage.

Next, PLN involves specific mathematical formulas for calculating the probability value of the conclusion of an inference rule based on the probability values of the premises plus (in some cases) appropriate background assumptions. It also involves a particular approach to estimating the confidence values with which these probability values are held (weight of evidence, or second-order uncertainty). Finally, the implementation of PLN in software requires important choices regarding the structural representation of inference rules, and also regarding "inference control" – the strategies required to decide what inferences to do in what order, in each particular practical situation.

Here we will not be concerned at all with PLN's probability formulas – they are absolutely critical for performing practical inferences and getting useful answers, but here we will only be concerned with exploring the *forms* of various inferences, and so we will refer the reader to the *Probabilistic Logic Networks* book (Goertzel *et al.*, 2008) for discussion of quantitative formulas. In our examples here, we will omit quantitative truth values so as to focus on the forms of inferences. In fact, the quantitative truth value associated with an inference may come out differently depending on the particular parameters of the truth value formulas, as clarified in the PLN book.

12.2   Term and Predicate Logic in PLN

One of the distinguishing features of PLN is the way its inference rules combine predicate logic and term logic. As briefly reviewed above, predicate logic and term logic are two different but related forms of logic, each of which can be used both for crisp and uncertain logic.

Predicate logic is the most-familiar kind, where the basic entity under consideration is the "predicate," a function that maps argument variables (which are quantified universally or existentially) into truth values.

On the other hand, in term logic, which dates back at least to Aristotle and his notion of the syllogism, the basic element is a subject-predicate statement, denotable in many ways, for instance

$$A \rightarrow B$$

where $\rightarrow$ denotes a notion of inheritance or specialization. Logical inferences take the form of "syllogistic rules," which give patterns for combining statements with matching terms. (We don't use the → notation much in PLN, because it's not sufficiently precise for PLN purposes since PLN introduces many varieties of inheritance; but we will use the → notation in this section since here we are speaking about inheritance in term logic in general rather than about PLN in particular).

Example term logic inference rules are the deduction, induction, and abduction rules:

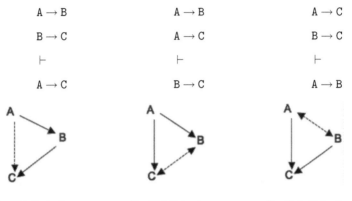

Fig. 12.1 Deduction   Fig. 12.2 Induction   Fig. 12.3 Abduction

These rules are simple schematically but subtler when one matches them with uncertain truth value formulas. For instance, when one does so, one finds that deduction is infallible, in the case of absolutely certain premises, but uncertain in the case of probabilistic premises; while abduction and induction are always fallible, even given certain premises. In fact, in PLN one derives abduction and induction from the combination of deduction with a simple rule called inversion

$$A \rightarrow B$$
$$\vdash$$
$$B \rightarrow A$$

whose truth value formula derives from Bayes' rule.

Predicate logic is generally felt to deal more naturally with deduction than with induction, abduction and other uncertain, fallible inference rules. On the other hand, term logic can deal quite elegantly and simply with all forms of inference. Furthermore, as argued in (Goertzel et al., 2008) the predicate logic formulation of deduction proves less amenable to "probabilization" than the term logic formulation. It is for these reasons, among others, that the foundation of PLN is drawn from term logic rather than from predicate logic. PLN begins with a term logic foundation, then adds on elements of probabilistic and combinatory logic, as well as some aspects of predicate logic, to form a complete inference system, tailored for easy integration with software components embodying other (not explicitly logical) aspects of intelligence.

Sommers and Engelbretsen (Englebretsen & Sommers, 2000) have given an excellent defense of the value of term logic for crisp logical inference, demonstrating that many pragmatic inferences are far simpler in term logic formalism than they are in predicate logic formalism. On the other hand, the pioneer in the domain of uncertain term logic is Pei Wang (Wang, 1996), to whose NARS uncertain term logic based reasoning system PLN owes a considerable debt. To frame the issue in terms of our above discussion of PLN's relation to traditional probabilistic logic approaches, we may say we have found that many things are significantly easier in a term logic rather than predicate logic context, including:

1) the formulation of appropriate heuristics to guide probabilistic inference in cases where adequate dependency information is not available,
2) and the creation of appropriate methods to extend first-order extensional inference rules and formulas to handle other sorts of inference.

In these respects, the use of term logic in PLN is roughly a probabilization of the use of term logic in NARS; but of course, there are many deep conceptual and mathematical differences between PLN and NARS, so that the correspondence between the two theories in the end is more historical and theory-structural, rather than being a precise correspondence on the level of content.

12.3   Knowledge Representation in PLN

PLN knowledge representation is conveniently understood according to two dichotomies: extensional vs. intensional, and first-order vs. higher-order. The former is a conceptual (philosophical/cognitive) distinction, between logical relationships that treat concepts according to their members versus those that treat concepts according to their properties. In PLN extensional knowledge is treated as more basic, and intensional knowledge is defined in terms of extensional knowledge via the addition of a specific mathematics of intension (somewhat related to information theory). This is different from the standard probabilistic approach which contains no specific methods for handling intension, and also different from Wang's approach in which intension and extension are treated as completely symmetric with neither of them being more basic or derivable from the other.

The first-order versus higher-order distinction, on the other hand, is essentially a mathematical one. First-order, extensional PLN is a variant of standard term logic, as originally introduced by Aristotle in his Logic and more recently elaborated by theorists such as Wang (Wang, 1996) and Sommers and Engelbretsen (Englebretsen, 2000). First-order PLN involves logical relationships between terms representing concepts, such as

```
Inheritance cat animal
ExtensionalInheritance Pixel_444 Contour_7565
```

(where the notation is used that R A B denotes a logical relationship of type R between arguments A and B). A typical first-order PLN inference rule is the standard term-logic deduction rule

$$A \rightarrow B$$
$$B \rightarrow C$$
$$\vdash$$
$$A \rightarrow C$$

which in PLN looks like

```
ExtensionalInheritance A B
ExtensionalInheritance B C
⊢
ExtensionalInheritance A C
```

As well as purely logical relationships, first-order PLN also includes a fuzzy set membership relationship, and specifically addresses the relationship between fuzzy set membership and logical inheritance, which is closely tied to the PLN concept of intension.

Higher-order PLN, on the other hand, has to do with functions and their arguments. Much of higher-order PLN is structurally parallel to first-order PLN: for instance, implication between statements is largely parallel to inheritance between terms. However, a key difference is that most of higher-order PLN involves either variables or higher-order functions (functions taking functions as their arguments). So for instance one might have

```
ExtensionalImplication
    Inheritance $X cat
```

```
Evaluation eat ($X, mice)
```

(using the notation that

R

    A

    B

denotes the logical relationship R applied to the arguments A and B). Here Evaluation is a relationship that holds between a predicate and its argument-list; so that e.g.

```
Evaluation eat (Sylvester, mice)
```

means that the list *(Sylvester, mice)* is within the set of ordered pairs characterizing the *eat* relationship. The parallel of the first-order extensional deduction rule given above would be a rule

```
ExtensionalImplication A B
ExtensionalImplication B C
⊢
ExtensionalImplication A C
```

where the difference is that in the higher-order inference case, the tokens A, B and C denote either variable-bearing expressions or higher-order functions. Some higher-order inference rules involve universal or existential quantifiers as well.

While first-order PLN adheres closely to the term logic framework, higher-order PLN is better described as a mix of term logic, predicate logic and combinatory logic (though the latter aspect will not be emphasized here). The knowledge representation is kept flexible as this seems to lead to the simplest and most straightforward set of inference rules.

12.4 PLN Truth Values and Formulas

Next, one of the less conventional aspects of PLN – which will not play a major role in this book, but still merits brief mention – is the quantification of uncertainty using imprecise truth values that contain at least two components, and usually more (in distinction from the typical truth value used in probability theory, which is a single number: a probability). PLN's indefinite probability approach is related to earlier multi-component truth-value approaches due to Wang and Walley [Wang 2006b; Walley 1991] and others, but is unique in its particulars.

The simplest kind of PLN truth value, called a SimpleTruthValue, consists of a pair of numbers <s,w> called a strength and a confidence. The strength value is a probability; the confidence value is a measure of the amount of uncertainty attached to the strength value. Confidence values are normalized into $[0, 1]$.

For instance <.6,1> means a probability of .6 known with absolute certainty. <.6,.2> means a probability of .6 known with a very low degree of certainty. <.6,0> means a probability of .6 known with a zero degree of certainty, which is equivalent to <x,0> for any other probability value x.

Another type of truth value, more commonly used as the default within PLN, is the IndefiniteTruthValue. We introduce the mathematical and philosophical foundations of IndefiniteTruthValues in Chapter 3. Essentially a hybridization of Walley's imprecise probabilities and Bayesian credible intervals, indefinite probabilities quantify truth values in terms of four numbers <L,U,b,k>: an interval [L,U], a credibility level b, and an integer k called the lookahead. IndefiniteTruthValues provide a natural and general method for calculating the "weight-of-evidence" underlying the conclusions of uncertain inferences.

Beyond the SimpleTruthValues and IndefiniteTruthValues mentioned above, more advanced types of PLN truth value also exist, principally "distributional truth values" in which the strength value is replaced by a matrix approximation to an entire probability. Note that this then provides for three different granularities of approximations to an entire probability distribution. A distribution can be most simply approximated by a single number, a somewhat better approximation being provided by a probability interval, and an even better approximation given by an entire matrix.

(Goertzel et al., 2008) defines the various inference rules of PLN, and also associates with each of them a "strength value formula" with each of them (a formula determining the strength of the conclusion based on the strengths of the premises). For example, the deduction rule mentioned above is associated with two strength formulas, one based on an independence assumption and the other based on a different "concept geometry" based assumption. The independence-assumption-based deduction strength formula looks like

B $< s\_B >$

C < s_C >

ExtensionalInheritance A B < s_AB >

ExtensionalInheritance B C < s_BC >

⊢

ExtensionalInheritance A C < s_AC >

where

$$s_{AC} = s_{AB}\, s_{BC} + (1 - s_{AB})(s_C - s_B\, s_{BC})/(1 - s_B)$$

This particular rule is a straightforward consequence of elementary probability theory. Some of the other formulas are equally straightforward; but some are subtler and (as explained in detail in (Goertzel *et al.*, 2008)) require heuristic reasoning beyond standard probabilistic tools like independence assumptions.

Since simple truth values are the simplest and least informative of our truth value types, they provide quick, but less accurate, assessments of the resulting strength and confidence values. A valuable enterprise is extending the simple truth value formulas to IndefiniteTruthValues. A careful consideration of this matter shows that indefinite truth values provide a natural approach to measuring weight-of-evidence. IndefiniteTruthValues can be thought of as approximations to entire distributions, and so provide an intermediate level of accuracy regarding strength and confidence. Finally, PLN inference formulas may also be modified to handle entire distributional truth values. Distributional truth values provide more information than the other truth value types. As a result, they may also be used to yield even more accurate assessments of strength and confidence.

12.5   Some Relevant PLN Relationship Types and Inference Rules

In this section we briefly review the specific PLN relationship types and inference rules that will be used in the inference examples given in later chapters. Contextual, spatial and temporal relationships will not be covered here, as these will be described later on in the appropriately specialized chapters.

As seen above the PLN formalism allows one to express relationships over predicates and relationships. For this purpose it uses higher order operators (comparable in some ways to first order logic connectives and quantifiers), such as Implication, Equivalence, Average and ThereExists (there is also a ForAll operator but as it is not used in the inference examples we will not elaborate further on it). The semantics of Equivalence and Implication are easily definable using the SatisfyingSet operator that we define below.

12.5.1 *SatisfyingSet and Member*

The SatisfyingSet operator allows us to express the concept of a set whose members are all elements that satisfy the predicate. We also recall the Member relationship type that expresses how much an element belongs to a concept (with a truth value that is fuzzy rather than probabilistic).

Let's for instance consider the predicate FriendOfBob, defined by the three elements Jack, John and Jill as follows:

```
Evaluation < .7 >
       FriendOfBob
       Jack
Evaluation < .6 >
       FriendOfBob
       John
Evaluation < .8 >
       FriendOfBob
       Jill
```

According to the definition of the SatisfyingSet operator, we would then have:

```
Member < .7 >
       Jack
       SatisfyingSet(FriendOfBob)
Member < .6 >
       John
       SatisfyingSet(FriendOfBob)
Member < .8 >
       Jill
       SatisfyingSet(FriendOfBob)
```

12.5.2   *Equivalence and Implication*

Now we can define Equivalence and Implication as follows:

```
Equivalence
      A
      B
```

is equal to

```
Similarity
      SatisfyingSet(A)
      SatisfyingSet(B)
```

and

```
Implication
      A
      B
```

is equal to

```
Inheritance
      SatisfyingSet(A)
      SatisfyingSet(B)
```

We have defined the mixed versions of Equivalence and Implication. The extensional and intensional versions are analogously defined, we give only the definition of ExtensionalEquivalence:

```
ExtensionalEquivalence
      A
      B
```

is equal to

```
ExtensionalSimilarity
      SatisfyingSet(A)
      SatisfyingSet(B)
```

12.5.3 *Quantifiers, Average and ThereExists*

Quantification in uncertain logic is a somewhat subtle matter. PLN handles it largely via the Average construct, which is a kind of "average quantifier": the truth value of

```
AverageLink
      $X
      F($X)
```

can be defined as the weighted average of the truth value of F($X), i.e. as

$$\frac{\sum_x w(x)F(x)}{\sum_x w(x)}$$

(Note that this approach has been elaborated in detail only for finite domains, as the intended application is to the set of knowledge contained explicitly within an AI system. Extension to infinite domains is thought to be possible but would require additional theoretical elaboration.)

There may be other ways to define the truth value of Average, possibly more advantageous in various respects, but the one outlined above has the advantage of being rather tractable, and it is the approach taken in the current PLN software system.

ThereExists is an existential quantification; it is the dual of the quantifier *ForAll* and we will not recall it in detail here (see the PLN book for more information (Goertzel *et al.*, 2008)). Informally let's just say that the truth value of *ThereExists* $XF($X)$ quantifies how much it exists an X such that $F($X)$ is essentially not zero, i.e. lying within [e,1], where e is a margin of error.

From the detailed treatment of *Average* and *ThereExists* given in (Goertzel *et al.*, 2008), it follows that the truth value of *ThereExists* $XF($X)$ must be equal to or greater than the truth value of *Average* $XF($X)$, *at least assuming that e is equal or smaller than the truth value of Average* $XF($X)$. This will be useful in the inference examples given later on.

12.5.4   *Some Inheritance rules*

The following rule is also useful in examples given later on; it basically says that if all elements that inherit F, also inherit G, then as a consequence F inherits G:

```
Average $X
        ExtensionImplication
                Inheritance $X F
                Inheritance $X G
Inheritance F  G
```

12.5.5   *Intensional Inheritance*

As stated earlier in the section, intensional inheritance quantifies how much the patterns of a concept inherits from the patterns of another. There is not a unique way to define the notion of pattern. Here our working definition is that the set of patterns of A is the set of concepts which contribute to define A and which are simpler than A itself. Formally P is a pattern of A if

```
1) ExtensionaInheritance
        A
        P
```

```
2) NotLink
        ExtensionalInheritance
                NotLink
                        A
                P
```

3) $c(P) < c(A)$, where c is a measure of complexity (for instance some variant of Kolmogorov complexity).

The reason we require both 1 and 2 is to avoid patterns that are too general to be useful, for instance a concept like BeingPartOfTheUniverse will not be retained as an interesting pattern because it does not help to define A, since both A and Not A are part of the universe.

Let us denote PAT(A) the set of patterns of A, then

```
IntensionalInheritance
    A
    B
```

is just equivalent to

```
ExtensionalInheritance
    PAT(A)
    PAT(B)
```

Not that this definition works just as well if we have an intensional implication instead of inheritance due to equivalence between implication and inheritance (implication is used for predicates and inheritance is used for concepts).

12.6 Applying PLN

To sum up: the goal underlying the theoretical development of PLN has been the creation of practical software systems carrying out complex, useful inferences based on uncertain knowledge and drawing uncertain conclusions. Toward that end we have implemented most of the PLN theory described in the PLN book, in a "PLN module" incorporated in the Novamente Cognition Engine (NCE), an integrative artificial intelligence software framework (Goertzel, 2006), and the OpenCog engine [Goertzel, 2008; Hart & Goertzel, 2008], an open-source offshoot of the NCE.

By far the most difficult aspect of designing a PLN implementation is inference control – which is really a foundational conceptual issue rather than an implementational matter per se. The PLN framework just tells you what inferences can be drawn, it doesn't tell you what order to draw them in, in which contexts. The current PLN implementation utilizes the standard modalities of forward-chaining and backward-chaining inference control. However, the vivid presence of uncertainty throughout the PLN system makes these algorithms more challenging to use than in a standard crisp inference context. Put simply, the search trees expand unacceptably fast, so one is almost immediately faced with the need to use clever, experience-based heuristics to perform pruning.

The issue of inference control leads into deep issues related to automated reasoning and cognitive science; we briefly mention some of these issues in these pages, but do not fully explore, because that would lead too far afield from the focus of the book. In the final chapter we visit this theme in the specific context of exploring exactly how commonsense knowledge about spatial and temporal events may help guide PLN inference to perform scalably on large stores of real-world knowledge.

The practical application of PLN is still at an early stage; but so far, we have applied PLN to several areas. We have applied it to process the output of a natural language processing subsystem, using it to combine together premises extracted from different biomedical research abstracts to form conclusions embodying medical knowledge not contained in any of the component abstracts (Goertzel *et al.*, 2006). We have also used PLN to learn rules controlling the behavior of a humanoid agent in a 3D simulation world: for instance, PLN learns to play "fetch" based on simple reinforcement learning stimuli (Goertzel *et al.*, 2007). Our current research involves extending PLN's performance in both of these areas, and bringing the two areas together by using PLN to help the NCE and OpenCog carry out complex simulation-world tasks involving a combination of physical activity and linguistic communication; and, additionally, pursuing the sorts of inferences described in this book, applying PLN to scalable inference on real-world spatiotemporal knowledge stores.

12.7   Deploying PLN in the OpenCog System

With the above comments in mind, we here briefly describe how PLN has been integrated with OpenCog. OpenCog is a complex framework with a complex underlying theory, and here we will only hint at some of its key aspects. OpenCog is an open-source software framework designed to support the construction of multiple AI systems; and the current main thrust of work within OpenCog is the implementation of a specific AGI design called OpenCogPrime (OCP), which is presented in the online wikibook (Hart & Goertzel, 2008). Much of the OpenCog software code, and many of the ideas in the OCP design, have derived from the open-sourcing of aspects of the proprietary Novamente Cognition Engine, which has been described extensively in previous publications (Goertzel *et al.*, 2004).

The first key entity in the OpenCog software architecture is the AtomTable, which is a repository for weighted, labeled hypergraph nodes and hyperedges. In the OpenCog implementation of PLN, the nodes and links involved in PLN are stored here. OpenCog also contains an object called the CogServer, which wraps up an AtomTable as well as (among other objects) a Scheduler that schedules a set of MindAgent objects that each (when allocated processor time by the Scheduler) carry out cognitive operations involving the AtomTable.

The essence of the OCP design consists of a specific set of MindAgents (including some carrying out various PLN inference operations) designed to work together in a collaborative way in order to create a system that carries out actions oriented toward achieving goals (where goals are represented as specific nodes in the AtomTable, and actions are represented as Procedure objects indexed by Atoms in the AtomTable, and the utility of a procedure for achieving a goal is represented by a certain set of probabilistic logical links in the AtomTable, etc.). OpenCog is still at an experimental stage but has been used for such projects as statistical language analysis, probabilistic inference, and the control of virtual agents in online virtual worlds (see opencog.org). We believe it could also be of significant value in the many other RWR applications.

Chapter 13

Temporal and Contextual Reasoning in PLN

In this chapter we review the temporal and causal PLN relationship types and rules that are used to guide these sorts of inference in PLN, and give some simple examples to illustrate how they are used. In the following chapters we will present more elaborate examples of spatiotemporal reasoning, using these constructs and ideas.

13.1 Temporal relationship types

First, the notation

```
AtTimeLink  < TV >
        T
        E
```

means that the event E holds during T, where T is a time interval.

So for example:

```
AtTimeLink  < .9, .8 >
        [10:March:2007, 14:March:2007]
        Evaluation
            Sick
            Bob
```

means that Bob is sick with degree 0.9 at confidence 0.8 from the 10th of March 2007 to the 14th of March 2007.

The time format in the examples is arbitrary and matters little, in practice it is an integer corresponding to the number of time units – a time unit could be 10ms for instance – that have passed since a referential beginning date, the zero time.

The relationships intiatedAt and terminatedAt represent respectively when an event starts and stops. So for instance the example above can be similarly expressed by:

```
And
        initiatedAt  < .9,.8 >
            10:March:2007
            Evaluation Sick Bob
        terminatedAt  < .9,.8 >
            14:March:2007
            Evaluation Sick Bob
```

Sometimes, that notation is not enough to characterize the temporal aspect of an event. For instance one may want to express that an event has started within an interval, or similarly ended within an interval. For that the temporal relationships initiatedTroughout and terminatedThroughout are used:

For instance if Bob has gotten progressively sick and healed progressively too:

```
And
        initiatedThroughout  < .9,.8 >
            [10:March:2007, 11:March:2007]
            Evaluation Sick Bob
        terminatedThroughout  < .9,.8 >
            [13:March:2007, 14:March:2007]
            Evaluation Sick Bob
```

means that the 10th of March Bob was sick with degree 0 and then that degree progressively increased till the 11th of March.

Given these primitives it is possible to express other temporal relationships like OverlapTime which represents how much 2 time intervals overlap:

```
OverlapTime  < .8 >
        [Monday, Wednesday]
```

```
[Tuesday, Friday]
```

Or During which represents how much an interval is included in another one:

```
During < 1 >
        [Tuesday, Wednesday]
        [Monday, Friday]
```

These two relationships can be considered as shorthands as they can be expressed using initiatedAt and terminatedAt.

13.2   PLN Temporal Inference in Action

Next we give a concrete example of PLN doing temporal inference, according to the representational mechanisms described above.

Suppose a user has submitted to a logical knowledge based system a query regarding which people were in the same place as Jane last week. Suppose Susie and Jane use the same daycare center, but Jane uses it everyday, whereas Susie only uses it when she has important meetings (otherwise she works at home with her child). Suppose Susie sends a message stating that Tuesday she has a big meeting with a potential funder for her business. Inference is needed to figure out that on Tuesday she's likely to put her child in daycare, and hence (depending on the time of the meeting!) potentially to be at the same place as Jane sometime on Tuesday. To further estimate the probability of the two women being in the same place, one has to do inference based on the times Jane usually picks up and drops off her child, and the time Susie is likely to do so based on the time of her meeting.

So: how do we use PLN to infer the truth value of the proposition that Susie was at the same Place as Jane last week?

Formally, in PLN notation our target theorem looks like:

```
ThereExists $Place, $TimeInterval1, $TimeInterval2
        And
                AtTime($TimeInterval1, AtPlace(Susie, $Place))
                AtTime($TimeInterval2, AtPlace(Jane, $Place))
                OverlapTime($TimeInterval1, $TimeInterval2)
```

```
During($TimeInterval1, LastWeek)
During($TimeInterval2, LastWeek)
```

where atPlace is a predicate that indicates if a given person is at a given place. Note that since temporal reasoning has not been fully implemented yet we will not include the numerical values in that example.

We make the following assumptions for the purpose of the example inference:

Axioms

Axioms related to Jane:

1) "Jane is at the daycare center everyday of the week between 7am and 7:30am and between 16pm and 16:30pm (when she brings and fetch her child)."

    1.a) ```Average $Day
            And
              IsWeekDay($Day)
              AtTime([$Day:7am, $Day:7:30am], AtPlace(Jane, daycare))
    ```

    1.b) ```Average $Day
            And
              IsWeekDay($Day)
              AtTime([$Day:16am, $Day:16:30am], AtPlace(Jane, daycare))
    ```

Axioms related to Susie:

2) "When Susie has an important meeting at time interval T, she will be in the daycare center during 30 minutes an hour before the beginning of T and after the end of T"

```
Implication
        AtTime(T, ImportantMeeting(Susie))
        And
            AtTime
                [beginning(T)-1h, beginning(T)-1:30h]
                AtPlace(Susie, daycare)
```

```
AtTime
        [end(T)+1h, end(T)+1:30h]
        AtPlace(Susie, daycare)
```

3) "Susie had an important meeting last Tuesday between 1:30pm and 3:15pm"

```
AtTime
        [LastTuesday:1:30pm, LastTuesday:3:15pm]
        ImportantMeeting(Susie)
```

Inference chain:

1) "Susie was at the daycare center Tuesday between 4:15pm and 4:45pm". Using axioms 2 and 3:

```
And
        AtTime
                [LastTuesday:12:30pm, LastTuesday:1pm]
                AtPlace(Susie, daycare)
        AtTime
                [LastTuesday:4:15pm, LastTuesday:4:45pm]
                AtPlace(Susie, daycare)
```

Then using PLN inference rules to deal with And

```
AtTime
        [LastTuesday:4:15pm, LastTuesday:4:45pm]
        AtPlace(Susie, daycare)
```

2) "Jane was at the daycare center Tuesday between 4:pm and 4:30pm". Using axioms 1.b

```
And
        isWeekDay(Tuesday)
        AtTime
                [LastTuesday:4pm, LastTuesday:4:45pm]
```

```
                AtPlace(Jane, daycare)
```

Then using PLN inference rules to deal with And

```
AtTime
        [LastTuesday:4pm, LastTuesday:4:45pm]
        AtPlace(Jane, daycare)
```

3) Then we can infer an instance of the target theorem using the conclusion of inference step 1 and 3+ other axioms related to temporal relationships

```
And
        AtTime
                [LastTuesday:4:15pm, LastTuesday:4:45pm]
                AtPlace(Susie, daycare)
        AtTime
                [LastTuesday:4pm, LastTuesday:4:45pm]
                AtPlace(Jane, daycare)
        OverlapTime
                [LastTuesday:4:15pm, LastTuesday:4:45pm]
                [LastTuesday:4pm, LastTuesday:4:45pm]
        During
                [LastTuesday:4:15pm, LastTuesday:4:45pm]
                LastWeek
        During
                [LastTuesday:4pm, LastTuesday:4:45pm]
                LastWeek
```

4) And the target theorem is reached using step 3 and PLN existential quantifier axioms, by setting

```
$Place=daycare
$TimeInterval1=[LastTuesday:4:15pm, LastTuesday:4:45pm],
$TimeInterval2=[LastTuesday:4pm, LastTuesday:4:45pm]
```

and thus concluding

```
ThereExists $Place, $TimeInterval1, $TimeInterval2
        And
                AtTime($TimeInterval1, AtPlace(Susie, $Place))
                AtTime($TimeInterval2, AtPlace(Jane, $Place))
                OverlapTime($TimeInterval1, $TimeInterval2)
                During($TimeInterval1, LastWeek)
```

13.3   PLN Causal Relationship Types

PLN represents the notion of causality with the PredictiveImplication relationship and some variants thereof.

Formally PredictiveImplication is defined as follows:

```
PredictiveImplication < TV >
        T
        A
        B
```

is equal to

```
IntensionalImplication < TV >
        A
        SequentialAnd
                T
                A
                B
```

where T is a time (or a time interval) representing the delay between A and B. Which more formally can be expressed as

```
Average < TV >
        t
        And
```

```
           AtTime
                t
                A
           AtTime
                t+T
                B
```

13.4   PLN Contextual Inference in Action

Finally, in this section, we run the contextual inference example given in Chapter 7 above using PLN rather than the more traditional contextual inference approach explored earlier.

First we enumerate the assumed axioms, describing each one in natural language and then formally in PLN terms:

Axioms for Music Context

1) In the context of music Alice frequently mentions Canadian place names

```
Context  < .5, .9 >
        Music
        Evaluation
                Mention
                List
                        Alice
                        CanadianPlaceNames
```

2) In the context of music Bob frequently mentions Canadian place names

```
Context  < .5, .9 >
        Music
        Evaluation
                Mention
                List
```

```
                Bob
                CanadianPlaceNames
```

3) In the context of music Clark does not frequently mention Canadian place names

```
Context  < .01, .9 >
        Music
        Evaluation
                Mention
                List
                        Clark
                        CandianPlaceNames
```

Axioms for Accounting Context

4) In the context of accounting Alice does not frequently mention Canadian place names

```
Context  < .01, .9 >
        Accounting
        Evaluation
                Mention
                        List
                                Alice
                                CanadianPlaceNames
```

5) In the context of accounting Bob frequently mentions Canadian place names

```
Context  < .5, .9 >
        Accounting
        Evaluation
                Mention
                List
                        Bob
                        CanadianPlaceNames
```

6) In the context of accounting Clark frequently mentions Canadian place names

```
Context  < .6, .9 >
        Accounting
        Evaluation
                Mention
                List
                        Clark
                        CanadianPlaceNames
```

Non-Context-Specific Axioms

7) Accounting is associated with Money

```
ExtensionalInheritance  < .7, .9 >
        Accounting
        Money
```

8) CanadianPlaces is associated with Canada

```
Inheritance  < .8, .9 >
        CanadianPeople
        CanadianPlacesNames
```

9) If X frequently mentions Y then he/she is highly involved with Y

```
Average  < .9, .8 >
        List $X, $Y
        Implication
                Evaluation
                        Mention
                        List
                                $X
                                $Y
```

```
        Evaluation
            Involved
                $X
                $Y
```

10) Non Canadian People involved with Canadian people in the context of Money have a
    chance of being associated with log trafficking activities

```
AverageLink  < .6, .8 >
        ListLink
            $X
        ImplicationLink
            AndLink
                SubsetLink
                    $X
                    NotLink
                        CanadianPeople
                ContextLink
                    Money
                    EvaluationLink
                        Involved
                        ListLink
                            $X
                            CanadianPeople
            InheritanceLink
                X
                LogTrafficking
```

11) Clark is not Canadian

```
ExtensionalInheritance  < .9, .9 >
        Clark
        Not
            CanadianPeople
```

12) It is also necessary to define the truth value of the following concepts

    Accounting $< .2, .9 >$
    Music $< .3, .9 >$
    CanadianPlaceNames $< .1, .8 >$
    Money $< .2, .9 >$
    CanadianPeople $< .25, .8 >$

Question to answer :
What is the chance of Clark being involved with log trafficking?

    IntensionalInheritance $<? >$
        Clark
        LogTrafficking

Next we show one possible inference trail via which PLN's inference rules may estimate the truth value of the target logical relationship, based on the assumption of the above axioms. Of course, there exist many other inference trails as well, and in reality an automated PLN inference system (such as the ones implemented in the NCE or OCP AI systems) will find many of these and produce an overall truth value formed by revising their various conclusions. However, for expositional purposes, it seems sufficient to recount a single inference trail in detail, just show "how such inferences go." The problem of inference control – i.e. of how an inference engine may be guided to create inferences like this in a reasonable amount of time – will be discussed in a later chapter.

This inference is a very detailed one as it actually has been directly extracted from a real run of PLN (with manually inference control).

Inference trail

1) Instantiation of axiom 9, with $X=Clark and $Y=CanadianPlaceNames

    Implication $< .9, .9 >$
        Evaluation
            Mention

```
        List
                Clark
                CanadianPlaceNames
        Evaluation
                Involved
                        Clark
                        CanadianPlaceNames
```

2) This step is necessary so that all TVs are correctly contextualized in the Accounting context, using rule to contextualize a context knowledge

```
ContextLink < .9, .54 >
        Accounting
        ImplicationLink
                EvaluationLink
                        Mention
                        ListLink
                                Clark
                                CanadianPlaceNames
                EvaluationLink
                        Involved
                        ListLink
                                Clark
                                CanadianPlaceNames
```

3) Using Modus Ponens in the context of Accounting with return of step 1 as the implication and axiom 6 as the antecedent.

```
ContextLink < .45, .48 >
        Accounting
        EvaluationLink
                Involved
                ListLink
                        Clark
```

```
                    CanadianPlaceNames
```

4) Decontextualize the result of step 3

```
ExtensionalInheritance  < .45, .48 >
        Accounting
        SatisfyingSetLink
                EvaluationLink
                        Involved
                        ListLink
                                Clark
                                CanadianPlaceNames
```

5) Apply PLN deduction rule on axiom 7 and the result of step 4

```
ExtensionalInheritance  < .45, .48 >
        Money
        SatisfyingSetLink
                EvaluationLink
                        Involved
                        ListLink
                                Clark
                                CanadianPlaceNames
```

6) Contextualize step 5

```
ContextLink  < .45, .48 >
        Money
        EvaluationLink
                Involved
                ListLink
                        Clark
                        CanadianPlaceNames
```

7) Using a PLN rule substitute terms given their inheritnace relation and axiom 8 to infer how much Clark in involved with CanadianPeople in the context of Money

```
ContextLink  < .45, .3 >
        Money
        EvaluationLink
                Involved
                ListLink
                        Clark
                        CanadianPeople
```

8) Infer the conjunction of axiom 11 and the previous step

```
AndLink  < .4, .27 >
        InheritanceLink
                Clark
                NotLink
                        CanadianPeople
        ContextLink
                Money
                EvaluationLink
                        Involved
                        ListLink
                                Clark
                                CanadianPeople
```

9) Instantiate axiom 10 with X = Clark

```
ImplicationLink  < .6, .8 >
        AndLink
                InheritanceLink
                        Clark
                        NotLink
                                CanadianPeople
                ContextLink
```

```
                    Money
                    EvaluationLink
                         Involved
                         ListLink
                              Clark
                              CanadianPeople
              InheritanceLink
                    Clark
                    LogTrafficking
```

10) Apply modus ponens with step 9 as implication and step 8 as antecedent

```
InheritanceLink  < .24, .27 >
        Clark
        LogTrafficking
```

So we can conclude that with probability 0.24 and confidence 0.27 Clark is involved with log trafficking. One could run similar inferences for Bob and Alice and see that they have less change to be related to log trafficking.

Chapter 14

Inferring the Causes of Observed Changes

In this chapter we consider the specific question of how the ideas of the previous chapters contribute to carrying out reasoning regarding the potential causes of salient changes in large knowledge stores. The following would be three sorts of examples of change-related inference, in the Twitter domain:

- Looking for changes in a particular person's patterns of social interaction (a significant new contact, a number of casual acquaintances with similar profiles, etc.), and potential causes of these changes
- Looking for groups with changes in sentiment toward a certain person or organization (say, the Tory party), and potential causes of these changes
- Looking for places with a significant change in their relationship to some specific place (say, East Anglia), and potential causes of these changes

Corresponding examples on other application areas, such as robotics, are obvious to formulate. In this section we give a detailed exposition of an inference regarding the first of these example cases. The others would be handled similarly.

We will make use of the PLN logic framework here, although others could have been utilized as well. In fact no existing logic framework has been fleshed out in great detail in the context of precisely this sort of application, so whatever logical formalism one chooses, in order to approach examples like this, one is going to be carrying out a certain amount of creative improvisation. Due to our prior experience with PLN we felt most comfortable carrying out this invention in this context.

Specifically, we consider the following scenario :

- Before March 2007, Bob never had any Canadian friends except those who were also friends of his wife.

- After March 2007, Bob started acquiring Canadian friends who were not friends of his wife.
- In late 2006, Bob started collecting Pokemon cards. Most of the new Canadian friends Bob made between March 2007 and Late 2007 are associated with Pokemon cards
- In late 2006, Bob started learning French. Most of the new Canadian friends Bob made between March 2007 and Late 2007 are Quebecois.

These are the sorts of patterns that might be identified via the pattern mining algorithms discussed above, for finding surprising relationships in large logical knowledge bases. The question we consider here is: suppose such a pattern has been identified, then how do we figure out what its cause might be? We will consider two cases of the above scenario, one involving temporal reasoning only, and one involving both spatial and temporal reasoning.

The importance of this sort of question should be clear: it is not a matter of doing obscure analytical detective work, it's a matter of figuring out whether a pattern that arises from a pattern-mining algorithm is actually interesting enough to merit anyone paying attention to it. Pattern mining algorithms tend to find a lot of patterns, and most of them are pretty uninteresting. When a pattern arises from such an algorithm, it is worthwhile to know whether there is an obvious cause for the pattern – and if so, whether the cause is the kind of cause that is interesting to the humans who are receiving the output of the pattern mining algorithm. Thus, causal inference may actually be viewed as an integral part of the pattern mining process. We may in fact posit a repeated process such as:

(1) Mine patterns from the knowledge base, biased by a set of concepts and patterns called the "focus"
(2) Perform causal inference to find a set P of patterns that are significant but have no known cause, or have causes believed to be interesting to the human users
(3) If any of the patterns in P are estimated to be sufficiently interesting to any of the human users, report them to these human users
(4) Add these interesting patterns to the focus and return to Step 1

We have already discussed the pattern-mining portion of this process; now we turn to the causal inference aspect.

14.1   The Case of Bob and His New Friends, with Temporal Inference Only

In this section, we will formalize the above example in PLN, and then use PLN inference to assess the strength of a few possible causal relationships that can explain why Bob
has gotten new friends from Canada apart from his wife's (after March 2007).

14.1.1   *Axioms*

Here we will use probabilities without confidences. As temporal reasoning has not
been fully implemented yet we are not going to compute the actual truth values so these
probabilities are just indicative. Before starting enumerating the axioms let us define the
following predicates, this will make the axioms much more readable.

1) Bob's Canadian friends

```
Def CanadianFriendBob
=
AndLink
        EvaluationLink
                FriendOf
                ListLink
                        Bob
                        $X
        ExtensionalInheritance
                $X
                CanadianPeople
```

2) Bob's wife friends

```
Def BobWifeFriend
=
EvaluationLink
        FriendOf
                ListLink
                        BobWife
                        $X
```

3) Canadian Friend of Bob but Not His Wife

```
Def CanadianFriendBobNotWife
=
AndLink
        CanadianFriendBob
        NotLink
                BobWifeFriend
```

4) Bob collecting Pokemon cards

```
Def BobCollectingPokemonCards
=
EvaluationLink
        Collecting
                ListLink
                        Bob
                        PokemonCards
```

5) Bob learning French

```
Def BobLearningFrench
=
EvaluationLink
        Learning
                ListLink
                        Bob
                        FrenchLanguage
```

Now we are ready to enumerate the axioms

1) Before March 2007, Bob never had any Canadian friends except those who were also friends of his wife.

```
AtTime  < 0 >
```

```
Before_March_2007
AverageAll
    $X
    CanadianFriendBobNotWife
```

2) After March 2007, Bob started acquiring Canadian friends who were not friends of his wife.

```
InitiatedThroughout  < .3 >
        Between_March_2007_And_Late_2007
        AverageLink
            $X
            CanadianFriendBobNotWife
```

3) In late 2006, Bob started collecting Pokemon cards.

```
InitiatedAt  < .9 >
        Late_2006
        BobCollectingPokemonCards
```

4) The process of collecting $Y shares associations with $Y

```
AverageLink  < .7 >
        $X, $Y
        ImplicationLink
                EvaluationLink
                        Collecting
                        ListLink
                            $X
                            $Y
                Inheritance
                        $X
                        $Y
```

5) Most of the new Canadian friends Bob made after March 2007 (who are not friends of his wife) are associated with Pokemon cards.

```
AtTime  < .6 >
        March2007_till_late2007
        AverageAll
            X
        ImplicationLink
                CanadianFriendBobNotWife
                InheritanceLink
                    X
                    PokemonCards
```

6) In late 2006, Bob started learning French.
   So we can now define the axiom:

```
initiatedAt  < 1 >
        Late_2006
        BobLearningFrench
```

7) If $X learns $Y then $X shares associations with $Y

```
AverageLink  < .7 >
        $X, $Y
        ImplicationLink
                Evaluation
                        Learning
                        List
                            $X
                            $Y
                Inheritance
                        $X
                        $Y
```

8) Most of the new Canadian friends Bob made after March 2007 (who are not friends of his wife) are Quebecois.

```
AtTime  < .7 >
        March_2007_Till_Late_2007
        AverageLink
            $X
            ImplicationLink
                    CanadianFriendBobNotWife
                    SubsetLink
                        $X
                        Quebecois
```

9) Quebecois are associated with French language

```
InheritanceLink  < .7 >
        Quebecois
        FrenchLanguage
```

14.1.2   *Inference Trails*

We now describe three PLN inference trails, aimed at evaluating the validity of the following inference targets:

Theorem 14.1. *"Bob's Pokemon cards interest is the cause of his new Canadian friendships":*

```
PredictiveImplicationLink  <? >
        3_Months_To_1_Year
        BobCollectingPokemonCards
        AverageLink
            X
            CanadianFriendBobNotWife
```

Theorem 14.2. *"Bob starting learning French is the cause of his new Canadian friend-ships":*

```
PredictiveImplicationLink <?>
        3_Months_To_1_Year
        BobLearningFrench
        AverageLink
            X
            CanadianFriendBobNotWife
```

Theorem 14.3. *"The conjunction of Bob starting learning French and collecting Pokemon cards is the cause of his new Canadian friendships"*

```
PredictiveImplicationLink <?>
        3_Months_To_1_Year
        AndLink
            BobCollectingPockemonCards
            BobLearningFrench
        AverageLink
            X
            CanadianFriendBobNotWife
```

14.1.2.1   *Target Theorem 14.1*

Note that as of the time the writing, temporal reasoning is not yet fully implemented in OpenCog's PLN inference engine. So we have omitted the truth values in the inference and instead explains how such inferences would be constructed.

To illustrate one path for evaluating the truth value of Theorem 14.1 using PLN, we will begin by presenting four steps that go backward from the target theorem to the axioms.

1) Target 1: "Bob starting collecting Pokemon cards is the cause of his new Canadian friendships"

```
PredictiveImplicationLink <?>
        3_Months_To_1_Year
```

```
BobCollectingPokemonCards
AverageLink
      X
CanadianFriendBobNotWife
```

1) By the definition of PredictiveImplicationLink, the target is equivalent to

```
ImplicationLink
      BobCollectingPokemonCards
      SequentialAnd
            3_Months_To_1_Year
            BobCollectingPokemonCards
            AverageLink
                  X
                  CanadianFriendBobNotWife
```

To simplify, let us define a short hand for the sequentialAnd term

```
Def SeqAndTerm
=
SequentialAnd
      3_Months_To_1_Year
      BobCollectingPokemonCards
      AverageLink
            X
            CanadianFriendBobNotWife
```

So the above is equivalent to

```
ImplicationLink
      BobCollectingPokemonCards
      SeqAndTerm
```

2) An ImplicationLink encapsulates both extensional and intensional implication, that is the above is equivalent to

```
OrLink
        ExtensionalImplicationLink
                BobCollectingPokemonCards
                SeqAndTerm
        IntensionalImplicationLink
                BobCollectingPokemonCards
                SeqAndTerm
```

2.1) To infer the extensional part

```
ExtensionalImplicationLink
        BobCollectingPokemonCards
        SeqAndTerm
```

we can rewrite SeqAndTerm according to the definition of SequentialAnd (see Section 13.3).

```
ExtensionalImplicationLink
        BobCollectingPokemonCards
        Average  < TV >
                t
                And
                        AtTime
                                t
                                BobCollectingPokemonCards
                        AtTime
                                t+3_Months_To_1_Year
                                AverageLink
                                        X
                                        CanadianFriendBobNotWife
```

2.2) Then we can evaluate that directly from the axioms 2 and 3. But since BobCol-lectingPokemonCards happens only once the truth value of such implication will have a very low confidence.

This is where intensional reasoning may come handy, when little data are available intensional inference can lead to less biased and more confident results.

3) To infer the intensional implication part one can expand it into an extensional inheri-tance of the set of patterns of

BobCollectingPokemonCards

and

SeqAndTerm

as explained in Section 12.5.5.

3.1) Using axiom 4, that if X collects Y then shares associations with Y, we can infer that Pokemon cards is a pattern of BobCollectingPokemonCards (assuming that the complexity of Pokemon cards is less than the one of BobCollectingPokemon-Cards), formally

MemberLink
    PokemonCards
    PAT(BobCollectingPokemonCards)

3.2) Next, using axiom 5 (and few more steps involving the definition of SequentialAnd that we do not detail), we can infer that Pokemon card is also a pattern of

SeqAndTerm

that is formally

MemberLink
    PokemonCards
    PAT(SeqAndTerm)

4) Given the above we can conclude that

```
ExtensionalInheritance
        PAT(BobCollectingPokemonCards
        PAT(SeqAndTerm)
```

Which is equivalent to the intensional part of the predictive implication we were trying to infer.

Here we have only used one possible pattern, Pokemon cards, in practice there might be hundreds or even thousands of patterns.

14.1.2.2   *Target Theorem 14.2*

The inference of target 2 "Bob starting learning French is the cause of his new Canadian friendships":

```
PredictiveImplicationLink <?>
        3_Months_To_1_Year
        BobLearningFrench
        AverageLink
              X
              CanadianFriendBobNotWife
```

is very similar but instead it uses axiom 6 and axiom 2 to infer the extensional implication. It uses axiom 7 to infer that FrenchLanguage is a pattern of BobLearningFrench, and axiom 9 to infer that FrenchLanguage is a pattern of Quebecois.

14.1.2.3   *Target Theorem 14.3*

Then the target 3 "The conjunction of Bob starting collecting Pokemon cards and learning French is the cause of his new Canadian friendships"

```
PredictiveImplicationLink <?>
        3_Months_To_1_Year
        AndLink
              BobCollectingPockemonCards
              BobLearningFrench
        AverageLink
```

X

`CanadianFriendBobNotWife`

is the most interesting because it involves both patterns, Pokemon cards and French language for the intensional implication part. Note that the extensional implication part will provide a confidence as low as for target theorem 14.1 and 14.2 because the conjunction Bob starting collecting Pokemon cards and learning French, with respect to the data, is just as a rare event, it happens only once. But the intensional part however will have an increase of confidence because 2 patterns instead of one are involved in the implication.

14.2   Incorporating Spatial Inference into Analysis of Change

In this section we consider a variation of the inference given above, modified to include spatial reasoning involving Canada and its neighbors. This is an illustration of how temporal and spatial inference rules may be combined to carry out commonsense reasoning regarding potential causes of changes in large knowledge bases. See Figure 14.1 for the map used in the example.

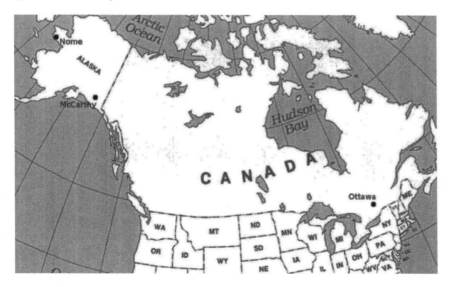

Fig. 14.1   Canada and its neighbors

We consider a query similar to one discussed above, but slightly relaxed; instead of the causes of Bob's new Canadian friendships we are interested in the causes of Bob's new friends who are Canadian and associated with Canadian; that is more, formally speaking, who inherit extensionally and/or intensionally from Canadian (instead of only extensionally as in the previous inference).

So, the definition of Bob's Canadian friend in the previous inference is replaced by:

```
Def CanadianFriendBob

=

AndLink
        EvaluationLink
                FriendOf
                ListLink
                        Bob
                        $X
        InheritanceLink
                $X
                CanadianPeople
```

Then we introduce some spatial knowledge by adding the predicate near(X,Y) and a "curried" version of it, nearCanada(X)=near(X,Canada), represented by a fuzzy grid in Figure 14.2, where the level of opacity of each cell of the grid corresponds to the degree of its proximity to Canada. And we extract from that grid two regions, Canada and Ottawa as shown in Figure 14.3, to illustrate the use of the Region Connection Calculus (RCC) as discussed above. And finally we add an axiom that relates geographic proximity and intensional association.

14.2.1 *New Axioms*

We can now formalize the above knowledge in PLN (one should consider it as a set of additional axioms, to be added to the ones from the previous example, which is why they are numbered from 11):

10) Nome Alaska is not near Canada

Let's first define the predicate nearCanada:

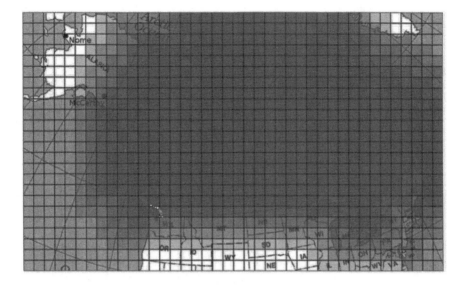

Fig. 14.2   Fuzzy Grid of the predicate near Canada

```
Def nearCanada

=

Evaluation

        near

        List

                $X

                Canada
```

and the axiom (according to the fuzzy grid of Figure 14.2):

```
Evaluation  < 0, .9 >

        nearCanada

        Nome
```

Actually in practice this knowledge would be deduced from lower-level knowledge such as the following:

```
Evaluation  < 0, .9 >
```

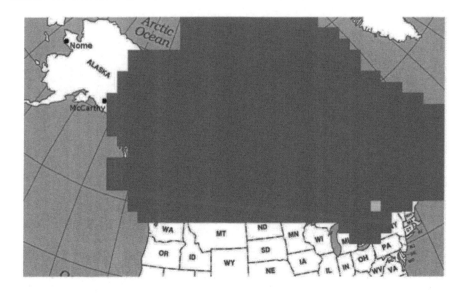

Fig. 14.3   Canada Region in dark gray, Ottawa Region in light gray

```
occupiesCell
List
        Nome
        Cell(8,8)
```

where the predicate occupiesCell indicates whether (or to what degree) a location occupies a cell of the grid, and using the axiom:

```
AverageLink  < 1,.9 >
        $X, $Y, $Z
        ExtensionalImplication
                Evaluation
                        occupiesCell
                        List
                                $X
                                Cell($Y,$Z)
        Evaluation
                nearCanada
```

```
                     $X
```

But for the sake of simplicity we will directly use the predicate nearCanada.

11) How near McCarthy Alaska is to Canada

```
Evaluation  < .6,.9 >
        nearCanada
        McCarthy
```

12) How near Northern Maine is to Canada (the north of ME as indicated in the map
Figure 14.1).

```
Evaluation  < .8,.9 >
        nearCanada
        NorthernMaine
```

13) Nearby locations have intensional similarity

```
AverageLink  < .5,.9 >
        $X, $Y
        ExtensionalImplication
                Evaluation
                        near
                               $X
                               $Y
                IntensionalSimilarity
                        $X
                        $Y
```

14) People of a given location intensionally inherit from that location

```
AverageLink  < .7,.9 >
        $X, $Y
        ExtensionalImplication
                Evaluation
```

```
            liveIn
            List
                    $X
                    $Y
        IntensionalInheritance
            $X
            $Y
```

15) Canadians live in Canada

```
Evaluation  < .9, .9 >
        liveIn
        List
            Canadian
            Canada
```

16) The disjunction of NTPP (Non-Tangential Proper Part) and TPP (Tangential Proper Part) is transitive (from the Region Connection Calculus defined above)
Let's define first PP for Proper Part

```
AverageLink  < 1, .9 >
        $X, $Y
        ExtentionalEquivalence
            Evaluation
                    PP
                    List
                            $X
                            $Y
            OR
                    Evaluation
                            NTPP
                            List
                                    $X
                                    $Y
```

```
                    Evaluation
                        TPP
                        List
                                $X
                                $Y
```

And then axioms stating the transitivity of PP

```
AverageLink  < 1,.9 >
        $X, $Y, $Z
        ExtensionalImplication
                And
                        Evaluation
                                PP
                                List
                                        $X
                                        $Y
                        Evaluation
                                PP
                                List
                                        $Y
                                        $Z
                Evaluation
                        PP
                        List
                                $X
                                $Z
                                                $Z
```

17) If someone is a proper part of a place he/she lives there

```
AverageLink  < .9,.9 >
        $X, $Y
        ExtensionalImplication
```

```
              Evaluation
                    PP
                    List
                          $X
                          $Y
              Evaluation
                    liveIn
                    List
                          $X
                          $Y
```

18) Jack lives in McCarthy

```
Evaluation  < .9, .9 >
        liveIn
        List
              Jack
              McCarthy
```

19) Jim lives in Nome

```
Evaluation  < .9, .9 >
        liveIn
        List
              Jim
              Nome
```

20) John lives in Ottawa

```
Evaluation  < .9, .9 >
        liveIn
        List
              John
              Ottawa
```

21) Ottawa is a proper part of Canada (as represented in Figure 14.3)

```
Evaluation < .9, .9 >
        PP
        List
                Ottawa
                Canada
```

22) Someone living in Canada is Canadian

```
AverageLink < .8, .9 >
        $X
        ExtensionalImplication
                Evaluation
                        liveIn
                        List
                                $X
                                Canada
                ExtensionalInheritance
                        $X
                        Canadian
```

And that's it for the axioms. The target theorems are unchanged from the prior example. We will not describe the entire inference here, but only the additional steps dealing with the spatial knowledge introduced and connecting them to the previous inference.

What we will show is how to infer that Jack (living in McCarthy) and John (living in Ottawa) inherit from Canadian, but Jim (living further away in Nome) does not. Then this knowledge might be used as sub-step to infer what was defined as axiom 2 in the previous inference, that is that new friends on Bob are Canadian or related to Canada.

14.2.2 Evaluating the Theorems

As previously, we now have the following 3 sub-target theorems:

```
Inheritance <? >
        Jack
```

```
        Canadian

Inheritance <?>
        John
        Canadian

Inheritance <?>
        Jim
        Canadian
```

We now discuss each of these, using the new spatial information available.

14.2.2.1   *Evaluation of Theorem 14.1*

1) Using the definition of near and axiom 11

```
    Evaluation < .6,.9 >
            near
            List
                    McCarthy
                    Canada
```

2) Using the conclusion of step 1 and an instantiation of axiom 13 with $X=McCarthy and $Y=Canada and the PLN deduction rule

```
    IntensionalSimilarity < .5,.9 >
            McCarthy
            Canada
```

3) Using axiom 18, an instantiation of axiom 14 with $X=Jack and $Y=McCarthy and the PLN deduction rule

```
    IntensionalInheritance < .9,.9 >
            Jack
            McCarthy
```

4) Using the definition of IntensionalSimilarity and the conclusion of step 2

```
And < .5, .9 >
        IntensionalInheritance
                McCarthy
                Canada
        IntensionalInheritance
                Canada
                McCarthy
```

5) Using the conclusion of step 4 (stripping away the second term of the conjunction), the conclusion of step 3 and the PLN deduction rule

```
IntensionalInheritance < .7, .8 >
        Jack
        Canada
```

6) Using axioms 15 as antecedent of the implication gotten from instantiating axiom 14 with $X=Canadian and $Y=Canada

```
IntensionalInheritance < .67, .9 >
        Canadian
        Canada
```

7) Using the conclusions of steps 5, 6 and the PLN abduction rule

```
IntensionalInheritance < .56, .6 >
        Jack
        Canadian
```

8) Using the definition of Inheritance (disjunction of Extensional and Intensional inheritance) and the results of step 7 and

```
Inheritance < .56, .6 >
        Jack
        Canadian
```

So due to the additional items of spatial knowledge we can conclude that Jack inherits from Canadian, therefore assuming that after March 2007 Jack is a friend of Bob and not a friend of his wife – knowledge which may have an influence in the calculation of the axiom 2 of the inference of the previous section, even though Jack isn't in fact from Canada strictly speaking. Of course it is clear that Jack inherits from Canadian with a lower strength than a real Canadian individual because the latter extensionally inherits from Canadian, but nevertheless Jack's (mixed) inheritance from Canadian has a non null strength.

A similar inference could be built for someone living in northern Maine.

14.2.2.2   Evaluation of Theorem 14.2

1) Using axiom 20 and an instantiation of axiom 17 with $X=John, $Y=Ottawa

```
Evaluation  < .9, .9 >
        PP
        List
                John
                Ottawa
```

2) Using step 1, axiom 21 and the axiom 16 of the transitivity of PP

```
Evaluation  < .9, .9 >
        PP
        List
                John
                Canada
```

3) Using step 2, axiom 17 with $X=John, $Y=Canada

```
Evaluation  < .8, .9 >
        liveIn
        List
                John
                Canada
```

4) Using step 3 and an instantiation of axiom 22 with $X=John

```
ExtensionalInheritance  < .72, .9 >
        John
        Canadian
```

5) Using the definition of Inheritance (disjunction of extensional and intensional inheritance)

```
Inheritance  < .72, .9 >
        John
        Canadian
```

So using the Region Connection Calculus within PLN, one can conclude that John is Canadian and assuming that John is a friend of Bob after March 2007 and not a friend of his wife may have a influence over the strength of axiom 2 in the initial example.

14.2.2.3   Evaluation of Theorem 14.3

This inference is essentially identical to the inference of Theorem 1, so we will not recall it. The only difference is that the strength of (IntensionalInheritance Jim Canadian) is null, and since Nome is not in Canada this ExtensionalInheritance is null as well, therefore

```
Inheritance  < 0, .9 >
        Jim
        Canada
```

Chapter 15

Adaptive Inference Control

As the discussion in the above chapters has hopefully made clear, every one of the tasks involved in logic-based RWR has been carefully approached by computer scientists, using various formalisms and software prototypes. We have produced more fully fleshed-out examples using PLN than other formalisms, because PLN is the inference framework we're most familiar with and because we believe it most adequately integrates rich uncertainty representations with powerful inference mechanisms; but similar explorations could be produced using other inference formalisms, and of course one could also go into far greater detail than has been done above.

But there's a catch, of course: None of the formalisms or prototypes described in the literature (including PLN) comes along with fully confident theoretical or empirical knowledge telling one how to deal effectively with real-world-scale data stores. This is not just a quantitative problem: it's a qualitative problem. Addressing this problem adequately requires the implementation and adoption of fundamentally new ideas, complementing existing approaches,

Assuming a logic-based approach, scalability of pattern mining, query processing and analysis boils down to *efficient inference control*. Which of course, is in general terms a monstrously hard problem. Making inference control generally efficient across all possible large knowledge stores is almost surely impossible.

The need for efficient inference control should be very clear via looking at the detailed PLN inference trails supplied above. At each step in any one of those inference trails, there were many other inferences that could have been done, aside from the ones shown. The question becomes how to choose these exact ones, or others with similar effect. If there are 20 steps in an inference, and 100 possibilities for each step (actually a terrible underestimate of the real situation), then there are 100^{20} possible inference trails to be theoretically considered. If there are several thousand viable possibilities for each step, which is more likely the case in an inference involving a large knowledge store, then the number of possible inference trails becomes even more astronomical. Fortunately there are also many paths leading to useful conclusions, not just one – but even so, if you view it as a search problem, finding useful inference trails amidst the space of all possible ones is a lot worse than finding a few needles in a planet-sized haystack.

Even without the complications of large and uncertain knowledge stores, the inference trail pruning problem is a very difficult one. This is the essential reason why automated theorem proving has not yet obsoleted human mathematicians. Automated theorem provers, using formal logic, can carry out individual inference steps adeptly (and without making the "stupid mistakes" that even smart humans are sometimes prone to), but in most cases they are vastly inferior to humans at choosing which inference steps to take. Some of the biggest successes in automated theorem proving have occurred in highly restricted contexts (where there aren't that many possibilities to choose from) or else using a semi-automated methodology, where a human expert intervenes to make choices at places where the AI gets confused at the variety of choices and lacks the experience to make an informed decision.

So, clearly, in its fully general scope, the problem of inference control is practically unsolvable! But, does that mean the whole research programme outlined in this book is infeasible? No, because we don't need to solve the general problem. To make the programme described here work, the problem needs to be solved only in the context of commonsensical inferences involving the types of knowledge actually stored in the knowledge store. And, to put the point mathematically, it's clear that real-world temporal and spatiotemporal knowledge stores have special *statistical properties*, which have mostly not been carefully characterized. So, we suggest that a key focus for research going forward must be the creation of inference control mechanisms that *adaptively exploit the statistical structure of real-world temporal and spatiotemporal data, so as to achieve efficient inference control over large real-world knowledge stores.*

15.1   Specific Examples Requiring Adaptive Inference Control

The above point may sound like a very abstract one, so to make it concrete, let's consider a couple inference steps drawn from one of the above inference trails: the proof of Theorem 1 given above.

Quoting directly from there (but leaving out a small amount of explanatory text), we had the following inference step

3) To infer the intensional implication part one can expand it into an extensional inheritance of the set of patterns of

```
BobCollectingPokemonCards
```

and

```
SeqAndTerm
```

as explained in Section 12.5.5.

3.1) Using axiom 4, that if X collects Y then shares associations with Y, we can infer that Pokemon cards is a pattern of BobCollectingPokemonCards (assuming that the complexity of Pokemon cards is less than the one of BobCollectingPokemon-Cards), formally

```
MemberLink
        PokemonCards
        PAT(BobCollectingPokemonCards)
```

3.2) Next, using axiom 5 (and few more steps involving the definition of SequentialAnd that we do not detail), we can infer that Pokemon card is also a pattern of

```
SeqAndTerm
```

that is formally

```
MemberLink
        PokemonCards
        PAT(SeqAndTerm)
```

4) Given the above we can conclude that

```
ExtensionalInheritance
        PAT(BobCollectingPokemonCards)
        PAT(SeqAndTerm)
```

The above is perfectly straightforward once you've decided to do it, but where does that decision come from? Basically the decision in moving from Step 3 to Step 4 in this inference is to expand the IntensionalImplication in 3 into an ExtensionalInheritance as shown in 4. However, the utility of this step is obvious only in hindsight. One doesn't always want to handle an IntensionalImplication by expanding it into an ExtensionalInheritance. Sometimes, for instance, one might want to try to produce it via deduction from other IntensionalImplication – or via unification by binding values to variables in some other IntensionalImplication with a similar form and some overlapping terms, but a lot more free variables. One could also try to derive it using Bayes rule from some other existing IntensionalImplications. Et cetera.

In many contexts, expanding an IntensionalImplication into an ExtensionalInheritance may be viewed as a "tactic of last resort", because it's often going to devolve into a detailed analysis of many special cases. So in many contexts (not necessarily all) it will be an advantageous strategy to first try to evaluate an IntensionalImplication via first-order-inference-style rules from other IntensionalImplications, or via unification from more abstract knowledge, before resorting to the reduction to extensionality. But even if this strategy is followed, there's the question of how much effort to expend on other methods before resorting to extensionality. And this is bound to be context-dependent. For instance, it may happen that in certain contexts, reasoning purely on the level of intensional relationships has systematically proved difficult, and reductions to extensionality have proved necessary very frequently; whereas in other contexts, reduction to extensionality has rarely proved necessary.

The other interesting aspect of that inference is the computation of the set of patterns of BobCollectingPokemonCards. As explained this set could be much larger and actually potentially contains all concepts of the knowledge base. So without some kind of mechanism to restrict focus, the inference process will consume an excessive amount of computational resources evaluating irrelevant associations. An example of the kind of mechanism that can be helpful here is activation spreading (see e.g. (Collins *et al.* , 1975; Anderson, 1983; Crestani, 1997; Nilsson, 1998)), which is carried out in various existing AI systems using a variety of mechanisms (for instance, in neural nets it uses activation spreading; in the NCE/OpenCog architecture it uses artificial economics methods (Goertzel *et al.*, 2007); etc.). Using activation spreading, if all the terms involved in Steps 1-4 were to spread some sort of activation to the terms and relationships related to them, and this activation were to then further propagate to the relatives of *these* terms and relationships (and so forth) –

then, quite likely, PokemonCards would get more activation than nearly any other category in the overall knowledge store, and would be nominated for investigation as indicated in the above text.

Note that in principle one could do the above purely by inference, without introducing an external mechanism such as activation spreading. For instance, one could do inference on links such as (Association A B) denoting generic associative semantics, using probabilistic inference rules designed for such inference. In fact the NCE/OpenCog design contains this possibility. However, unless one adopts an extremely constrained control mechanism for this associational inference, then one is faced once again here with a potential combinatorial explosion problem. And if one does adopt an extremely restrained control mechanism here, then in effect one is basically using uncertain inferential algebra to carry out spreading activation (which may be a fine thing to do).

If such an associative link exists, and there is an inference control heuristic biasing PLN toward building inferential links that generally follow the path laid down by associational links, then the above inference step would indeed emerge as obvious.

We could similarly "psychoanalyze" every step in the above inference trails, studying the various alternatives and how they could be explored using intelligent inference control heuristics. However, we will restrict ourselves to giving two more examples, intended to illustrate the way in which commonsense knowledge about time and space is important for inference control.

15.1.1   *Using Commonsense Knowledge about Space in Inference Control*

As an example of using commonsense knowledge about spatial relations to control inference, let us first recall the following axiom from the above spatial PLN inference:

17) If someone is a proper part of a place he/she lives there

```
AverageLink  < .9, .9 >
      $X, $Y
      ExtensionalImplication
            Evaluation
                  PP
                  List
                        $X
                        $Y
```

```
            Evaluation
                liveIn
                List
                        $X
                        $Y
```

This axiom was used in the following inference step:

2) Using step 1, axiom 21 and the axiom 16 of the transitivity of PP

```
Evaluation  < .9, .9 >
        PP
        List
                John
                Canada
```

3) Using step 2, axiom 17 with $X=John, $Y=Canada

```
Evaluation  < .8, .9 >
        liveIn
        List
                John
                Canada
```

The question here pertaining to inference control is: why would a PLN inference engine choose to make this step rather than some other one? Obviously, not every proper-part relationships is going to be equally promising for hypothetical transformation into a live-in relationship. The answer here however is conceptually obvious: where people and places are concerned, living-in is a common variety of proper-part relationship. This conceptually obvious answer may however be expressed formally in a number of different ways.

It could be expressed explicitly as an implication, e.g.

17') If someone is a proper part of a place he/she lives there

```
AverageLink  < .9, .9 >
        $X, $Y
        ExtensionalImplication
```

```
        And
            Inheritance $X Human
            Inheritance $Y Place
            Evaluation
                PP
                List
                        $X
                        $Y
    Evaluation
            liveIn
            List
                    $X
                    $Y
```

In this case, this more specialized axiom 17' could be used instead of Axiom 17. It would be more likely to be chosen if there were an inference control heuristic in use stating that: The weight assigned to an application of the variable unification rule between a more general Atom A and a more specific Atom B, should be proportional to how surprising it is to find Atoms that bind with A as well as B does. In this case, the point would be that the assignment $X=John, $Y=Canada matches 17' surprisingly well (relative to most possibly assignments); and that it matches 17' more surprisingly well than it matches 17.

However, the same effect could be achieved via an activation spreading mechanism. All one needs is for associative linkages such as the following to exist:

- Association John Human
- Association Canada Place
- Association Human liveIn
- Association Place liveIn

Of course many other variants are also possible; for instance one could have Inheritance relations in place of the first two Association relations in the above list; or one could have an association

Association (Human And Place) liveIn

and so forth. This is a simpler approach than the approach of introducing 17' in place of 17, but ultimately, in this context, the two achieve the same thing.

One way or another, the key here is that the system has specialized knowledge about the connections between spatial relationships (ProperPart in this case) and specific content (people living in places, in this case), and that it deploys this specialized knowledge to guide it along the right inference trail, thus avoiding the combinatorial explosion of getting dragged down irrelevant trajectories.

15.1.2 *Using Commonsense Knowledge about Time in Inference Control*

Time plays a role quite similar to space in inference control, yet even more fundamental. Without inference control heuristics that specifically take into account the habitual connections between temporal relationships and specific content, doing scalable temporal reasoning is not likely to be possible.

Let us consider the following inference step, drawn from Step 2.1 in Theorem 1 in Section 14.1.2.1 above

To infer the extensional part

```
ExtensionalImplicationLink
        BobCollectingPokemonCards
        SeqAndTerm
```

we can rewrite SeqAndTerm according to the definition of SequentialAnd (see Section 13.3).

```
ExtensionalImplicationLink
        BobCollectingPokemonCards
        Average  < TV >
            t
        And
                AtTime
                    t
                    BobCollectingPokemonCards
                AtTime
                    t+3_Months_To_1_Year
                    AverageLink
```

X

CanadianFriendBobNotWife

The question here, control-wise, is why the decision would be made to expand the Sequen-tialAnd into its finer grained definition. Again this should be a last resort choice because computing the Average of the above formula might be quite expensive. One may perhaps infer it using some less expensive first-order deduction rules, or some general temporal pattern to infer a more specific one. For instance, given

```
SequentialAnd
      Evaluation TurnOn ($X, CarOf($X))
      Evaluation Drive  ($X, CarOf($X))
```

on may infer

```
SequentialAnd
      Evaluation TurnOn (Ben, CarOf(Ben))
      Evaluation Drive  (Ben, CarOf(Ben))
```

To address this combinatorial explosion problem again one can use some assumptions to guess beforehand what temporal relationships are more likely to occur. And example of such assumptions could be:

Events of a given temporal scale relate more often to events of the same temporal scale.

For instance SleepingTonight might show a strong correlation with BeingInShapeTo-morrow. But one would consider absurd to temporally correlate SleepingTonight and Bein-gInShapeNextYear, or even more absurd SleepingTonight and IraqWar. An even better assumption might be that

Events of a given spatio-temporal scale relate more often to events of the same spatio-temporal scale.

One could then represent that knowledge using Association as explained above which would translate into more activation for events belonging to a given spatio-temporal time scale.

There are of course more assumptions one could find and use. This specific knowledge embodies the particular statistics of real-world knowledge stores, which is fortunately not the same as the statistics of a random knowledge store, or else real-world inference would not be feasible.

15.2   General Issues Raised by the Above Examples

A key point we wish to emphasize is that the full, realistic problem of inference control is not encountered when one runs inference engines as "toy systems" or prototypes. If one adds a relatively small number of knowledge into an inference engine, it's not terribly hard to supply it with simple, general inference control heuristics allowing it to do inferences like the examples given in previous chapters. The really hard part comes when you couple an inference engine with a massive knowledge store, because then the problem of drawing inferences becomes inextricably tangled up with the problem of figuring out which data items are relevant enough to be sensibly used in a given inference.

To handle the "scalable inference control problem," we have hypothesized, will require a combination of specialized heuristics (such as the ones described in the immediately preceding sections) and the integration of inference with non-inferential methods such as activation spreading. But whether or not this hypothesis is correct, what is plain is that any logic-based approach that is going to handle large knowledge stores (especially large, complex spatiotemporal knowledge stores) is going to need to deal with this problem some-how – and there is not much current research explicitly addressing this area.

As noted above, the idea of "exploiting the statistics implicit in real-world knowledge stores" arises here implicitly. For instance, if drawing inferences that follow the lines of associations works effectively, this is an example of "special statistics" – in a general, math-ematically random knowledge store, this kind of heuristic would provide little if any value. And if there are certain contexts in which, systematically, reducing intensional relations to extensional ones is differentially more useful than in the average context – again, this is an example of "special statistics" that would not likely occur in a random knowledge store. To the extent that appropriate heuristics and design principles can be created, implicitly or explicitly representing systematic biases that tend to be present in real-world data, the inference control problem will be solvable.

15.2.1 *Inference Control and Cognitive Architectures*

Work in the area of cognitive architecture also has some relevance here; architectures like SOAR (Wray & Jones, 2005) and ACT-R (Stewart & West, 2006) are specifically aimed at processing information in a way that avoids combinatorial explosions via restricting cognition's attention to information items that are directly relevant to the tasks at hand. Underlying such architectures is the idea of implicitly embedding assumptions about the statistical regularities of the real world in the cognitive architecture itself. However, these architectures have not yet been neither applied in a really scalable way, nor have they been tested in combination with highly powerful formal inference systems. SOAR has been used in conjunction with real-world spatiotemporal data in some contexts, e.g. the TacAir flight simulator project (Jones *et al.*, 1993), which is promising.

So it seems that, to some extent, the final solution to the all-important inference control problem may involve a fusion of ideas from the temporal, spatial and uncertain logic literatures with ideas from the cognitive architecture literature. This is one way of describing aspects of the direction we've taken in our own work with the NCE and OpenCog; but of course it's an idea that can be fleshed out in many different ways. However, the elaboration of the ways that various cognitive architectures might enable effective scalable inference control would lead us too far beyond the scope of this book.

15.3   Inference Control in the OpenCog Cognitive Architecture

We end this chapter with some brief remarks about the specific flavor that adaptive inference control takes in the OpenCog cognitive architecture, within which PLN is currently embedded.

15.3.1 *Activation Spreading and Inference Control in OpenCog*

A number of our remarks on inference control above mentioned "activation spreading." This is a general notion with a long history in cognitive science and AI, which may be implemented in many different ways. In this section we will briefly describe one such way, ECAN, which is implemented in the OpenCog framework and is currently being integrated with the PLN inference engine.

ECAN, or Economic Attention Networks, constitutes a novel method for simultaneously storing memories and allocating resources in AI systems. It bears some resemblance to the spread of activation in attractor neural networks, but differs via explicitly differentiating two kinds of "activation" (Short Term Importance, related to processor allocation; and Long Term Importance, related to memory allocation), and in using equations that are based on ideas from economics rather than approximative neural modeling.

An ECAN is a graph, consisting of untyped nodes and links, and also links that may be typed either HebbianLink or InverseHebbianLink. It is also useful sometimes to consider ECANs that extend the traditional graph formalism and involve links that point to links as well as to nodes. The term Atom will be used to refer to nodes and links collectively. Each Atom in an ECAN is weighted with two numbers, called STI (short-term importance) and LTI (long-term importance). Each Hebbian or InverseHebbian link is weighted with a probability value.

The equations of an ECAN explain how the STI, LTI and Hebbian probability values get updated over time. The metaphor underlying these equations is the interpretation of STI and LTI values as (separate) artificial currencies. The motivation for this metaphor has been elaborated somewhat in (Goertzel *et al.*, 2007) and will not be recapitulated here. The fact that STI (for instance) is a currency means that the total amount of STI in the system is conserved (except in unusual instances where the ECAN controller decides to introduce inflation or deflation and explicitly manipulate the amount of currency in circulation), a fact that makes the dynamics of an ECAN dramatically different than that of, say, an attractor neural network (in which there is no law of conservation of activation).

Conceptually, the STI value of an Atom is interpreted to indicate the immediate urgency of the Atom to the ECAN at a certain point in time; whereas the LTI value of an Atom indicates the amount of value the ECAN perceives in the retention of the Atom in memory (RAM). An ECAN will often be coupled with a Forgetting process that removes low-LTI Atoms from memory according to certain heuristics.

STI and LTI values will generally vary continuously, but the ECAN equations we introduce below contain the notion of an AttentionalFocus (AF), consisting of those Atoms in the ECAN with the highest STI value. The AF is given its meaning by the existence of equations that treat Atoms with STI above a certain threshold differently.

Conceptually, the probability value of a HebbianLink from A to B is the odds that if A is in the AF, so is B; and correspondingly, the InverseHebbianLink from A to B is weighted with the odds that if A is in the AF, then B is not. A critical aspect of the ECAN equations is that Atoms periodically spread their STI and LTI to other Atoms that connect to them via Hebbian and InverseHebbianLinks; this is the ECAN analogue of activation spreading in neural networks.

In an OpenCog context, ECAN consists of a set of Atom types, and then a set of MindAgents carrying out ECAN operations such as HebbianLinkUpdating and ImportanceUpdating. OCP also requires many other MindAgents carrying out other cognitive processes such as probabilistic logical inference according to the PLN system (Goertzel, 2008) and evolutionary procedure learning according to the MOSES system (Looks, 2006). The interoperation of the ECAN MindAgents with these other MindAgents is a subtle issue that will be briefly discussed in the final section of the chapter, but the crux is simple to understand.

The CogServer is understood to maintain a kind of central bank of STI and LTI funds. When a non-ECAN MindAgent finds an Atom valuable, it sends that Atom a certain amount of Stimulus, which results in that Atom's STI and LTI values being increased (via equations to be presented below, that transfer STI and LTI funds from the CogServer to the Atoms in question). Then, the ECAN ImportanceUpdating MindAgent carries out multiple operations, including some that transfer STI and LTI funds from some Atoms back to the CogServer – keeping the flow of money going.

All this represents one among many possible ways of implementing the general notion of activation spreading mentioned in the above inference control examples. A key point is that making activation spreading work well for inference control will likely require extremely tight integration between the inference engine and the association-spreading engine; and the OpenCog approach presents one way of providing such integration.

15.3.2 *Working around the Frame Problem via Integrative AGI*

We noted in Chapter 2 that nonmonotonic logic is not the only route for circumventing the frame problem; and in fact in our own work with PLN in the NCE and OpenCog, we have taken a significantly different approach. Our own approach involves two key ingredients:

- Heavy use of activation spreading to guide inference, as illustrated in several of the examples given in the previous section. This mitigates against a reasoning system actually spending its time doing inferences that are useless because they pertain to assumptions that are implicit and considered obvious. The idea is that these background assumptions just don't get stimulated with much "juice" (which may formally be an activation level, an importance value, or take some other form depending on the AI system in question; in NCE or OCP it is a ShortTermImportance currency value, as briefly discussed above).

- Use of a hierarchical ontology within inference control, to provide a form of "default logic" that is contained in the inference control mechanism rather than, in nonmonotonic logic, in the logical formalism itself. Effective use of the hierarchical ontology relies on the existence of a robust activation spreading mechanism, in a way that will be described below.

To exemplify the notion of default inheritance, consider again the case of penguins, which do not fly, although they are a subclass of birds, which do fly. When one discovers a new type of penguin, say an Emperor penguin, one reasons initially that they do not fly – i.e., one reasons by reference to the new type's immediate parent in the ontological hierarchy, rather than its grandparent. In standard default logic frameworks, the notion of hierarchy is primary and default inheritance is wired in at the inference rule level. But this is not the case with PLN – in PLN, correct treatment of default inheritance must come indirectly out of other mechanisms, this can be achieved in a fairly simple and natural way.

Consider the two inferences

A)
```
Implication penguin fly < 0 >
Implication bird penguin < .02 >

Implication bird fly
```

B)
```
Implication penguin bird < 1 >
Implication bird fly < .9 >

Implication penguin fly
```

The correct behavior in these cases, according to the default inheritance idea is that, in a system that already knows at least a moderate amount about the flight behavior of birds and penguins, inference A should be accepted but inference B should not. That is, evidence about penguins should be included in determining whether birds can fly – even if there is already some general knowledge about the flight behavior of birds in the system. But evidence about birds in general should not be included in estimating whether penguins can fly, if there is already at least a moderate level of knowledge that in fact penguins are atypical birds in regard to flight.

But how can the choice of A over B be motivated in terms of PLN theory? The essence of the answer is simple: in case B the independence assumption at the heart of the deduction rule is a bad one. Within the scope of birds, being a penguin and being a flier are not at all independent. On the other hand, looking at A, we see that within the scope of penguins, being a bird and being a flier are independent. So the reason B is ruled out is that if there is even a moderate amount of knowledge about the truth-value of (Inheritance penguin fly), this gives a hint that applying the deduction rule's independence assumption in this case is badly wrong.

On the other hand, what if a mistake is made and the inference B is done anyway? In this case the outcome could be that the system erroneously increases its estimate of the strength of the statement that penguins can fly. On the other hand, the revision rule may come to the rescue here. If the prior strength of (Inheritance penguin fly) is 0, and inference B yields a strength of .9 for the same proposition, then the special case of the revision rule that handles wildly different truth-value estimates may be triggered. If the 0 strength has much more confidence attached to it than the .9, then they won't be merged together, because it will be assumed that the .9 is an observational or inference error. Either the .9 will be thrown out, or it will be provisionally held as an alternate, non-merged, low-confidence hypothesis, awaiting further validation or refutation.

What is more interesting, however, is to consider the implications of the default inference notion for inference control. It seems that the following may be a valuable inference control heuristic:

1. Arrange terms in a hierarchy; e.g., by finding a spanning DAG of the terms in a knowledge base, satisfying certain criteria (e.g., maximizing total strength*confidence within a fixed limitation on the number of links).
2. When reasoning about a term, first do deductive reasoning involving the term's immediate parents in the hierarchy, and then ascend the hierarchy, looking at each hierarchical level only at terms that were not visited at lower hierarchical levels.

This is precisely the "default reasoning" idea – but the key point is that in PLN it lives at the level of inference control, not inference rules or formulas. In PLN, default reasoning is a timesaving heuristic, not an elementary aspect of the logic itself. Rather, the practical viability of the default-reasoning inference-control heuristic is a consequence of various other elementary aspects of the logic, such as the ability to detect dependencies rendering the deduction rule inapplicable, and the way the revision rule deals with wildly disparate estimates.

One way to embody the above ideas in concrete AI system design is to define a notion of OntologicalInheritance, based on the spanning DAG mentioned above. One can build a default logic based on the spanning DAG G, as follows. Suppose X lies below A in the DAG G. And, suppose that, for predicate F, we have

$$F(A) < TV >$$

meaning that F applies to A with truth value tv. Then, we may say that "If $\sim F(X)$ is not known, then $F(X)$". In other words, we may assume by default that X possesses the properties of the terms above it in the hierarchy D. More formally, we might propose a "default inference rule" such as:

```
Implication
        And
            OntologicalInheritance X A
                Evaluation F A
                Not
                        Known( Not (Evaluation F X ) )
        Evaluation F X
```

There is no reason that a rule like this can't be implemented within PLN. Note that implementing this rule within PLN gives you something nice, which is that all the relationships involved (OntologicalInheritance, Known, Not, etc.) may be probabilistically quantified, so that the outcome of the inference rule may be probabilistically quantified. The "Known" predicate is basically the K predicate from standard epistemic logic (commonly denoted K_a, where a is the reasoning system itself in this case) (Fagin *et al.*, 2003; Rescher, 2005).

The hierarchy G needs to be periodically rebuilt as it is based on abstracting a DAG from a graph of probabilistic logical relations. And, the results of the above default inference rule may be probabilistic and may be merged with the results of other inference rules.

The results from using this rule, in principle, should not be so different from if the rule were not present. However, the use of an ontological hierarchy in this way leads to a completely different dynamics of inference control, which in practice will lead to different results.

And, note finally that for this sort of ontological approach can also be used in the context of activation spreading. In this case, it may take the form (for example) of ontology-based pruning of Assocation relationships. The Association between pigeon and flyer may be pruned because it is essentially redundant with a set of two Association relationships that are implicit in the hierarchy:

```
Association pigeon bird
Association pigeon flyer
```

Using an ontology-pruned set of Association links to guide inference that is partially based on ontology-driven default inference rules, provides an alternative approach to solving the frame problem, that doesn't require introducing a notion of hierarchy into the underlying logic.

In this section we have already, perhaps, ventured too far from the focus of this book, which is logic, into the domain of integrative cognitive architecture. But we have done so with a purpose – to illustrate our belief that, in fact, the most likely route to effective control of RWR lies in integrative cognitive architecture, i.e. in mixing up reasoning with other cognitive processes that are not explicitly inferential. This may be done in different ways within different cognitive architectures, and is in our view an extremely important subject of research in the quest for effective RWR for both AGI and near-term application purposes.

Chapter 16

Conclusion

As emphasized from the start, the main purpose of this book has been to serve as a sort of "thought experiment." We began with a very general problem of "querying, mining and analyzing huge real-world knowledge stores" – i.e., Real-World Reasoning. We then made the choice to characterize this problem in terms of formal logic, and in this context considered its various aspects:

- How to represent real-world knowledge in logical form?
- How to pragmatically translate knowledge from other formats into logical form?
- How to store, retrieve and manipulate large amounts of logical knowledge?
- How should software applications query large logical knowledge stores?
- How to best manage the uncertainty that is rampant in real-world knowledge and conclusions?
- How to represent and reason about time, space and context within an uncertain logic based system?
- How to mine patterns from large logical knowledge stores, and how and why to interface pattern-mining algorithms with inference algorithms
- How to control and direct inference algorithms so as to make them scalable to large knowledge stores?

For each of these questions, we have surveyed the available literature, and in some cases introduced our own ideas when the literature appeared insufficient.

As we have not (yet) actually constructed a scalable, uncertain logic-based system for querying, mining and analyzing large stores of real-world knowledge, we cannot claim any definitiveness for the original ideas we've introduced here, following our extensive literature review. But we do believe we have demonstrated, at least, that this is an extremely promising area for future investigation. Having pursued the RWR thought-experiment as

far as we have done in these pages, we have little doubt that the construction of scalable uncertain logic based systems would constitute a viable approach to the problem of querying,
mining and analyzing changes and other relevant patterns in large real-world knowledge
stores.

References

Aehlig, K., & Beckmann, A. (2007). Propositional Logic for Circuit Classes. Proceedings of the 21st International Workshop, CSL 2007, 16th Annual Conference of the EACSL, Lausanne, Switzerland, September 11–15, 2007.

Aiello, M. & Pratt-Hartmann, I. & van Benthem, J. editors (2007). Handbook of Spatial Logics, pp. 497–564. Springer.

Akman, V., & Surav, M. (1996). Steps toward formalizing context. AI Magazine 17 (3), 55–72, 1996.

Allen, J. F. (1983). Maintaining Knowledge about Temporal Intervals. Communications of the ACM 26, 11, 832–843, November 1983.

Allen, J. F. (1984). Towards a general theory of action and time, Artificial Intelligence, volume 23, pages 123–154, 1984.

Anderson, J. (1983). "A spreading activation theory of memory." Journal of Verbal Learning and Verbal Behavior.

Angrist, J.D. & Imbens G.W. & Rubin, D.B. (1996). Identification of Causal Effects Using Instrumental Variables: Rejoinder. Journal of the American Statistical Association, Vol. 91, No. 434., pp. 468–472, 1996.

Åqvist, L. (2005). Combinations of tense and deontic modality: On the Rt approach to temporal logic with historical necessity and conditional obligation. J. Applied Logic 3(3-4): 421–460 (2005)

Bacchus, F., Tenenberg, J.D., Koomen, J.A.G.M. (1991). A Non-Reified Temporal Logic. Artif. Intell. 52(1): 87–108 (1991)

Barrett, C. & Sebastiani, R. & Seshia, S.A. & Tinelli C. (2009). Satisfiability Modulo Theories. In: Handbook of Satisfiability 2009.

Batson, B., Lamport, L. (2003). High-Level Specifications: Lessons from Industry, Formal Methods for Components and Objects, Lecture Notes in Computer Science number

2852, 242–262, Springer, 2003.

Bettini, C. & Brdiczka, O. & Henricksen, K. & Indulska, J. & Nicklas, D. & Ranganathan, A. & Riboni, D. (2010). A survey of context modelling and reasoning techniques. Pervasive and Mobile Computing 6(2): 161–180 (2010)

Bloch, I., & Saffiotti, A. (2003). On the Representation of Fuzzy Spatial Relations in Robot Maps. In: B. Bouchon-Meunier, L. Foulloy and R.R. Yager (eds) Intelligent Systems for Information Processing, pp. 47–57. Elsevier, NL, 2003.

Blostein, D., E. Lank, R. Zanibbi, "Treatment of Diagrams in Document Image Analysis", Lecture Notes in Computer Science, vol. 1889, pages 330–344, 2000

Blostein, D., J.R. Cordy, R. Zanibbi, "Applying Compiler Techniques to Diagram Recognition", Proc. 16th IAPR International Conference on Pattern Recognition, 2002

Bollobás, B. (1998). Modern Graph Theory. Springer, 1998

Bennacer, N. (2006). Formalizing Mappings for OWL Spatiotemporal Ontologies. Lecture Notes in Computer Science, Springer Berlin / Heidelberg.

Bouquet, P., Ghidini, C., Giunchiglia, F., & Blanzieri, E. (2001). Theories and uses of context in knowledge representation and reasoning. Technical Report DIT-02-010, Informatica e Telecomunicazioni, University of Trento, 2001.

Bresina J.L., Jonsson A.K., Morris P.H., Rajan K. (2005). Activity Planning for the Mars Exploration Rovers. Proceedings of the International Conference on Automated Planning and Scheduling/Artificial Intelligence Planning Systems - ICAPS(AIPS), 2005.

Brezillon, P. (1999). Context in problem solving: A survey. The Knowledge Engineering Review 14 (1), 1–34, 1999.

Bry, F. & Jacquenet, F. (2005). First Order Logic for Learning User Models in the Semantic Web: Why Do We Need It? Workshop on Machine Learning for User Modeling: Challenges, Edinburgh, Scotland, 2005, http://www-connex.lip6.fr/~artieres/UM2005/

Broersen J., Dignum F., Dignum, V., & Meyer, J-J. Ch. (2004). Designing a Deontic Logic of Deadlines. 7th International Workshop on Deontic Logic in Computer Science, DEON 2004, Madeira, Portugal, May 26–28, 2004.

Burke, R. (2000). Knowledge-based recommender systems, Encyclopedia of Library and Information Science, Vol. 69(32), 2000.

Buvac, S., & Mason, I. (1993). Propositional logic of context. Proc. of the 11th American National Conference on Artificial Intelligence (AAAI-93), 412–419, 1993.

Samulowitz, M., Michahelles, F., Linnhoff-Popien, C. (2001). CAPEUS: An Architecture for Context-Aware Selection and Execution of Services. Conference on New Developments in Distributed Applications and Interoperable Systems, 2001.

Chakrabarti, S., S. Sarawagi, and B. Dom (1998) Mining surprising patterns using temporal description length. Proceedings of the 24th International Conference on Very Large Data Bases.

Cheng, J. (2006). Temporal Deontic Relevant Logic as the Logical Basis for Decision Making Based on Anticipatory Reasoning. IEEE International Conference on Systems, Man and Cybernetics, 2006. SMC '06.

Claypool, M., Le, P., Waseda, M., & Brown, D. (2001). Implicit interest indicators. In Proceedings of Intelligent User Interfaces 2001, pages 33–40, 2001.

Cohn, A.G., Bennett, B., Gooday, J.M., Gotts, N. (1997). RCC: a calculus for Region based Qualitative Spatial Reasoning. GeoInformatica 1(3):275–316 (1997)

Collins, A. Loftus, E. (1975). "A spreading-activation theory of semantic processing", Psychological Review. 1975 Nov Vol 82(6) 407–428.

Copi, I., & Cohen, C. (1998). Introduction to Logic. Prentice Hall College Div; 10th edition (August 1998).

Cowie J. & Wilks Y. (2000). Information Extraction. Handbook of natural language processing, edited by Robert Dale, Hermann Moisl, H. L. Somers, 2000. Marcel Dekker.

Craven, M., DiPasquo, D., Freitag, D., McCallum, A., Mitchell, T., Nigam, K., & Slattery, S. (1998). Learning to Extract Symbolic Knowledge from the World Wide Web, CMU-CS-98-122, Carnegie Mellon University, September 1, 1998

Crestani, F. (1997). "Application of Spreading Activation Techniques in Information Retrieval". Artificial Intelligence Review

Danks, D. (2006). Causal Statistical Inference, Carnegie Mellon Summer School, 2006.

Delgrande, J., & Schaub, T. (2003). A Consistency-Based Approach for Belief Change, Artificial Intelligence Journal 151, 1-2, 2003, pp. 1–41.

Dieterich, H., Malinowski, U., Kühme, T., & Schneider-Hufschmidt M. (1993). State of the art in Adaptive User Interfaces, in Schneider-Hufschmidt M., Kuehme T., Malinowski U. (eds), Adaptive User Interfaces, Elsevier, 1993, pp. 13–48.

Dignum, F., & Kuiper, R. (1997). Combining dynamic deontic logic and temporal logic for the specification of deadlines. Proceedings of the Thirtieth Hawaii International Conference on System Sciences, 1997.

Dimopoulos, Y., Kakas, A. (1996). Abduction and Induction: an AI Perspective. Proceedings of the ECAI '96 Workshop on Abductive and Inductive Reasoning.

Dinsmore, J. (1991). Partitioned Representations. Kluwer Academic Publishers, 1991.

Emerson, E.A. (1991). Temporal and modal logic, Handbook of theoretical computer science (vol. B): formal models and semantics, MIT Press, 1991.

Englebretsen, G., & Sommers, F.T. (2000). An Invitation to Formal Reasoning - The Logic of Terms. Ashgate Pub Ltd, 2000.

Fagin, R., J. Halpern, Y. Moses, M, Vardi (2003). Reasoning about Knowledge. Cambridge: MIT Press.

Farquhar, A., Dappert, A., Fikes, R., & Pratt, W. (1995). Integrating Information Sources Using Context Logic. In: Proceedings of AAAI Spring Symposium on Information Gathering from Distributed Heterogeneous Environments, 1995.

Fox, S., Karnawat, K., Mydland, M., Dumais S.T., & White T. (2005). Evaluating implicit measures to improve web search. ACM Transaction of Information System, 23(2):147–168, 2005.

Frank, A. (1991). Qualitative spatial reasoning with cardinal directions. In Proceedings of the Seventh Austrian Conference on Artificial Intelligence.

Gallo, A., T. De Bie, N. Cristianini (2007). MINI: Mining Informative Non-redundant Itemsets. Proceedings of the 11th conference on Principles and Practice of Knowledge Discovery in Databases (PKDD07), Warsaw, September 2007.

Galton, A. (1991). Reified temporal theories and how to unrelfy them, In Proc IJCAI-91, pp 1177–1182, (1991)

Ghidini, C., Giunchiglia, F. (2001). Local Models Semantics, or Contextual Reasoning = Locality + Compatibility. Artificial Intelligence 127 (4), 221–259, 2001.

Giunchiglia, F., & Serafini, L. (1994). Multilanguage hierarchical logics. Artificial Intelligence 65, 29–70, 1994.

Goertzel, B. (2008). Achieving Advanced Machine Consciousness through Integrative, Virtually Embodied Artificial General Intelligence. Nokia Workshop on Machine Consciousness 2008.

Goertzel B., & Bugaj, S.V. (2008). Stages of Ethical Development in Artificial General Intelligence Systems. Proceedings of the First Conference on Artificial General Intelligence, 2008.

Goertzel, B. & de Garis, H. (2008). XIA-MAN: An Extensible, Integrative Architecture for Intelligent Humanoid Robotics. Biologically Inspired Cognitive Architectures, AAAI

2008 Fall Symposium Series: November 7–9, Arlington, Virginia, USA.

Goertzel, B., Iklé, M., Goertzel, I.F., Heljakka A. (2008). Probabilistic Logic Networks - A Comprehensive Framework for Uncertain Inference. Springer, 2008.

Goertzel, Ben, Ari Heljakka, CassProbabilistic Logic Based Reinforcement Learning of Simple Embodied Behaviors in a 3D Simulation World, Welter Silva, Cassio Pennachin, Andre Senna, Izabela Goertzel, Teemu Keinonen, Matthew Ikle', Sanjay Padmane, *Proceedings of International Symposium on Intelligence Computation and Applications* (ISICA) 2007

Goertzel, Ben (2007). Virtual Easter Egg Hunting: A Thought-Experiment in Embodied Social Learning, Cognitive Process Integration, and the Dynamic Emergence of the Self, in Advances in Artificial General Intelligence, IOS Press.

Goertzel, Ben, Hugo Pinto, Ari Heljakka, Michael Ross, Izabela Goertzel, Cassio Pennachin. *Using Dependency Parsing and Probabilistic Inference to Extract Gene/Protein Interactions Implicit in the Combination of Multiple Biomedical Research Abstracts,* Proceedings of BioNLP-2006 Workshop at ACL-2006, New York

Goertzel, B., Iklé, M., & Goertzel, I. (2006c). Indefinite Probabilities for General Intelligenge. AGIRI Workshop 2006.

Goertzel B., Looks M., Heljakka A. & Pennachin C. (2006a). Toward a Pragmatic Understanding of the Cognitive Underpinnings of Symbol Grounding. In Gudwin R and Queiroz J (eds), Semiotics and Intelligent Systems Development, Idea Group Publishing.

Goertzel, Ben, Ari Heljakka, Stephan Vladimir Bugaj,?Cassio Pennachin, Moshe Looks, Exploring Android Developmental Psychology in a Simulation World, Symposium "Toward Social Mechanisms of Android Science", Proceedings of ICCS/CogSci 2006, Vancouver.

Goertzel, Ben (2006). Patterns, Hypergraphs and General Intelligence. Proceedings of WCCI 2006, Vancouver.

Goertzel, B., Looks, M., & Pennachin, C. (2004). Novamente: An Integrative Architecture for General Intelligence. AAAI Fall Symposium on Achieving Human-Level Intelligence.

Goertzel, B., & Pennachin, C. (2006). Artificial General Intelligence. Springer.

Goertzel, B., Pennachin, C., de Souza Coelho, L., Gurbaxani, B., Maloney, E.M. & Jones, J.F. (2006b). Combinations of single nucleotide polymorphisms in neuroendocrine effector and receptor genes predict chronic fatigue syndrome. Pharmacogenomics. 2006

Apr;7(3):475–83.

Goertzel B. & Wang P (2006). Introduction: Aspects of Artificial General Intelligence. Proceedings of the AGIRI Workshop 2006.

Goethals, B. and Zaki, M. J. (2004). Advances in frequent itemset mining implementations: report on FIMI'03. SIGKDD Explor. Newsl. 6, 1 (Jun. 2004), 109–117.

Gong, Z. (2008). Parametric Potential-Outcome Survival Models for Causal Inference, PhD Thesis, University of Canterbury, 2008.

Gounder R. S., Esterline, A. C. (1998). Fuzzy Versions of Epistemic and Deontic Logic, NASA-URC98, Huntsville, AL.

Greenland, S. & Brumback B. (2002). An overview of relations among causal modelling methods. International Journal of Epidemiology 31:1030–1037, 2002.

Greenland, S. & Pearl, J. & Robins, J.M. (1999). Causal diagrams for epidemiologic research. Epidemiology, 10:37–48, 1999.

Grinberg, D., Lafferty J., & Sleator, D. (1995). A robust parsing algorithm for link grammars. Carnegie Mellon University Computer Science technical report CMU-CS-95-125, and Proceedings of the Fourth International Workshop on Parsing Technologies, Prague, September, 1995.

Grindrod, P. & Kibble, M. (2004). Expert Review of Proteomics, August 2004, Vol. 1, No. 2, Pages 229–238, DOI 10.1586/14789450.1.2.229 (doi:10.1586/14789450.1.2.229)

Grindrod, P. & Kibble, M. (2004). Review of the uses of network and graph theory concepts within proteomics, Expert Rev Proteomics, 1(2), 2004

Hart, D. and Goertzel, B. (2008). OpenCog: A Software Framework for Integrative Artificial General Intelligence. Proceedings of the First Conference on Artificial General Intelligence, 2008.

Hayes, B. (1997). Computing Science: Can't Get No Satisfaction. American Scientist, Vol. 85, No. 2, March-April 1997, pages 108–112.

Held, A., Buchholz, S., & Schill, A. (2002). Modeling of context information for pervasive computing applications. In Proceedings of SCI 2002/ISAS 2002, 2002.

Hill A. B. (1965). The environment and disease: association or causation? Proc Royal Soc Medicine 1965, 58:295–300.

Hitchcock, C. (2002). Probabilistic Causation, Stanford Encyclopedia of Philosophy, 2002, on-line at: http://plato.stanford.edu/entries/causation-probabilistic/

Hsu, W., Lee, M. L., & Wang, J. (2008). Temporal and Spatio-Temporal Data Mining. Igi Global, 2006.

Huang, B., & Claramunt, C. (2002). STOQL: an ODMG-based spatio-temporal object model and query language. In: D. Richardson, P. Oosterom (Eds.), Advances in Spatial Data Handling, Springer-Verlag, Berlin, 2002.

Ivancsy, R., & Vajk, I. (2005). A Survey of Discovering Frequent Patterns in Graph Data. Proceedings of Databases and Applications (DBA 2005).

Jones, R. Tambe, M., Laird, J., Rosenbloom, P. (1993). Intelligent automated agents for flight training simulators. In Proceedings of the Third Conference on Computer Generated Forces and Behavioral Representation. University of Central Florida. IST-TR-93-07.

Jurafsky, D. and J. Martin (2008). Speech and Language Processing, Prentice Hall

Kelly, D., & Belkin, N.J. (2004). Display time as implicit feedback: Understanding task effects. In Proceedings of SIGIR 2004, 2004.

Kelly, D., & Teevan, J. (2003). Implicit feedback for inferring user preference: A bibliography. SIGIR Forum, 37(2):18–28, 2003.

Kemerling, G. (2006). Philosophy Pages, on-line at http://www.philosophypages.com/, 2006.

Kluve, J. (2001). On the Role of Counterfactuals in Inferring Causal Effects of Treatments. University of Heidelberg and IZA, Bonn, Discussion Paper No. 354, 2001.

Kobsa, A. (1993). User Modeling: Recent Work, Prospects and Hazards, In Adaptive User Interfaces: Principles and Practise. Elsevier, 1993.

Kobsa A. (2007). Generic User Modeling Systems, In: P. Brusilovsky, A. Kobsa, W. Nejdl, eds.: The Adaptive Web: Methods and Strategies of Web Personalization. Berlin, Heidelberg, New York: Springer Verlag, 136–154, 2007.

Kontchakov, R. & Kurucz, A. & Wolter, F. & Zakharyaschev, M. (2007). Spatial logic + temporal logic =? In M. Aiello, I. Pratt-Hartmann and J. van Benthem, editors, Handbook of Spatial Logics, pp. 497–564. Springer, 2007.

Kontchakov, R. & Pratt-Hartmann, I. & Wolter, F. & Zakharyaschev, M. (2010). Spatial logics with connectedness predicates. Logical Methods in Computer Science 6(3), 2010.

Kontchakov, R. & Pratt-Hartmann, F. & Zakharyaschev, M. (2010). Interpreting Topological Logics over Euclidean Spaces. In F. Lin, U. Sattler and M. Truszczynski, editors, Proceedings of KR (Toronto, Canada, May 9–13), AAAI Press, 2010.

Kozen, D. (1983). Results on the Propositional μ-Calculus. Theoretical ComputerScience, 27 (1983).

Krötzsch, M., Hitzler, P., Vrandecic, D., & Sintek, M. (2006). How to reason with OWL in a logic programming system. In Thomas Eiter, Enrico Franconi, Ralph Hodgson, Susie

Stephens, eds.: Proceedings of the Second International Conference on Rules and Rule Markup Languages for the Semantic Web (RuleML-06), pp. 17–26. IEEE Computer Society 2006.

Lamport, L. (1994). The temporal logic of actions. ACM Transactions on Programming Languages and Systems, 16(3):872–923, 1994.

Laschi C., Dario P., Carrozza M.C., Guglielmelli E., Teti G., Taddeucci D., Leoni F., Massa B., Zecca M. & Lazzarini R. (2000). Grasping and Manipulation in Humanoid Robotics. S7: General Control & Simulation, First IEEE-RAS Workshop on Humanoids - Humanoids 2000, Boston, MA, September 7-8, 2000.

Lawlor, D.A. & Smith, G.D. & Ebrahim. S. (2004). The hormone replacement - coronary heart disease conundrum: is this the death of observational epidemiology? International Journal of Epidemiology, 33:464–467, 2004.

Lenat, D., & Sierra, C. (1999). The Dimensions of Context Space. Tech. rep. CYCorp, http://www.cyc.com/context-space.rtf,doc,txt., 1999.

Lewis, D. (2000). Causation as Influence, The Journal of Philosophy 97: 182–197, 2000.

Lightstone, S., T. Teorey and T. Nadeau (2007). Physical Database Design. Morgan Kaufmann

Lynce, I., & Marques-Silva, J. P. (2002). Building State-of-the-Art SAT solvers. In: Proceedings of the European Conference on Artificial Intelligence, July 2002.

Ma, J., & Knight, B. (2001). Reified Temporal Logics: An Overview, Artificial Intelligence Review, Volume 15, Number 3, pp. 189–217, 2001.

Manning, C. and H. Schuetze (1999). Foundations of Statistical Natural Language Processing, The MIT Press.

Martin, C., Moravec, H. P. (1996). Robot Evidence Grids. Technical rept., Robotics Institute, Carnegie-Mellon University.

McCarthy, J., (1958). Programs with common sense, Symposium on Mechanization of Thought Processes. National Physical Laboratory, Teddington, England, 1958.

McCarthy, J., & Hayes, P.J. (1969). Some philosophical problems from the standpoint of artificial intelligence. Machine Intelligence, 4:463–502.

McCarthy, J. (1987). Generality in Artificial Intelligence. Communications of ACM, 30(12):1030–1035, 1987.

McNamara, P. & Prakken, H. (1999). Norms, Logics and Information Systems: New Studies in Deontic Logic and Computer Science. Amsterdam: IOS Press.

Mendelson, E. (1997). Introduction to Mathematical Logic. Fourth Edition. International Thomson Publishing, 1997, 440 pp.

Meulen, A. (2001), Logic and Natural Language, in Goble, Lou, ed., The Blackwell Guide to Philosophical Logic. Blackwell.

Mitra, D. (2004). Modeling and Reasoning with Star Calculus. Eighth International Symposium on Artificial Intelligence and Mathematics (AMAI 2004).

Moszkowski, B. (1994). Some very compositional temporal properties. In E.-R. Olderog, editor, Programming Concepts, Methods and Calculi, volume A-56 of IFIP Transactions, pages 307–326. IFIP, Elsevier Science B.V. (North-Holland), 1994.

Muller, M. (2001). Inducing Content Based User Models with Inductive Logic Programming Techniques, UM2001 Workshop on Machine Learning for User Modeling, 2001.

Myaeng, S. H., & Korfhage, R. R. (1986). Towards an intelligent and personalized retrieval system. In Proceedings of the ACM SIGART international symposium on Methodologies for intelligent systems, pages 121–129, Knoxville, Tennessee, United States. ACM Press, 1986.

Mylopoulos, J., & Motschnig-Pitrik, R. (1995). Partitioning Information Bases with Contexts. In: Third International Conference on Cooperative Information Systems. Vienna, 1995.

Nilsson, N. (1998). "Artificial Intelligence: A New Synthesis". Morgan Kaufmann Publishers, Inc., San Francisco, California, 1998, pages 121–122

Nurnberger, A., & Detyniecki, M. (2005). Adaptive Multimedia Retrieval: From Data to User Interaction, In Do Smart Adaptive Systems Exist? Studies in Fuzziness and Soft Computing, Volume 173, pp. 341–370, Springer, 2005.

Palermiti R., & Polity, Y. (1995). Desperately seeking user models in information retrieval systems : benefits and limits of cognitivist and marketing approaches, The new review of information and library research, vol 1, 1995, p. 57–65.

Pani A. K., & Bhattacharjee, G. P. (2001). Temporal representation and reasoning in artificial intelligence : A review, Mathematical and computer modelling, 2001, vol. 34, number 1-2, pp. 55–80.

Pearl, J. & Russel, S. (1998). "Bayesian Networks", 1998.

Pearl, J. (2000). Causality: Models, Reasoning and Inference. Cambridge University Press, 2000.

Pnueli, A. (1977). The temporal logic of programs. Proceedings of the 18th IEEE Symposium on Foundations of Computer Science, pages 46–67, 1977.

Pohl, W., & Hohle, J. (1997). Mechanisms for Flexible Representation and Use of Knowledge in User Modeling Shell Systems. In Anthony Jameson, Cécile Paris, and Carlo Tasso (Eds.), User Modeling: Proceedings of the Sixth International Conference, UM97, CISM, 1997.

Pohl, P. (1999). Logic-Based Representation and Reasoning for User Modeling Shell Systems, User Modeling and User-Adapted Interaction 9: 217–282, 1999.

Przulj, N. (2005). Graph Theory Analysis of Protein-Protein Interactions, a chapter in "Knowledge Discovery in Proteomics", edited by Igor Jurisica and Dennis Wigle, CRC Press, 2005.

Radlinski, F., & Joachims, T. (2005). Query chains: Learning to rank from implicit feedback. In Proceedings of SIGKDD 2005.

Reiter R. (1980). A logic for default reasoning. Artificial Intelligence, 13:81–132.

Rescher, Nicolas (2005). Epistemic Logic: A Survey Of the Logic Of Knowledge. University of Pittsburgh Press.

Rich, E. (1979). Building and Exploiting User Models. PhD. Thesis, Department of Computer Science. Pittsburgh, PA: Carnegie-Mellon University, 1979.

Richardson, M. & Domingos, P. (2006). Markov logic networks. Machine Learning, Volume 62, Numbers 1-2, February 2006, pp. 107–136 (30).

Robins, J.M. (2001). Data, design, and background knowledge in etiologic inference. Epidemiology 12:313–20, 2001.

Rothman, K.J. (1976). Causes. Am J Epidemiol. 104:587–92, 1976.

Rothman, K.J. & S. Greenland & C. Poole, T. & Lash (2008). Causation and Causal Inference. In: *Modern Epidemiology (3rd edition)*. Wolter Kluwer, 2008.

Schockaert Steven, De Cock Martine, Cornelis Chris and Kerre Etienne E. (2008). Fuzzy region connection calculus: Representing vague topological information. Approx. Reasoning, Volume 48, Number 1, 2008, pages 314–331, Elsevier Science Inc.

Scott, D., & De Bakker, J. (1969). A theory of programs. Unpublished manuscript, IBM, Vienna, 1969.

Shanahan, M.P., & Baars, B.J. (2005). Applying Global Workspace Theory to the Frame Problem, Cognition, vol. 98, no. 2 (2005), pages 157–176

Sheng L., Ozsoyoglu, Z.M. & Ozsoyoglu, G. (1999). A graph query language and its query processing. Proceedings of the 15th International Conference on Data Engineering, 1999.

Shoham, Y. (1987). Temporal logics in AI: Semantical and ontological considerations. Artificial Intelligence, 33(1):89–104, 1987.

Smigrodzki R., Goertzel B., Pennachin C., Coelho L., Prosdocimi F. & Parker W.D. Jr. (2005). Genetic algorithm for analysis of mutations in Parkinson's disease. Artif Intell Med. 2005 Nov;35(3):227-41. Epub 2005 Oct 3.

Stewart, T. C. & West, R. L. (2006). Deconstructing ACT-R. In Proceedings of the Seventh International Conference on Cognitive Modeling (pp. 298–303). Trieste, Italy.

Strang T., & Linnhoff-Popien, C. (2004). A Context Modeling Survey. Workshop on Advanced Context Modelling, Reasoning and Management, 2004.

Sugiyama K., Hatano K., & Yoshikawa, M. (2004). Adaptive web search based on user profile constructed without any effort from users. In Proceedings of WWW 2004, pages 675–684, 2004.

Sutcliffe G., Gao Y. & Colton S. A Grand Challenge of Theorem Discovery. In Proceedings of the CADE-19 workshop on Grand Challenges and Novel Applications of Automated Reasoning, 2003.

Tarski, A. (1994). Introduction to Logic and to the Methodology of the Deductive Sciences. (New edition of book originally published in Polish in 1936), New York, Oxford University Press.

Thiele, H. (1993). On the Definition of Modal Operators in Fuzzy Logic. In Proceedings of the 23rd IEEE International Symposium on Multiple-Valued Logic, 1993: 62–67.

Lewis, D. (2000). Causation as Influence, The Journal of Philosophy 97: 182–197, 2000.

Van Gils, B., & Schabell, E. D. (2003). User-profiles for Information Retrieval, In Proceedings of the 15th Belgian-Dutch Conference on Artificial Intelligence.

Vilain, M., Kautz, H., & van Beek, P. (1989). Constraint propagation algorithms for temporal reasoning: a revised report. Readings in Qualitative Reasoning about Physical Systems.

Walley, P. (1991). Statistical reasoning with imprecise probabilities. London; New York: Chapman and Hall, 1991. Monographs on statistics and applied probability : 42.

Wang, P. (1996). Heuristics and normative models of judgment under uncertainty. International Journal of Approximate Reasoning, Vol. 14, No. 4, Pages 221–235, 1996.

Wang, P. (2006a). From NARS to a Thinking Machine. Proceedings of the Artificial General Intelligence Research Institute Workshop, Washington DC, May 2006.

Wang, P. (2006b). Rigid Flexibility - The Logic of Intelligence. Springer, 2006.

Weischedel R.M. (2006). Challenges in Natural Language Processing. Cambridge University Press, 2006.

Westervelt E.R., Grizzle J.W., Chevallereau C., Choi J.H. & Morris B. (2007). Feedback control of dynamic bipedal robot locomotion (Control & automation, Vol. 1). Taylor & Francis/CRC, 2007.

Weyhrauch, R., 1980. Prolegomena to a Theory of Mechanized Formal Reasoning. Artificial Intelligence 13 (1), 133–176, 1980.

Wheeler R. & Aitken S. (2000). Multiple algorithms for fraud detection. Knowledge-Based Systems, Volume 13, Issues 2-3, April 2000, Pages 93–99.

Wieringa, R. J. & Meyer, J-J. Ch. (1993). Applications of deontic logic in computer science: A concise overview. in Deontic Logic in Computer Science: Normative System Specification (1994).

Wood, W.G. (1989). Temporal Logic Case Study, Technical Report CMU/SEI-89-TR-024, Carnegie Mellon University, 1989.

Wray, R.E., & Jones, R.M (2005). An introduction to Soar as an agent architecture. In, R. Sun (ed), Cognition and Multi-agent Interaction: From Cognitive Modeling to Social Simulation, Cambridge University Press, pp. 53–78, 2005.

Yeung, Albert K.W. & Hall, G. Brent (2007). Spatial Database Systems: Design, Implementation and Project Management, edited by Albert K.W. Yeung, Springer, 2007.

Ying, M.S. (1988). On a standard models of fuzzy modal logics. Fuzzy Sets and Systems.

Zadeh, L. A. (1965). Fuzzy sets. Inf. Control 8, 338–353, 1965.

Zadeh, L. A. (1978). Fuzzy sets as a basis for a theory of possibility, Fuzzy Sets and Systems 1, 3–28, 1978.

Zanibbi, R. & Blostein, D. & Cordy, J.R. (2003). A Survey of Table Recognition: Models, Observations, Transformations, and Inferences International Journal of Document Analysis and Recognition, 2003.

Zanibbi, R. & Blostein, D. & Cordy, J.R. (2004). A survey of table recognition Models, observations, transformations, and inferences, International Journal on Document Analysis and Recognition, Volume 7, Number 1, 2004.

Zanibbi, R. & Blostein, D. & Cordy, J.R. (2006). Decision-Based Specification and Comparison of Table Recognition Algorithms, Western New York Image Processing Workshop, 2006.

Looks, M. (2006). Competent Program Evolution, Doctoral Dissertation, Washington University in St. Louis, 2006.

Cohn, A. & Renz, J. (2008). Qualitative Spatial Representation and Reasoning, in: F. van Hermelen, V. Lifschitz, B. Porter, eds., Handbook of Knowledge Representation, Elsevier, 551-596, 2008.

van Beek, P. & Manchak D. (1996). The Design and Experimental Analysis of Algorithms for Temporal Reasoning, Volume 4, pages 1-18, 1996.

Emerson, E. (1995). Efficient Automation of Temporal Reasoning. CONCUR 1995: Pages 393-394

Rothman, K. & Greenland, S. & Lash, T. (2008). Modern Epidemiology, Lippincott Williams & Wilkins; Third edition (March 14, 2008).

Szabó R. (2004). Topological navigation of simulated robots using occupancy grid, International Journal of Advanced Robotic Systems, Vol. 1. No. 3. I-II. pp. 201-206., 2004.

Tarski, A. (1929). Foundations of the Geometry of Solids, reprinted in his. Logic, Semantics and Metamathematics (Oxford: Clarendon Press, 1956), 24-9